The Queen

Also by Michelle Morgan

Marilyn Monroe: Private and Undisclosed
Hollywood Scandals
Madonna
The Battered Body Beneath the Flagstones and Other Victorian Scandals
When Marilyn Met the Queen: Marilyn Monroe's Life in England

The Queen

100 Years, 100 Stories

Michelle Morgan

ROBINSON

ROBINSON

First published in Great Britain in 2026 by Robinson

1 3 5 7 9 10 8 6 4 2

Copyright © Michelle Morgan, 2026

The moral right of the author has been asserted.

All rights reserved.

No part of this publication may be reproduced, stored in a retrieval system, or transmitted, in any form, or by any means, without the prior permission in writing of the publisher, nor be otherwise circulated in any form of binding or cover other than that in which it is published and without a similar condition including this condition being imposed on the subsequent purchaser.

Photo p. vi: Tim Graham/Getty Images

A CIP catalogue record for this book is available from the British Library.

ISBN: 978-1-40878-346-7 (hardback)
ISBN: 978-1-40878-347-4 (trade paperback)

Typeset in Electra LT Std by SX Composing DTP, Rayleigh, Essex
Printed and bound in Great Britain by Clays Ltd, Elcograf S.p.A.

Papers used by Robinson are from well-managed forests and other responsible sources.

Robinson
An imprint of
Little, Brown Book Group
Carmelite House
50 Victoria Embankment
London EC4Y 0DZ

The authorised representative
in the EEA is
Hachette Ireland
8 Castlecourt Centre, Dublin 15,
D15 XTP3, Ireland
(email: info@hbgi.ie)

An Hachette UK Company
www.hachette.co.uk

www.littlebrown.co.uk

For my beautiful niece, Angelina.
May your crown always shine diamond bright.
I love you!

Queen Elizabeth as the world will always remember her.

Contents

	Acknowledgements	xi
	Introduction	1
1.	One of the Prettiest Babies	3
2.	'Baby Betty' Visits Her Grandparents	6
3	The Most Popular Baby in the Land	9
4	Margaret Rose Makes Four	12
5	Lilibet Loves Animals	15
6.	The Little House with the Straw Roof	18
7.	The Quiet Before the Storm	22
8.	The Heavy Burden of Responsibility	25
9.	Times Are Changing	29
10.	The Coronation . . . 'a Pageant, a Show'	32
11.	Camp Fires and Map Reading at Buckingham Palace	35
12.	Accidents, Illness and a Trip to the Zoo	39
13.	'The King Will Never Leave'	42
14.	'I Am Glad We Have Been Bombed'	45
15.	'All Will Be Well'	48
16.	All the World's a Stage	51
17.	Princess 230873	55
18.	Conga at the Palace	58
19.	Joy and Good Fortune in Northern Ireland	61
20.	The Princess Meets a Prince	64
21.	'I Declare Before You All . . .'	67

22.	Wedding Plans at Buckingham Palace	70
23.	An Ivory Gown and Nine-Foot Wedding Cake	74
24.	Parties in Paris	77
25.	A Baby at Buckingham Palace	80
26.	A 'Normal' Life in Malta	83
27.	How Do You Clean a Kettle?	86
28.	Cheering Crowds, Tea and a Gold-mounted Riding Crop	89
29.	The Scandal of Marion 'Crawfie' Crawford	92
30.	'An Extremely Strenuous Tour Awaits'	96
31.	The King Is Dead	99
32.	Gold Lace and Diamonds at the Opening of Parliament	103
33.	The Death of Queen Mary	106
34.	'I Name this Ship *Britannia*'	109
35.	Bunting, Tea Parties, Crowns and Complaints	112
36.	'I Shall Strive to Be Worthy of Your Trust'	115
37.	The Princess and the Equerry	118
38.	A Surge of Crowds in Scotland	122
39.	Aureole, a Difficult Horse	125
40.	Princess Margaret Decides Between Love and Duty	128
41.	Rain, No Umbrellas and a Dirty Red Carpet	131
42.	When the Queen Met Marilyn	135
43.	Scandal on *Britannia*, and a Trip to Portugal	138
44.	Opening Parliament in Canada	141
45.	The Queen Meets the President	144
46.	Happy Christmas from Sandringham	147
47.	Thunder, Umbrellas and the Magna Carta in Lincoln	150
48.	The Queen Meets the Kennedys	153
49.	Trees, Tea and Soapy Suds in Corby	156

50.	Sympathy and Kindness at Addenbrookes	159
51.	Prince Charles and the Cherry Brandy	161
52.	One More Baby at Buckingham Palace	163
53.	When the Beatles Met the Queen	166
54.	Heartache at Aberfan	168
55.	A Royal Photo Scandal	171
56.	Prince Charles Comes of Age	174
57.	Eggs and Bomb Threats at the Investiture	177
58.	A Different Side to the Royal Family	180
59.	Walkabouts and Ruined Frocks in Coventry	183
60.	The Princess Anne Kidnap Attempt	187
61.	A Most Boring Dresser in the USA	191
62.	Street Parties and Downpours at the Silver Jubilee	194
63.	Stray Dogs and Gigantic Cheese in Chester	197
64.	Prince Charles Finds a Wife	200
65.	A Trip to the Cobbles	203
66.	'It's Always Lovely to Have a New One'	205
67.	An Intruder at Buckingham Palace	208
68.	Controversy at the Opening of Parliament	211
69.	Faux Pas and 'Dowdy' Clothes in Canada	214
70.	Complaints and Crying Children in Scotland	217
71.	Eggs and Demonstrations Down Under	221
72.	The Mayor Collapses in Canterbury	224
73.	Working Against the Tide at Heysham	226
74.	The Fire at Windsor	229
75.	Annus Horribilis	232
76.	The Gate of Romantic Candyfloss	234
77.	Breaking Records, and a Visit to the Fame School	237

78.	The Role of Grandmother versus Queen	240
79.	'He Has Been My Strength and Stay'	243
80.	'We Must Now Say Goodbye to *Britannia*'	246
81.	A Very Precious One Hundredth Birthday	249
82.	Walking into the 'Danger Zone' at Berwick	251
83.	'In Loving Memory, Lilibet'	254
84.	The Queen Meets James Bond	257
85.	The Happiest of Happy Birthdays	259
86.	Why Doesn't the Queen Like Tennis?	262
87.	A Royal Wedding and a Familiar Ring	265
88.	'Good Evening, Mr Bond'	268
89.	The Queen's Horse Wins the Gold Cup	271
90.	'A Source of Inspiration and Pride for Us All'	273
91.	Time Marches On	276
92.	The Queen . . . 'Quite Cantankerous' But Also Hilarious	279
93.	'Better Days Will Return'	282
94.	Princess Beatrice Borrows a Dress	285
95.	'With Grateful Hearts, We Remember'	287
96.	'Thank You, Ma'am . . . For Everything'	289
97.	One Last Time on the Balcony	292
98.	The Passing of the Queen	295
99.	'Sleep, Dearie, Sleep'	298
100.	The Queen's Lasting Legacy	301
	Bibliography	304
	Index	331

Acknowledgements

I would first of all like to say a big thank you to all those who have shared information, memories and advice for the research of this book. It has all been extremely useful to me, and your support has been invaluable.

I would also like to thank my family and friends, who all celebrated this book with me, and especially my husband, Richard. Not only has he always been supportive of my writing career, but he was especially excited about this book, because he had his own sweet memory of the Queen to share. My daughter Daisy has been a sounding board for this and so many other projects. Daisy, I love you so much. Remember that all my dreams came true because of you.

Finally, I'd like to thank Tamsin English, Lucy Buchan, Ella Garrett, Howard Watson and everyone at Robinson/Little, Brown for all the help and enthusiasm I have received for this book. Tamsin, when I sent this idea to you, I did so in the hope that you might give it some consideration. To receive such love for it has been one of the biggest thrills of my career. I am forever grateful to you for that. Thank you so much.

Introduction

Who was the Queen? To millions of people, she was the head of state, a woman on a stamp or a coin. She was a figure on the television screen, seen opening a school, or a hospital, or launching a ship. To those lucky enough to see her in the flesh, she was a flash of bright colour, rushing past in a Rolls-Royce, or the shake of a gloved hand, a smile or a polite – and sometimes funny – word or two. She was also a wife, a mother, a grandmother, a great-grandmother, a daughter, a sister and a friend. No matter who you are, or where you live, there is little doubt that you will have at least one memory of the Queen, even if it is from a Christmas Day speech or a mention in a newspaper.

I never had the opportunity of meeting Her Majesty in person, though I did see her in a car in 1982, waving on her way to open a local school. Unknown to me at the time, she spoke to my future husband – then a student at that school – and that has been his proud claim to fame ever since.

In recent years, the Queen has been something of a ray of light to me. In 2022, my book, *When Marilyn Met the Queen*, was published six days after I was diagnosed with cancer. Publicising the book – the story of Marilyn Monroe's life in England, during which time she met Her Majesty – gave me a reason to get up every day, and allowed me to feel normal if just for a couple of hours. I wanted to let the Queen know how much she had inspired me over the years, and how she was helping me at that particular time, so I sent a copy of the book to her at Windsor Castle.

About a month later, I received a letter from her lady-in-waiting, to tell me that the Queen was very touched to receive the book and my accompanying note. The letter arrived on the same day as I lost my hair to chemotherapy, and it became the only bright spark in an otherwise dark and lonely time.

Several years have gone by since then, but that letter still holds a special place in my heart. To now have the opportunity of writing this book is one of the biggest joys of my life. I mean that most sincerely.

The Queen: 100 Years, 100 Stories does not pretend to read the Queen's mind, or reveal her innermost secrets. Instead, it is a celebration of our experience of Her Majesty, and Her Majesty's experience of us. Here, you can read about her personal milestones, such as her engagement to Prince Philip, the loss of her father and the birth of her children. But in addition to that, you can read about the most important part of Her Majesty's job – touring the country and the world, and meeting the public . . . her public.

You can time-travel your way from the birth of Princess Elizabeth all the way to her funeral, almost one hundred years later. Along the way, you can discover the pomp, the ceremony, the celebrations and the complaints. The flags, the bunting, the gun salutes and the marching bands. This is a journey of one hundred moments. The Queen's greatest hits, if you will. It has been an honour to write these stories. I hope you enjoy them as much as I have, and I hope they bring you a sense of nostalgia, on the occasion of our Queen's one hundredth birthday.

Michelle Morgan

1

One of the Prettiest Babies

When Princess Elizabeth Alexandra Mary was born at 2.40 a.m. on the morning of 21 April 1926, nobody could have had any idea that this baby would go on to become one of the most famous women in history. Born to the Duke and Duchess of York (the son and daughter-in-law of King George V and Queen Mary), the little girl was in direct line to the throne, but was never likely to be crowned, especially if the Duke and Duchess went on to have a boy, or if the Duke's elder brother, the Prince of Wales, was to marry and have children. Interestingly, when the Princess's astrological chart was read a couple of years after her birth, it was predicted that she would live a long life, and would one day become the Queen of England.

The British public were absolutely enthralled at the news that Princess Elizabeth had been born. Newspapers were full of articles about her arrival, flags were flown around the country, and gun salutes were heard all over London. For many hours after the birth of Princess Elizabeth, visitors to 17 Bruton Street – the Duke and Duchess's London home – came and went, telegrams and elaborate, colourful bouquets arrived, and the doorbell was buzzed so many times that it finally broke.

THE QUEEN

By the time King George V and Queen Mary pulled up outside, the street was alive with a mostly female cheering crowd, perched on balconies, hanging out of windows, and balanced on their tiptoes on the pavement. Wearing cloche hats and long, spring jackets, they all had one thing in common – a wish to see the Princess for themselves.

A sighting would come later, but for now they had to be satisfied with a bulletin from Buckingham Palace, giving an update of sorts: 'The Duchess of York has had some rest since the arrival of her daughter. Her Royal Highness and the infant Princess are making very satisfactory progress.' The statement went on to say that the birth had come after 'a certain line of treatment was successfully adopted'.

For those desperate to see the baby, they were dutifully rewarded on 26 May 1926, when she attended the birthday party of her grandmother, Queen Mary, at Buckingham Palace. Extraordinarily, Her Majesty requested that Elizabeth's nanny take the baby to the gates of the palace, where a number of sightseers had the opportunity of meeting her.

Days later, on 29 May 1926, it was time for the baby's christening, which was held at the private chapel in Buckingham Palace. This came as a surprise, as most people had no idea that the palace even had a chapel. It was, however, a favourite place for the royals, with Queen Victoria spending a lot of time there during her reign.

On the day of the christening, crowds crammed into the Mall, and climbed on to the Queen Victoria Memorial for a better look. They were rewarded with a glimpse of the baby princess and her parents, arriving at the palace just after 2.30 p.m. To appease the well-wishers, the nanny held Princess Elizabeth high in her arms, before the car swung through the gates.

Once inside, a select number of family, friends and staff gathered in the private chapel, where the baby (dressed in a gown passed down through generations) was christened by the Archbishop of York. 'Elizabeth Alexandra Mary, I baptise thee in the name of the Father, and of the Son, and of the Holy Ghost. Amen.' The congregation then sang 'Father of All to Thee We Pray' and 'Praise the Lord ye Heavens Adore Him'.

While it was thought that the Duchess of York would return to society quickly after giving birth, she made the decision to stay away from public life for a time, and instead took herself and the baby to stay with her mother, the Countess of Strathmore. They first headed to Hertfordshire, before settling comfortably at Glamis Castle, Scotland. There, they visited relatives and walked in the garden, before joining the King and Queen at Balmoral. Newspaper reporters decided that the Duchess must be enamoured by her baby daughter, and that's why she had not returned to work yet.

It soon became apparent that everyone who met the baby felt the same way. With a resemblance to Queen Mary at the same age, and wearing ribboned frocks of pink and blue, Princess Elizabeth quickly became the bright spark of anywhere she visited. One unnamed visitor was quick to tell a reporter that she thought the new baby was one of the prettiest she had ever seen . . . 'And not in the heavy manner of advertised fine babies, but with a charming effect of energy and intelligence.'

Gifts poured in from around the country, but one proved to be especially popular. During a ceremony held at the family home, an engraved silver porringer was presented by Mr G. L. Joseph, chairman of the National Association of Jewellers.

'We hope,' he said, 'that this porringer will take its place in due time upon the breakfast table of the first baby in the land, and may even be banged imperiously upon the table by her infant hands.'

The baby princess put out her arms to take it, and the Duchess smiled. 'You see she likes it at once,' she said.

2

'Baby Betty' Visits Her Grandparents

As 1926 rolled into 1927, the Duke and Duchess of York readied themselves for an official trip to Australia and New Zealand. Tasks included shopping for clothes suitable for all eventualities, and spending time with Princess Elizabeth, who would remain in Britain under the care of her grandparents and nurses. By all accounts, the decision to leave the baby behind did not come lightly to the Duchess, who worried about her wellbeing for the entirety of the trip. And who could blame her, since the trip was to be six months in length, cover 35,000 miles, and would mean missing her daughter's first birthday.

On 6 January 1927, the Duke and Duchess said goodbye to Princess Elizabeth, who was held up at the drawing-room window for one final wave. They then headed to Victoria Station, where the King, Queen Mary and the Duchess's parents kissed them farewell. The upcoming tour was a huge deal, and dozens of people crowded into the station to watch the royal couple board the train, waving an array of handkerchiefs as the locomotive departed the station. From Victoria, the couple travelled to Portsmouth, where the sailors and staff on board HMS *Renown* waited to greet them with much pomp and ceremony.

'BABY BETTY' VISITS HER GRANDPARENTS

As the ship left the port, escorted by destroyers and seaplanes, Princess Elizabeth was at Bruton Street with her nannies. The announcement that Queen Mary would have charge of the baby caused confusion, with some folk imagining that she would have full custody for six months. Not so, said a spokesperson from Buckingham Palace. Instead, the Princess would stay at Bruton Street, for the present, under the close supervision of her maternal grandmother, the Countess of Strathmore. The King and Queen Mary, meanwhile, headed off to Sandringham.

For a time, it was believed that the baby would stay with her grandparents in Norfolk, but when Elizabeth caught a cold, and numerous cases of mumps were recorded at Sandringham, the trip was postponed. Instead of travelling, the baby continued her regular routine of being pushed around the royal gardens in her pram. When it was revealed that the baby was often seen in Kensington Gardens with her nurse, local mothers began taking their children, too. Occasionally, they would win a glimpse of the Princess's face, usually wearing a bonnet and peeping through the window of her car.

Finally, in early February, the King and Queen Mary returned to London, and Princess Elizabeth and her mother's golden retriever, Rex, were taken to greet them at Buckingham Palace. Under the Queen's guidance, the former rooms of Prince George, the Duke of Kent, were decorated for the Princess, with a wall full of silhouettes depicting elephants, polar bears, lions, camels, bison and zebras.

Princess Elizabeth's first birthday was spent at Windsor Castle, where the Duke and Duchess of York cabled their congratulations. Still on their trip, the couple were surrounded by well-wishers and gift-givers, all anxious to hear about the baby princess. When presented with a large doll from some Australian girl guides, the Duchess's reply was quite revealing. 'Thank you,' she said. 'I am terribly thrilled. I am sure Betty will adore it.' Back in England, Baby Betty, as the press began calling her, was in the care of her aunt, Princess Mary, at

Windsor while the King and Queen Mary visited Cardiff. Boxes of birthday presents arrived throughout the day, and included a rocking horse, soft toys and a talking doll.

For the remainder of spring and early summer 1927, Princess Elizabeth spent time between both sets of grandparents, and her travels included St Paul's Walden Bury in Hertfordshire, Windsor Castle, Buckingham Palace and then finally 145 Piccadilly, which was to be the York family's new home.

On 27 June 1927, the Duke and Duchess of York returned from their long but successful trip. It was raining heavily as the couple arrived in London, but that didn't stop royal fans, who left their homes and crowded into the Mall, hiding under brollies, waving handkerchiefs and cheering emphatically as the couple passed by. Inside Buckingham Palace, there was an emotional reunion between the Duke, the Duchess and Princess Elizabeth, and they then all stepped out on to the balcony, where they waved to the waiting crowds below. The Duchess of York beamed while holding her daughter, while Queen Mary held an umbrella over them. It had been a long separation for them all, but now the York family looked forward to a quiet summer in Scotland.

3

The Most Popular Baby in the Land

The public obsession with Princess Elizabeth was something to behold. Mothers dressed their children in bonnets and pretty pink dresses so that they could be just like her, crowds followed her wherever she went, and her social life was better than most adults. Indeed, the Princess was so loved that newspapers dubbed her 'the most popular baby in the land'.

Mr C. Herbert Bedells, president of the Institution of Surveyors, confirmed just how well-liked the baby was, when he attended a dinner in Belfast. During a toast to the Royals, he added, 'We must not forget the youngest member of the Royal Family who has increasingly of late endeared herself to the hearts of every one of us.'

It wasn't just the fact that she was a beautiful princess that led Elizabeth to have so many fans. She was popular because her personality was fun, friendly and adorable. She would wave at people in the street, and salute soldiers outside the palace. She would smile at sightseers walking past her pram in the park. She would peer over the balcony to gaze at the people standing outside her Piccadilly home. She was also funny. When the Princess sat for photographer Marcus Adams he described her as, 'the most remarkable child I've ever seen – and certainly the most entertaining.' He decided that her comic side could often be to the detriment of the photos being taken, but fans of the pictures did not agree.

So popular was the Princess that in 1930 a book was published about her. Entitled *The Story of Princess Elizabeth* by Anne Ring, the volume sold 50,000 copies in two weeks, and was published with the consent of the Duke and Duchess. Interestingly, it was in this book that readers discovered the Princess's nickname. Lilibet (or Lillibeth as written in the book) was how she was known to her parents, her grandparents and close members of the family.

During a 1928 visit to Glamis Castle in Scotland, friends, tenants of the estate, estate employees and local tradespeople were invited to spend time with the royal family. Princess Elizabeth was the most popular person there, and spent her time making comments about the people she met. 'Nice man,' she exclaimed to one young gentleman, before pointing out that a lady was wearing a blue hat. One child sneaked a look at the Princess while hiding behind his mother's legs, and she tugged on her own mother's skirt. 'Speak to pretty boy, mamma!' she said, but the boy refused to converse with her. Mothers were seen whispering to each other about how 'bonny' the child was, and commenting on everything from her eyes to her 'enchanting' smile.

Perhaps the most entertaining of Elizabeth's personality traits – for the press and public at least – was her cheekiness. During a visit with her mother to see the doll's house Titania's Palace, the Princess took great delight in studying the nursery, but was appalled by the toys all over the floor. 'How frightfully untidy,' she exclaimed, before complaining that her nanny aways made her pick up her own toys.

Another 'cheeky' moment was revealed in Anne Ring's official book about the Princess. Describing a dull night when the Duchess was sitting quietly by the fire, the Princess turned the light on and was told to switch it off again. Elizabeth then took it upon herself to create a disco vibe by switching the light on and off as fast as she could. When she was forcibly removed from the switch by her mother, Princess Elizabeth squealed, 'Naughty Mummy!' and proceeded to attempt a return to the switch.

Also amusing for onlookers was the little princess's temper. She was sometimes spotted stamping her feet when forced to stand on the balcony longer than she wished to, and during one visit to a dressmaker, she threw a tantrum when asked to try on hats. It was only when her frustrated nanny told her that 'all grown-up ladies wear hats' that the little girl relented, and let the dressmaker place a bonnet on her head.

But it wasn't all tantrums. The Princess was also a great comic, and by 1928 she had begun imitating members of the household. She would march up and down like the soldiers she saw outside, and then amuse everyone by copying her grandmother's bows and waves. When Queen Mary told her to sit up like a royal princess, Elizabeth repeated the request to her nanny, and added a bow from left to right, for good measure.

The child was very fond of her grandfather, King George V, but even he fell foul of her bossiness on occasion. One day when he was convalescing from an illness, Elizabeth visited him in his room, and then refused to leave. The King was forced to go into the hall to try and find someone to take her back to the nursery, but was perturbed to hear the Princess shouting from behind him.

He rushed back into the room, and asked what the matter was, to which she replied, 'You forgot to shut the door after you.'

4

Margaret Rose Makes Four

On 21 August 1930, Princess Margaret Rose was born to the Duke and Duchess of York. A sister for Princess Elizabeth, the baby was born in Glamis Castle, the ancestral home of the Duchess. The couple had been staying there for a while, and locals were so excited, they were frequently seen standing around the gates, trying to catch a glimpse of the growing family. Sometimes they'd be disappointed, but other times they'd see Princess Elizabeth out in the car with her grandmother, and would always be rewarded by her jumping up from her seat and giving a wave.

There was a definite sense of pride that the new princess was born in Scotland, but while many celebrated, the newspapers weren't sorry to disclose their opinion that it would have been nice if the 'fine chubby-faced little girl' had been a baby prince.

To celebrate the birth of the as yet unnamed baby, bells rang at Westminster Abbey, flags were hung all over the West End, and a royal salute of thirty-one guns was heard at Hyde Park and the Tower of London. 'Three cheers for the Duchess!' became a familiar cry all over London, and the public showed their appreciation for the newcomer by sending gifts and cards from all over the country and the world.

MARGARET ROSE MAKES FOUR

As the King and Queen Mary readied themselves for a trip to Scotland, three local girls were asked to light a beacon at Glamis, using the same torch that was used when the Duke and Duchess of York were married. As the flames reached over two hundred feet high, a thousand well-wishers travelled from around Scotland, climbed the muddy hill and cheered the new princess. Pipers played 'The Highland Lassie', the crowd danced and sang, and the Earl of Strathmore donated two barrels of beer for refreshment.

Back in the castle, Princess Elizabeth – fresh from welcoming her baby sister – strained to see the flames from a high window in one of the towers, while the Duchess got out of bed and watched for a while from her window.

So popular was the birth announcement that extra telephonists and telegraphists were employed just to deal with the number of enquiries coming into the royal residences. Some would ask about the Duchess's health, while others were keen to know who the Princess looked like, or how much she weighed. The most popular question, however, was what her name would be. No answers were immediately forthcoming about that, but the mystery kept the public fascinated for a month.

When the King and Queen Mary arrived at Balmoral, the Duke of York visited them to discuss what to call his new baby daughter. It was decided that Margaret should certainly be included, but it took a great deal of discussion between both families, before the name Rose was added. Rose was after the Duchess's sister, Lady Rose Leveson-Gower, while Margaret was an old Scottish name, which funnily enough had been bandied about by locals as the most popular choice. The name was made official when the Duke popped into the general store at Glamis to register the name with the registrar working there.

Princess Elizabeth soon decided that Margaret Rose should have a nickname – Bud – which the Duchess disliked immediately. 'Oh, but why Bud?' she asked. 'Well, she's not a real rose yet, is she? She's only a bud!' Elizabeth replied.

The christening of Princess Margaret Rose came on 30 October 1930, when the York family had returned to London. Well-wishers crowded around the Piccadilly address, and whooped their joy as the Duchess – wearing a bottle-green coat trimmed with a fur collar – exited the home, followed by Princess Margaret in the arms of her nurse, and Princess Elizabeth, who jumped into the car, followed by her father.

As with Princess Elizabeth, the ceremony was held in the private chapel at Buckingham Palace, which was decorated with white marguerites, roses and heather. As the family reached the gates of the palace, Princess Elizabeth rushed to the window of the car to wave to the crowd, while Princess Margaret Rose was held up to the window by her nurse, and received a cheer.

Inside, there was a small but beautiful celebration, with family, friends and staff in attendance. The baby wore the Queen Victoria christening robe, and showed a variety of emotions as the Archbishop of Canterbury conducted the ceremony. An organ was played, hymns sung and blessings recited, and then afterwards, the Duchess cut into one of the cakes, while another was delivered to the family home in Piccadilly, where it was the centrepiece for a small afternoon tea party.

As gifts of poems, flowers, jewellery and winter woollies were sent to various royal palaces, an argument raged in several corners as to whether or not the baby should be classed as Scottish or English. While it was announced that no matter what area she was born in, the Princess would be British, locals in Glamis, Scotland, could be forgiven for gloating a little bit when each household received a box through the post, holding a dainty piece of christening cake.

5

Lilibet Loves Animals

Princess Elizabeth was introduced to a variety of animals from her early years. Dogs, horses, ponies and birds fascinated her, and spending so much time in the country meant that animals became the loves of her life.

The Princess's third birthday was to prove very important, as it was on this day that she was presented with her first dog – a cairn terrier puppy – gifted by Elizabeth's uncle, the Prince of Wales. Not only that, but the Duke and Duchess gave their daughter a Shetland pony, which she excitedly spent time with in the garden.

Shortly after, the Duke and Duchess of York visited the Bristol Settlement during a tour of the city. There they met sixteen-year-old Thomas Preen, who had spent a considerable amount of time working on a painting to give to the Princess. The picture was – of course – animal-themed, and depicted a caterpillar playing leapfrog with a rabbit and a mouse. The Duchess accepted it with a smile. 'Oh, how charming,' she said. 'I am sure she will love it.'

When the Duchess's brother John Bowes-Lyon passed away in February 1930, she stepped away from engagements, and instead spent much time with her daughter. Together they took long walks around the stables and fields of Naseby Hall, Northamptonshire, where they spoke about natural history and petted the horses. A couple of months later, on her fourth birthday, the King presented Elizabeth with a pony called Peggy. She immediately got to work, learning how to ride in the grounds of Windsor Castle, and waving to her parents as they cautiously watched from the sidelines. When away from her beloved Peggy, the Princess had Tommy, a toy pony on wheels, that she would pretend to stable behind the screen in the drawing room of her home.

Trips to the zoo were a regular occurrence for the child, and she would often be seen at London Zoo in the early morning, before the crowds arrived. There, she would refuse a guide, and instead rush around the grounds inspecting every animal. 'She always goes to the bird house,' reported one columnist, 'where she amuses herself feeding the birds.'

Even official duties were a time for Princess Elizabeth to think about her animals. When artist David P. Ramsay was given the task of painting her, the Princess found it hard to sit still. He later recalled: 'While I was painting her, I gave her a little desk, and she made her own drawings of animals in a little book, which she completely filled up.'

In April 1931, Princess Elizabeth celebrated her fifth birthday at Windsor Castle, and after opening her presents, and imitating the Irish Guards pipers marching up and down during the changing of the guard, off she went for a ride on her pony. She was still the proud owner of Peggy, and was becoming something of a professional rider. Of course, this hobby was reported widely in the press, with one newspaper – the *Civil and Military Gazette* – taking a special interest. 'Her tutors declare that she will turn out a fine horsewoman,' it said, before observing that she must surely get her skills from her grandmother, Queen Mary. She had been an excellent horsewoman when she was younger, and had often been spotted riding in Richmond Park.

LILIBET LOVES ANIMALS

The most famous pets in Princess (and later Queen) Elizabeth's life were her corgis. In 1933, the Princess met her first corgi when visiting the home of Viscount and Viscountess Weymouth. They introduced her to their new puppy, and Princess Elizabeth liked her so much that she asked her father if he would buy her one, too.

The Duke did some research, and discovered that the breed was considered suitable for children and should adapt well to country life. He bought one for the Princess, and from that moment on, Rozavel Golden Eagle (or 'Dookie' to his friends) went everywhere with her. Later in 1933, while visiting the Imperial Institute to see an exhibition of disabled men's work, the Duke and Duchess spotted some dog baskets. Asking what type of basket they should buy for Princess Elizabeth's puppy, they were confused when the stallholder told them that it all depended on how the dog curled up.

'Have you watched him?' he asked. There then followed a conversation on whether or not the dog curled up lengthways or sideways, before the Duke decided, 'Since it's a very long dog we'll have the larger size.'

Interestingly, in the early 1930s, the corgi breed was relatively unknown, with some branding them a type of fox or a mongrel, but as with everything related to Princess Elizabeth, as soon as it was revealed that she owned one, they became extremely popular. One newspaper printed a letter from the proud owner of Dookie's sister, while another reporter gave readers a detailed description of the dog and prophesied that, one day, they would be regarded with appreciation. 'And the enlightened public will no longer cast aspersions on his family tree.'

It would seem that Dookie himself often cast aspersions on his own family tree, because he was a bad-tempered pup who bit just about anyone who annoyed him. Governess Marion 'Crawfie' Crawford was one of his victims, and visitor to the palace Lord Lothian was another. The latter brushed aside any sympathy, and assured everyone that it didn't even hurt. 'All the same, he bled all over the floor,' Princess Elizabeth said.

6

The Little House with the Straw Roof

Most children enjoy playing house, but very often that includes hanging out in a creaky old wooden structure at the bottom of the garden, or under some strategically placed sheets set up in their bedrooms. However, in 1932, Princess Elizabeth became the envy of many children when she received not just a playhouse, but a miniature, liveable cottage.

The house was the idea of the lord mayor of Cardiff, and it was designed by architect Edmund Charles Morgan Willmott. Once plans were approved, construction began in 1931, as a secret gift from the Welsh people for the Princess's sixth birthday in April 1932. 'It is in no sense a doll's house,' one organiser said. 'It will be two-fifths of the size of an ordinary house. Small children will be able to move about comfortably in it, but it will be their domain entirely, for grown-ups will not even be able to get through the door.'

That wasn't strictly true because adults could just about fit inside, but it was certainly a squeeze. Built on a scale adapted for a six-year-old child, the home was fully habitable, 22 feet wide and 15 feet high. It was built of timber, with a thatched roof, and included a kitchen, dining room/living room, bedroom and bathroom, with a white hall and staircase leading up to a landing.

THE LITTLE HOUSE WITH THE STRAW ROOF

As if that wasn't fabulous enough, it included gas, electricity and water, and there would be a working bath, sink, telephone, fridge, cooker and boiler. The living room was panelled in white with an oak floor, with reproductions of old Welsh furniture, and a portrait of Princess Elizabeth's mother was displayed in the living room. The house was then given a Welsh name, Y Bwthyn Bach – meaning 'The Little Cottage' or 'The Little House with the Straw Roof'.

Before Princess Elizabeth received the house, it was first displayed at the Ideal Home and Building Exhibition in Cardiff to raise money for charity. It was then shown to the Duke and Duchess of York during a two-day visit to Wales in March 1932. The Duke thanked the lord mayor of Cardiff and then made a speech: 'We gladly accept it on behalf of our little daughter, to whom it will give the most intense pleasure. Indeed, it is difficult to find words in which to express our feelings. I cannot imagine any more delightful or interesting model for a child than "The Little House with the Straw Roof".' The Duchess herself turned on and off the taps and the light, and used the telephone. 'I could play in it for ever myself,' she said.

While everyone was excited about the gift, one reporter from the *Yorkshire Post* worried that certain dangers may arise, such as falling down the stairs, or electrocution from the lights. There was also the concern that it might catch fire, and the occupants would not be able to escape through the tiny doors. This observation proved valid, because while being transported from Cardiff to London on 21 March 1932, the house mysteriously caught fire.

An AA scout travelling with the steam wagon was first to see the flames, and he and the driver pulled over and tried to put it out, but the fire was too strong. While they struggled, villagers ran down the hills and, together with a policeman, formed a chain and collected buckets of water from the river. Unfortunately, it was a losing battle, and when the fire brigade arrived, the thatch and walls were well alight and the house was destroyed. The lord mayor was devastated, and his secretary told reporters, 'Everyone in Cardiff is terribly sorry that this has happened. The house was insured for £1250, but that, of course, is not the point.'

The destruction caused great concern in the newspapers, with the *Portsmouth Evening News* telling readers: 'One needs to be a child to understand what a disaster of this kind means to a little girl. Though I have no doubt the loss will be made up to her in some way or other, it will never be quite the same thing.'

Thankfully for Princess Elizabeth, she knew nothing about the house or the destruction, and the remains were taken to London and completely rebuilt. The cottage was then placed in a spot among the roses in the grounds of Royal Lodge in Windsor, and on her birthday, a delighted Princess Elizabeth was finally given the key and ran happily to her new 'home'.

It seemed as though the whole of the United Kingdom was fascinated by the house, and members of the Disabled Ex-servicemen's Handicraft Association wrote to Princess Elizabeth to ask if she would like a handmade woollen rug. In response they received a letter from Lady Helen Graham: 'The Duchess of York desires me to say that she is much touched by the desire of the disabled ex-service men. It will give her Royal Highness much pleasure to accept the kind offer. The rug will be much appreciated by Princess Elizabeth in her little house.'

A picture of Princess Elizabeth in the garden of her playhouse was even displayed at St George's Road Boy's School in Wallasey, where one boy – seven-year-old Derek Griffith – was so transfixed that he sent a letter about it to the 'Auntie Muriel's Treasure Chest' column at the *Liverpool Echo*. 'She is a very pretty little girl, and loves the garden and her house very much,' he wrote. 'She has golden hair and a white dress in the picture.'

Princess Elizabeth and her sister Princess Margaret Rose spent many happy hours playing in the cottage, and when they became adults, their own children played there, too. It is still in the grounds of the Royal Lodge, Windsor, and in 2012 was refurbished under the careful eye of Princess Beatrice and, of course, the Queen herself.

In 1990 – to celebrate her ninetieth birthday – the Queen Mother took an ITN news crew to the house. Showing them the working kitchen through the window, she laughed. 'I've had the most awful meals here,' she said. 'But you have to eat them.'

7

The Quiet Before the Storm

For the first ten years of her life, Princess Elizabeth was a carefree girl who loved many of the things other children loved. There were afternoons of playing with her dog, or reading in the nursery, walks in the park, visits to the local sweet shop, and games with her sister in the garden. Of course, being a princess also meant that she sometimes enjoyed the finer things, such as shopping trips with her mother or grandmother, visits to exhibitions, horse shows and museums, being a bridesmaid at a society wedding, garden parties, driving her toy motor around the Windsor Castle grounds, and the occasional appearance on the Buckingham Palace balcony.

Then there were the clothes. While most children only dressed in their finest outfits for trips to church on Sunday, Princess Elizabeth enjoyed a host of delicate gowns, riding wear, flowered cotton frocks, kilts and matching hats. There was even a sapphire-blue velvet cloak with a hood, which the Princess loved to wear to parties. The Duchess loved spoiling her daughter. One day while visiting the British Industries Fair at Olympia with Queen Mary and the Duke of York, the Duchess spied a children's pale blue crêpe de Chine bag, with a mirror inside. 'I must have that for Elizabeth,' she said, and she bought it, along with a large rocking horse and a wagon for gardening. The items were immediately packaged up and sent straight to 145 Piccadilly.

When it came to schooling, the princesses had lessons at home under the supervision of their governess, Marion 'Crawfie' Crawford. Subjects included reading, writing and arithmetic, and Princess Elizabeth was quite accomplished in French. She was also prone to a tantrum or two occasionally, such as the day when she became bored during French class, picked up the large inkpot, and placed it upside down on her head. 'She sat there with ink trickling down her face and slowly dyeing her golden curls,' Marion Crawford later wrote.

The Duchess took great interest in her daughters' education, and frequently called into the nursery. Together, the princesses would bellow out nursery rhymes while the Duchess played the piano, and then dance and practise military marches while records played on the gramophone – a present from the King. When weather permitted, the girls would leave the schoolroom and practise gardening, or ride on their ponies.

Princess Elizabeth's grandfather King George V was rarely in good health during her childhood but, even so, Elizabeth spent much time with him and Queen Mary. These visits included staying with them at various locations, including a time at Craigweil House, near Bognor Regis, while the King was recovering from septicaemia. There, she had tea parties with the children of the Duchess of Rutland, and played in a sandpit that Queen Mary had arranged to be built and filled with sand from the beach.

Birthdays were always special, and on her sixth, as well as being presented with the key to her playhouse, the Princess received a new pony from the King, and a gold and black bicycle from the British Cycle and Motor-Cycle Manufacturers and Traders Union. Inside the crate that housed the new bike was a letter from Jean Smith, the daughter of Major F. Walker Smith, president of the union. 'I am ten,' the girl wrote, 'and I often ride a bicycle. My Daddy taught me to ride my bicycle, and I hope you will soon learn to ride this one with your Nanny in the big Park at Windsor . . .'

Elizabeth's outings with her parents were always a fun treat. In 1934, the family turned heads when they visited a circus at Olympia. It was the first time Elizabeth had ever been to a big top, and wearing her red coat and matching hat, the child took a long time inspecting the horses before taking her seat to watch the performance. The visit was a secret one, but it took only moments for other audience members to recognise the royal family in the stand. When clown Whimsical Walker gave her a 'red hot' poker to hold, the crowd roared their amusement. A reporter from the *Western Mail* recounted that the Princess was not perturbed by the attention. Instead, the emotion of the audience 'greatly pleased the little Princess. Then she settled down to the performance and from first to last maintained a keen interest.'

The public maintained a fascination with the Princess throughout her childhood, and this was fed by the media, who were always keen to talk about her. 'The people, too, cannot help being interested in the life of so attractive and bonny a little girl,' expressed one reporter, on the occasion of the Princess's eighth birthday. Little did anyone know that, a couple of years later, her entire life would change for good.

8

The Heavy Burden of Responsibility

'The King is Dead! Long Live the King!' So said almost every newspaper in the land when it was announced that George V had passed away. The King had been unwell since Christmas Day 1935, almost immediately after his broadcast to the nation. However, it wasn't until just days before his death that the country discovered that he wasn't well, although the official line was that he had a cold and was to remain at Sandringham House during his recovery.

Questions were asked, and a further bulletin was released to say that he was actually suffering from bronchial catarrh and heart weakness. His health rapidly declined, and he passed away on 20 January 1936. At Sandringham at the time of the King's death were the Prince of Wales, the Duke of York, the Duke of Kent and the Princess Royal, who had all been summoned to pay their final respects. Now, with the announcement that King George V had passed away, his son was to take over as Edward VIII: 'God save our King – Long may he reign over us,' screamed the newspaper headlines.

As the Prince of Wales, Edward was an idol to many, and more popular than most monarchs had ever been. With his film-star looks and favourable personality, he spoke his mind, was interested in those less fortunate than himself, insisted on always being told the truth, was determined, and fiercely democratic. 'He has shared the sorrows and joys of the nation in war and in peace,' one newspaper wrote. 'He is loved as a comrade; he is loved as a Prince among men.' Now, with the death of his father, Edward was to be king. Not only that, but a bachelor king, and if he stayed that way, he'd be the first since William II took to the throne in 1087.

While the country wondered if the new king would marry and have an heir or two, Edward had already fallen in love with Wallis Simpson, an American woman who although now going through a divorce, was married when the couple met. Already known to the family (though George V was said to be outraged by the relationship), it was impossible for Simpson to be queen. In fact, the very idea caused a constitutional crisis when Edward refused to conduct the affair in secret, and instead told politicians that he intended to marry the woman. When the King would not let the idea go, statesman Stanley Baldwin brought up in parliament the prospect of the monarch marrying a divorcee, and it was dismissed immediately.

Initially, British newspapers were quiet about the relationship, but rumours of the affair bubbled away overseas. If those foreign magazines arrived in the UK, the offending pages were carefully removed for fear that the British people would find out exactly what was going on. This resulted in only a handful of people knowing what was being said about the new king.

The media carried on being muzzled until Mrs Simpson's divorce went to court, and a bizarre request ended up in the daily papers: 'The Associated Press requests all members to refrain from publishing the details of the case of Simpson v Simpson, which is due for the divorce side of the Courts shortly.' Sharp-eyed journalists noticed the announcement, and one Dublin correspondent received word from a London friend that the King was planning to marry a 'commoner', his choice possibly 'a middle-aged American brunette named Mrs Wallis Simpson'.

THE HEAVY BURDEN OF RESPONSIBILITY

The man went on to say that Simpson had been part of Edward's friend circle since he was still the Prince of Wales, and had recently accompanied him on a yachting cruise. Most telling was a quip that when the King entertained Simpson at Balmoral Castle, Queen Mary left as soon as the woman arrived.

By December 1936, the story had been ripped wide open; it was the headline in many British newspapers, and the topic of conversation around most – if not all – British dinner tables. When writer and suffragette Dr Maude Royden made a speech at the Guildhouse in London, she took the opportunity to praise the King for his straightforwardness and courage in challenging politicians. 'I ask everyone,' she said, 'to pray for The King and, also, not to forget the woman he loves, who needs your prayers.'

The government was less sympathetic. When the idea of marriage had been dismissed, Edward VIII was presented with three choices: to finish the relationship with Mrs Simpson; to go against the wishes of his government (who would be forced to resign); or to abdicate. The newspapers were not privy to the very private nature of the conversations between the two sectors, but they were not about to let the matter lie.

As a result, a statement was released from Downing Street, declaring that any suggestion of the government giving formal advice to the King was without foundation. 'It is emphasised that there has never been any clash between the Government and The King, the position never having approached such a point.' The statement also added that 'a major crisis is not anticipated'. The country didn't believe a word of it.

Sure enough, on 10 December 1936, Edward VIII made a broadcast to the nation, during which he announced his abdication. Noting that he had never wanted to withhold anything from the country, Edward told his subjects that, until that moment, it had not been possible for him to say anything, but he had now discharged his last duty as king and emperor. He had found it, he said, 'impossible to carry the heavy burden of responsibility, and to discharge my duties as King . . . without the help and support of the woman I love.'

Edward VIII would step down from the throne immediately. His brother, the Duke of York – to whom Edward pledged his allegiance – would now become king, and his niece, Princess Elizabeth, the heir presumptive to the throne.

9

Times Are Changing

The moment the Duke of York became King George VI, things changed rather dramatically for the two princesses. They moved into Buckingham Palace, and their parents became busier than they had ever been before. On advice from Queen Mary, the two girls had always had as much of a 'normal' childhood as they could manage, given that they were in the royal spotlight. 'After all,' said Queen Mary, 'childhood is short enough without deliberately reducing it, or allowing it to be overshadowed by future greatness.' Her main concern during the early years was making sure that the two girls kept in good health, away from public duties.

Now, however, circumstances had changed, and the princesses found themselves being seen in public more often, and even discussed in parliament. On 29 January 1937, the home secretary, Sir John Simon, was asked if he would consider introducing legislation to make it clear that, years from now, Princess Elizabeth would not have to share the throne with her sister, Margaret. Sir John assured MPs that there was no reason to change any laws or introduce any legislation. 'There is no doubt that in present circumstances her Royal Highness Princess Elizabeth would succeed to the throne as sole heir.'

Later in the year, there was another parliamentary discussion, this time about what kind of annuity she should receive, as heir to the throne. It was recommended that £6,000 seemed reasonable, and would likely increase to £15,000 when she reached the age of twenty-one, providing a son was not born to King George VI and Queen Elizabeth – the former Duke and Duchess of York.

The princesses were still schooled at home by governess Marion Crawford, but now Princess Elizabeth was aware that one day she might be queen and, in that regard, was educated on the subject of dedicating her service to the empire. There were all the regular subjects of maths, English, Bible studies, history and geography, but as well as those, there were studies into constitutional history, constitutional law and current affairs. On top of those was training in elocution, deportment and etiquette, all designed to help with her unusual position in society. There were also ballet, music and swimming lessons, all of which Princess Elizabeth enjoyed. '[I can] do six strokes without having to touch the bottom,' the ten-year-old said.

Inquisitive and eager to know all she could, the Princess soaked the information up. She even took many of her lessons standing up, in order to prepare herself for the years of speeches, ceremonies and events to come. In public Princess Elizabeth could be seen correcting her sister, and while Margaret was often seen gazing up to the sky, for the most part, Elizabeth seemed quite content to watch what was going on around her. As the child headed towards her eleventh birthday, it was evident that she was taking her royal duties most seriously.

One witness to the Princess's regal nature was Tom Smith, the station master at Euston Station, London. He had known the royals for many years, and had often spoken to them when coming in and out of the station. On the eve of his retirement, he revealed that, 'Princess Elizabeth is always a little chatterbox when she is going away by train or arriving home. She wants to know about everything, and it is a delight to satisfy her inquisitiveness.'

Another admirer was the Dean of Norwich. Talking of the royal family at the annual dinner of Norwich Cathedral Ex-Choristers' Guild, he spoke of his gratitude that the new king and queen were now in charge of the country. He also spoke animatedly about meeting Princess Elizabeth when she was five years old, while he was preaching at Sandringham. According to the Dean, the young girl was particularly interested in two parts of his sermon. He would not go into detail about what those pieces were, but did say that they discussed them afterwards. 'That shows her precocity,' he said. 'I do feel this, that if she comes to the Throne, we shall have a person quite equal in ability to her great predecessor, Queen Elizabeth of days gone by.'

10

The Coronation... 'a Pageant, a Show'

In the months leading up to King George VI's coronation, businesses across the country looked at ways to earn money from it. There were the usual cups, plates, flags, coins and bunting, but along with them there were also boxes of toffee, portraits of the young princesses, special wine, souvenir programmes, coronation-themed fabrics, engraved spoons, and even Princess Elizabeth and Princess Margaret dolls.

While visiting the British Industries Fair at Olympia, London, the King and Queen Elizabeth were shown the dolls, and revealed that they had already bought the Elizabeth one. The King then set his eye on some cards depicting a coronation procession. The idea, the stallholder said, was to hope that people would send them out the same way they sent Christmas greetings. 'That's a good idea,' the King said. 'Please send some of each to me at Buckingham Palace.'

Most market traders and shops draped their premises in a variety of decorations, not only to celebrate the coronation, but also to entice customers. Across the country, royalists bought traditional red, white and blue ornaments to hang around their homes. Some families couldn't get enough of the coronation joy, and one household in Thornton Heath, south London, boasted flags over the entire front of the home, and then covered their porch and their garden path, too.

THE CORONATION . . . 'A PAGEANT, A SHOW'

Gardeners strung lights around trees and bushes, and the fountains in some park ponds were illuminated, and featured coloured glass swans and waterlilies.

Parties, teas, sports, competitions, cabarets, concerts, balls and thanksgiving services were held all over the United Kingdom, and day and overnight trips to London were planned and booked. Some people, however, thought that the celebrations had gone a bit too far. One unnamed contributor sent his thoughts to the *Falkirk Herald*, prophesying that some people might feel that 'the Coronation could have taken place with less stirring of excitement. They are disturbed by evidence here and there of the obtrusion of the commercial spirit.'

It was also pointed out by some that while the coronation attracted lavish dinners, dances and celebrations around the country, there were some who could afford nothing at all. Writing to the editor of the *Worthing Gazette,* John M. Carrington put forward his idea to provide a banquet to those who were living on the streets. 'Cannot we just try and bring a little ray of light into their lives at Coronation time?' he wrote. 'The wider our area of sympathy the greater the reflex blessings upon ourselves.'

The coronation itself took place at Westminster Abbey on 12 May 1937, and was attended by ambassadors, princes, prime ministers, statesmen, clergymen and representatives of every nation. All eyes were on Princess Elizabeth when she arrived at the abbey, smiling widely as she greeted Earl Marshal the Duke of Norfolk. She had, said one reporter, 'a dignity and charm which had no trace of self-consciousness'. When she took her seat in the royal box, next to her sister Margaret Rose, her mother (waiting to be crowned) and her grandmother, the young princess was observed staring wide-eyed at the spectacle going on near her.

The ceremony took the same course as every other coronation before it, and included the recognition, whereupon the King must be accepted by the people, the oath, where the King promised to govern, and then the anointing with holy oil. After ceremonies delivering the Orb, the Ring, the Sceptre and the Rod of Equity, the King was crowned.

'God crown you with a crown of glory and righteousness,' the Archbishop of Canterbury recited as he placed St Edward's Crown on the King's head. When the prayer was finished, trumpets were sounded and the words 'God save King George' echoed around the abbey. Queen Elizabeth was then crowned in a less elaborate ceremony by the Archbishop of York.

Later that day, the King and Queen Elizabeth sent a message to the lord mayor of London. In it, they thanked the mayor and the citizens of London for their sentiments. 'Please convey to them our heartfelt thanks both for their good wishes and for the wonderful reception given to us in London on our Coronation Day,' it said.

After the coronation, there were a few negative views. Yes, the public had enjoyed the street parties, the balls and the spectacle of waving to the horse-drawn carriages as they trotted past on the street, but some of those who sat in the abbey from 8 a.m. until 3 p.m. saw it somewhat differently. One verbal critic was the Rev. J. G. Moelwyn Hughes, of Birkenhead. He told the General Assembly of the Presbyterian Church of Wales that the ceremony was decidedly wooden.

'There was only empty, ritualistic pomp, and the following of old, hoary-headed traditions in the Abbey,' he said. 'It was a pageant, a show, and an undevout emptiness.' He went on to say that he and his fellow clergymen were astounded by the extravagance, and by the end of it, he was rather glad to leave.

11

Camp Fires and Map Reading at Buckingham Palace

In 1937, Princess Elizabeth wished to join the Girl Guides. While she was keen to join any group, it was decided that for security reasons, it would not be a great idea for her to join a chapter outside the palace. Instead, an idea was put forward that the Westminster Division could become the parent of a palace-based Girl Guide group, and thus the 1st Buckingham Palace Guides company was born. The formation was overseen by the president of the Girl Guides Association, who just happened to be the Princess's aunt, Mary, the Princess Royal.

The membership was comprised of the friends, cousins and daughters of those already close to the royal family, and Princess Margaret as a Brownie in the Leprechaun Six. The fact that these girls were all considered to be privileged – and the princesses especially so – raised eyebrows, particularly as one part of the Guide Law requires the children to be 'a good friend and a sister to all Guides'. Some wondered how this could be possible, when the other girls in the group would be working with royals and curtsying to the princesses.

This was not considered a problem to secretary of the association, the Hon. Mrs C. Tufton. 'They will join just as ordinary children,' she said. This was, however, something of an exaggeration, considering that most of the girls were from the aristocracy. It was, noted one newspaper, 'the most exclusive little group of girls in the world'.

That aside, the Princess Elizabeth Company, or the Kingfisher Patrol as it was also known, was a successful one. Queen Elizabeth herself took a keen interest in everything the girls were doing, attended a dedication ceremony in the palace chapel, and gifted two flags – a Union Jack and a troop flag.

The Guides would meet in Buckingham Palace every Wednesday at 5 p.m. (though location was transferred to Windsor during the Second World War), and after paying their subscription, they would then play games, do tests, learn first aid, read maps, put together Christmas stockings for needy children, and take part in outdoor activities whenever the cold London weather allowed. Singing around the campfire was a popular activity, and this continued even when the weather forced the girls back to the schoolroom, where the fireplace would suffice. The idea behind every activity was that for all their privilege, the princesses would learn everything that other Guides learned, including sticking to the strict rules.

The operation was overseen by Guide leader Violet Synge, who would travel to the palace for every meeting, and inspect the uniforms in the headquarters of the princesses' schoolroom. Of course, Princess Elizabeth was keen to keep everyone in check, too, and could often be seen telling her friends where they had gone wrong with their uniforms or other equipment. She was also instrumental in running the company meetings, where minutes and notes would always be kept. This was an activity that the younger Princess Margaret desperately wanted to be involved in, but was deemed too young to attend.

So seriously did the girls take their Guide duties that even when on holiday at Sandringham or Balmoral they could be seen wearing their uniforms and practising their marches around the grounds. During one trip to Balmoral, Princess Elizabeth saw the opportunity to gain more knowledge about flowers by identifying them in the woods around the castle, and recording them intricately in her logbook. The girls also collected sphagnum moss, which at the time was used as emergency surgical dressing, thanks to its absorbent qualities.

In 1938, the princesses were thrilled when the King and Queen gave permission for the Buckingham Palace Guides to camp in Windsor Park. There, Princess Elizabeth took part in her fair share of duties, such as pitching tents and preparing meals. The troop also learned about lighting fires, woodcraft, nature lore, signalling and tying knots, while all the time remembering the Guide promise . . . 'To do my duty to God and The King. To help other people at all times. To obey the Guide Law.' They also observed the Girl Guides' National Service, which involved one thousand girls marching past the royal family, as Princesses Elizabeth and Margaret stood to attention.

In 1940, Princess Elizabeth was thrilled to have a letter published in the *Girl Guide Bulletin*. Written from Balmoral in 1939, the Princess explained that she and Margaret had gone to a meeting of the Balmoral Company. It was, she said, 'great fun, and we taught them some of our games. They have five evacuees from Glasgow attached to them.' She also revealed that they had been knitting for the Red Cross and evacuees, before concluding, 'Please would you send me the details of the War Service Badge?'

Princess Elizabeth never forgot her time in the Girl Guides, and held them in high regard throughout her adult life. During a tour of Scotland in 1947, twenty-one-year-old Princess Elizabeth was told about Nellie Clapperton, a bedridden Girl Guide who was desperate to catch a glimpse of Princess Elizabeth as she came past the house. Nellie's family had set up a series of mirrors so that she could watch the procession from her bedroom, and as the car drew parallel, Princess Elizabeth jumped out, stood before a mirror, and gave the Girl Guide salute. 'It was very nice of Princess Elizabeth,' Nellie said afterwards. 'She has proved a true Guide.'

In 1953, Princess Elizabeth (now the Queen) became the Girl Guides' patron, a position she held until her death in 2022.

12

Accidents, Illness and a Trip to the Zoo

In spring 1939, the King and Queen Elizabeth embarked on a mammoth seven-week tour of Canada, leaving their daughters in the care of their nannies, family and friends at home. To a child, the idea of not seeing their parents for two months is an abysmal one, but the two sisters kept themselves busy at Buckingham Palace and Windsor Castle.

One hobby that began at this time went on to become a lifelong pleasure. For her thirteenth birthday that year, Princess Elizabeth received a cine-camera, and while her parents were away, she practised taking clips of her sister and their corgis, and made plans to maybe one day produce a film for and about all of her friends.

One event that happened while the King and Queen were away could have easily become the plot of an adventure film, when Queen Mary got into a road traffic accident, days before her seventy-second birthday. While travelling in Putney, south-west London, her car was involved in a collision with a lorry and overturned. She was rushed back to her home, Marlborough House, where she was treated for a painful eye injury, bruising and shock. Princess Elizabeth immediately wrote a get-well-soon letter to her grandmother, while all around the house, crowds gathered to sign the visitors' book and try to catch a glimpse of the poorly queen.

Reporters, meanwhile, went in search of the lorry driver who had caused Queen Mary's car to overturn, but were met instead by his rather disgruntled boss, Mr H. W. R. Winter. Assuring the journalists that his employee wanted to avoid all publicity and would not wish his name to appear in the papers, he added, 'Apart from the fact that he was a little late this morning, he was on duty as usual. He is upset at having been involved in such an accident.'

Soon after, it was Princess Elizabeth who caused concern in the press, when it was reported that she would miss the annual Trooping the Colour parade because of a cold. While her sister and the still-recovering Queen Mary went out to watch, the Princess was kept inside Buckingham Palace as a precaution. This caused such a sensation in the newspapers that a statement of her recovery was hastily prepared and printed.

While life at home without their parents was marred somewhat by illness, the girls kept themselves busy with schoolwork, Girl Guide activities, riding and going on outings to museums, art galleries and even the Royal Mint to see a new coin being made. Perhaps the most famous of these trips was when they went to London Zoo first in May, and then again in June, shortly before their parents arrived home from the tour.

Accompanied by the wife of the foreign secretary, Lady Halifax, lady-in-waiting Mrs Geoffrey Bowlby and several friends, they arrived in the early morning and were greeted by Professor Julian Huxley, who was to act as tour guide for the visit. Of course, being royalty, the tour was not much like the ones a regular visitor would take, and the girls were able to go into many of the enclosures and see the animals up close. This included visiting a baby panda called Ming, who – with her rather unusual best friend Rex the Alsatian – had been a recent crowd-pleaser at the zoo.

Another stop was the sea lions, where Princess Margaret clapped and laughed as one of the animals continuously jumped off a rock in order to catch his breakfast. The older, more studious sister, Princess Elizabeth, wanted to know more about the animals' behaviour and lifestyle, asking the professor how they swam, and watching intently as he demonstrated.

However, older or not, Princess Elizabeth was happy to join in when both girls were offered the opportunity of feeding the sea lions themselves. This was not the only time the girls were given the chance to feed one of the animals, and Princess Elizabeth saw to it that they both bottle-fed baby antelopes, while Princess Margaret was butted by a rather impatient lamb.

Perhaps the most popular of the animals were, unsurprisingly, the ponies and donkeys in the children's corner. However, Princess Margaret was unimpressed by the penguins, particularly one called George, who was moulting. Photographs taken during one of the zoo visits show the two girls standing next to the birds; Princess Elizabeth looking in awe, while Margaret squirms as a penguin marches up to her leg.

Finally, on 22 June 1939, the King and Queen returned from their long trip. The two princesses left Waterloo Station for Portsmouth and, as their parents' ship approached, were taken out by a military boat to be reunited. While Princess Margaret was heard shouting an excited 'Hello,' her sister was seen kissing her father, and telling him all about their 'lively time' on the boat.

'One could imagine their excitement,' wrote one reporter, 'for they were not only reunited with their father and mother but they had had their first voyage on a destroyer.'

13

'The King Will Never Leave'

When war broke out in 1939, there was much talk about where the royal family should live for their own safety. Some imagined that it would be best for everyone if the princesses moved to Canada, while others pondered what would happen if they stayed in London. As dangerous as it was, the King was against moving out of England, and that ruled out anyone else going, either. 'The children won't go without me,' Queen Elizabeth said. 'I won't leave the King. And the King will never leave.'

In the end, the couple remained for the most part in London, while their daughters moved to Windsor Castle, which, while still considered a bomb risk, was far safer than the capital city. Indeed, Buckingham Palace was to suffer nine bombing attacks during the Second World War. The first of these was on 9 September 1940, when a delayed-action device was dropped into the garden. The device buried itself in the ground and, when discovered, was found to have landed in such a way that it could not be retrieved. Initially, nobody knew that it was a timebomb, and the King went about his business, even spending time in his sitting room, with the bomb just feet away from him.

Thankfully, the north-west part of the palace was evacuated before the bomb finally exploded on 10 September. The force demolished a wall, shattered windows (including some in the private apartments), damaged the swimming pool, and broke huge columns into pieces. This sent debris over the building and smashed the glass roof of the entrance to the Grand Hall. Another one-hundredweight piece of debris even lodged itself on the palace roof. The diving tower of the swimming pool was twisted and thrown into the water, and the roof above was caved in. In the garden, where so many parties had been held, glass was strewn all over the neatly cut lawn, while inside, glass splinters fell into the picture gallery.

'It went off like a 16-inch shell,' one witness told reporters. 'It was a really terrific bang. One of the pieces of masonry which fell in the quadrangle must have weighed a hundredweight.'

The King, Queen Elizabeth and the princesses were at Windsor Castle when the bomb exploded, but the couple later returned to London for lunch with Prime Minister Winston Churchill, and to survey the damage. Stunned but stoic, the couple wandered around the garden in their formalwear, picked up pieces of metal, clambered over piles of rubbish, talked to Air Raid Precautions staff, and pointed out the various damaged areas.

When the couple made a trip to bombed south-east London shortly after, both the King and Queen were visibly emotional. 'We think you are all wonderfully brave and we are very proud of you,' the Queen told a group of residents who had seen their homes destroyed, and families injured or killed. 'And we are proud of you,' an elderly lady replied.

Having their home bombed was a new experience for the King and Queen, and they added another one during their tour of south-east London. While they were talking to residents, the air-raid siren went off, and the couple found themselves in a shelter beneath a police station, sharing space with officers, court officials and various workers. There they sipped tea, spoke to their companions and, after given the all-clear, the King seemed hesitant to leave.

Later, a correspondent for the *Liverpool Daily Post* described how Queen Elizabeth had made no attempt to hide the emotion felt while touring the damaged community. 'There was something sisterly in the way she expressed her sympathy with bereft women who were brought to her,' wrote the correspondent. 'I have never seen her so motherly.' Indeed, Queen Elizabeth was seen consoling many of the people she met that day, and later described the visit as uplifting.

Meanwhile, German officials in Berlin denied that the palace was bombed deliberately: 'It is entirely possible, however, that a stray bomb may have fallen there.' Ending the statement was a rather ominous comment, boasting the fact that if they had really wanted to bomb the palace, 'it would have been a different matter from just one stray bomb'. The King and Queen Elizabeth would discover the truth of that, several days later.

14

'I Am Glad We Have Been Bombed'

The second bombing of Buckingham Palace came on the morning of 13 September 1940, when the King and Queen Elizabeth were in their private apartments. This time it was a direct strike, with bombs falling on to the palace chapel, the quadrangle (which had already been damaged from the bombing several days before) and the road outside the palace gates.

The bomb in the quadrangle caused a 10-foot-high fountain of water to shoot into the air, penetrating windows and ruining carpets, while the one just outside the gates caused a fire. Another timebomb fell just next to the Queen Victoria Memorial, and exploded the next day. Thankfully, it caused minimal damage, due to the police and the military placing sandbags around the bomb to minimise the explosion.

Queen Elizabeth later wrote to her mother-in-law, Queen Mary, about her experience of the bombing. She described how quickly everything had happened, and how the couple only had time to look at each other before the bomb hit and sent smoke and debris flying up from the quadrangle. They then rushed into the corridor, where they sheltered with two members of staff. When it was deemed safe to do so, the couple inspected the damage and spoke to their staff, before leaving for another tour of war-torn London.

A man walking outside the palace at the time had seen the strike, and later gave his story to reporters. 'I heard the plane coming down,' he said, 'and for a moment thought there must be something wrong with it . . . Then I heard several bangs – one of them very loud.'

While most of the damage could be repaired, the palace chapel was wrecked. It had held great sentimental value to the family, being a favourite place of Queen Victoria and the venue for many christenings, including those of Princess Elizabeth and Princess Margaret. When palace superintendent Mr T. D. Williams showed reporters the extent of the damage, they were shocked. Pillars were destroyed, the altar was completely shattered and the floor was caved in, causing tonnes of debris to be hurled into the basement. Three plumbers who had been working in the basement at the time, along with another who tried to rescue them, were injured, and one of the men sadly died just days later.

The lectern was buried upside down, but the family bible that had once sat on top of it was said to be quite undamaged, as were several tapestries, an organ, pews and electric candles. Nevertheless, 'It is an amazing scene of devastation,' wrote one reporter.

Along with the physical devastation caused by the bombs came the rodents. Huge rats, whose homes had been disturbed, infested the garden, terrifying Queen Elizabeth, though palace staff seemed to enjoy using them as target practice.

When Winston Churchill sent a wire to congratulate Their Majesties on escaping from the bombing, the King replied to give thanks. 'Like so many other people,' he wrote, 'we have now had a personal experience of German barbarity, which only strengthens the resolution of all of us to fight through to final victory.'

The bombing of Buckingham Palace was a stark reminder that nobody was safe from the tragedy of war. However, it was precisely because of this that the King and Queen Elizabeth somehow became more human to their subjects. They could relate to, and empathise with – in some ways at least – what others were going through.

'I AM GLAD WE HAVE BEEN BOMBED'

'We are impressed by the calm serenity of both,' wrote the *Walsall Observer*. 'They are in that akin to the humble folk of the East End of London who have had such a gruelling time.' Reporters who had rushed to the scene noted that the couple seemed quite unshaken as they left Buckingham Palace that day. However, while they may have been calm and serene on the outside, internally, both the King and Queen Elizabeth were traumatised by what they had witnessed, and the King wrote in his diary that he was unable to function properly for days after the event.

A couple of days later, the palace was targeted again. 'The German plane was flying very low when it dropped its bombs,' said one eyewitness. 'It appeared to be coming from the north.' Thankfully, there were no casualties this time, and minimal damage, which included a hole in the ceiling of the tapestry room, also used as the Queen's drawing room. Other devices caused small fires on the back lawn, which were put out quickly by palace staff.

The news of the bombings made headlines around the world, including the United States, where one reporter – Raymond Gram Swing – described the attack as a 'great psychological blunder . . . Now they all have shared this ordeal, King, Queen and everyone else. They are one.'

The family agreed. 'I am glad that we have been bombed,' said Queen Elizabeth. 'It makes me feel I can look the East End in the face.'

15

'All Will Be Well'

In 1935, a rumour had circulated that Princess Elizabeth would make her first radio broadcast, in celebration of the King's Silver Jubilee. Everyone at the BBC *Children's Hour* was enthusiastic about the prospect, and a representative told reporters, 'We should very much welcome the opportunity of broadcasting the voice of the Princess to the children. It is certainly a suggestion most welcome to the BBC.'

While the possibility of hearing Elizabeth on the radio was met with excitement, her first broadcast actually came four years later, in 1940. Still living at Windsor, and often away from her parents, Princess Elizabeth could empathise with those children living as evacuees away from home. This made her the perfect person to launch a new BBC weekly feature for children who had been evacuated to the States and Canada. The King and Queen Elizabeth agreed, and after weeks of talks, rehearsals and writing the speech, the Princess was ready to broadcast from Windsor Castle.

On 13 October 1940, Elizabeth sat at a desk used frequently by her father the King. Her parents stood nearby, and Margaret was by her side, as she waited for the red on-air light to flash. When it did,

'ALL WILL BE WELL'

she dived straight into her speech, as though her whole life had been leading up to that moment.

Princess Elizabeth began by recognising that thousands of children had left their homes and their parents. 'My sister, Margaret Rose, and I feel so much for you,' she said, 'as we know from experience what it means to be away from those we love most of all.' She continued by expressing how much the children at home thought about those who were away, and encouraged them not to forget about the old country. Before ending the speech, Elizabeth told listeners that all the children still in Britain were cheerful and courageous, and doing all they could to assist in the war effort. 'All will be well,' she said, before encouraging her little sister Margaret to say goodnight. This surprised everyone, because her appearance had been a well-kept secret.

BBC officials standing in the next room were surprised and relieved by the Princess's ease in front of the microphone, and the reaction from both sides of the Atlantic was positive. 'She speaks just like the Queen,' some listeners decided, while parents claimed that their children cheered at the end of the broadcast. The manager of the Gould Foundation in New York was encouraged by the speech, telling a reporter that the British children in his care had come in from playing long before the speech was due to begin. He worried that the homesick children would cry at the sound of the Princess's voice, but was happy when they seemed encouraged. 'I thought myself this young British girl did beautifully,' he said.

Derek McCulloch – known as Uncle Mac on *Children's Hour* – had coached and then introduced the Princess. He deemed the speech as 'One of the most important days in the history of "Children's Hour"', while a New York reporter described it as 'One of the most effective broadcasts ever received from Britain'. Most agreed that it gave a message of hope to children both at home and abroad.

The following Saturday, 'Uncle Charlie' from the 'Children's Corner' newspaper column, shared his thoughts. 'You will agree, I am

THE QUEEN

sure, that the Princess showed no sign of nervousness,' he said, before adding that while she may have had some assistance with writing her speech, 'it was the way she gave the message that counted'.

16

All the World's a Stage

If Princess Elizabeth hadn't been born into the royal family, she might have found her way on to stage and screen. Her love for the theatre began at an early age, when she was taken there by her parents, and she never lost the joy of performing.

From her early childhood, the Princess was always thrilled to watch plays, performances and shows. In 1934, she attended her first pantomime with her mother. It was entitled *Queen of Hearts*, and Elizabeth was thrilled to spend time with the other three thousand children in attendance. Clapping her hands and singing along to songs such as 'Oh, We All Went up the Mountain', the Princess was excited when actor George Jackley pulled a funny face just for her, and then she whooped in delight when the Queen of Hearts showed off a special crown that sported traffic lights on the top. She was also seen at the Cambridge Theatre watching the children's play, *Ever So Long Ago*, and while at Glamis Castle she saw the Children's Theatre Company from Glasgow in *The Land of Make-Believe*.

These events were fun and full of revelry, but Princess Elizabeth wasn't just interested in watching comedy, singing and dancing. At age nine she even found a love of Shakespeare, when her parents took her to a three-hour extravaganza at Drury Lane. Watching from the royal box, the Princess was gripped by the scenes playing out below her, and when actor George Robey bumped into the scenery on exiting the stage, she was seen laughing uncontrollably. One scene that wasn't so funny, however, was the murder from *Othello*. Knowing that this would likely traumatise their young daughter, the Duke and Duchess took her home shortly before it was due to begin.

While Princess Elizabeth enjoyed watching shows and films – and counted Bette Davis and Gary Cooper among her favourite actors – she was never far away from performing, herself. She would study other people in the palace, and imitate them accordingly, and after a trip to the zoo began acting out the noises made by the sea lions at feeding time. When staying at Birkhall in Scotland, her favourite pastime was to meet the mailcart, and then pretend to be the postwoman, delivering letters and packages to her amused parents. She produced plays with the help of a toy theatre gifted to her by her grandmother, took dance and singing lessons, and played out all kinds of scenarios with her friend, Sonia Graham-Hodgson. While a guest at a birthday party for the granddaughter of the Earl and Countess of Shaftesbury, Elizabeth even entertained everyone by acting the part of magician's assistant to party entertainer Mr A. Hay Prestowe.

When they grew old enough, Princess Elizabeth and Princess Margaret took everything they had learned and turned it all into performances for friends, family and locals. During the Second World War, these shows were performed while living at Windsor Castle, and often involved local schoolchildren. The two princesses became famous for their productions, and would riffle through cupboards, dressing-up boxes and attics to find old clothes and sets. The shows were always popular, though sometimes for the wrong reasons, such as playing instruments badly or suffering the curtain coming down on their heads.

At Christmas 1941, the girls found a sedan chair previously owned by Queen Anne, and used it as the coach in *Cinderella*. The King and Queen watched in awe as Elizabeth played Prince Charming and Margaret played Cinderella. Other parts were performed by friends, and local children danced in a ballet section. Margaret entertained everyone by singing several solo numbers, and encouraged the audience to join in with the choruses. The King especially enjoyed the dancing, and congratulated everyone afterwards, before providing a tea party for all involved in the production.

In 1942, Princess Elizabeth played the lead role in *Sleeping Beauty*, given in aid of the Royal Household Wool Fund. The cast was made up of the two princesses, evacuees and members of the household, while the dresses and scenery were supervised by Queen Elizabeth, herself a big supporter of the theatre. It was a huge success.

During a performance of *Aladdin*, in 1943, the princesses enrolled the help of Windsor Castle estate employee Cyril Woods to play the Dame, the Guards band to play the music, and the eight-year-old Duke of Kent and his sister Princess Alexandra in supporting roles. Forty village children were called upon to sing and dance, while local schoolmaster Hubert Tanner produced and stage managed the whole show.

Princess Elizabeth played the title role, and wearing long trousers and a kimono shirt, made her entrance by popping out of a laundry basket. The King and Queen sat in the front row, and clapped as Elizabeth tap-danced and sang 'In My Arms', while Princess Margaret sang 'Three Little Maids from School' with two other little girls. The princesses had even prepared jokes that poked fun at the royal family, and went through several costume changes during the course of the show.

The princesses loved entertaining, and the next year they performed in *Old Mother Red Riding Boots*, a story they created with Hubert Tanner. Wearing elaborate costumes and real tiaras, they sang 'Swinging on a Star', and ballet-danced their way around the stage with local schoolchildren. Princess Elizabeth even dressed as a

Victorian bathing belle during one particular routine, while Margaret was praised for her broad cockney accent.

When the war ended in 1945, the princesses more or less hung up their stage shoes. However, the delight in performing would stay with Elizabeth forever, and many years later, she would return to her roots, with the help of James Bond and then Paddington Bear!

17

Princess 230873

On 21 September 1944, while in Scotland with her parents, Princess Elizabeth visited an Auxiliary Territorial Service Training Centre, in Dalkeith, near Edinburgh. While the visit made scant mention in the newspapers, it was an important one because the Princess was hoping to join the ATS herself.

The eighteen-year-old was already interested in playing a role in the war effort, and just the week before had travelled to the Assembly Hall, Edinburgh, in order to collect donations for the YMCA appeal fund for overseas and POW work. There she had met with 180 people, representing groups, organisations, districts and the auxiliary service, all of whom had travelled to the hall to hand over the contributions collected in their areas. In the months ahead, she would launch a battleship, visit the Household Cavalry with her parents, and broadcast a message to the children of Belgium, thanking them for sending Christmas presents to British children affected by the war.

'It is so very hard to part with one's toys,' she said. 'I know that from experience – but you will believe me when I say that, for that very reason, your presents are all the more valuable to us.'

This interest in the war effort wasn't new, as in February 1942, the King had appointed her as colonel of the Grenadier Guards. This was her first link with the services, and many wondered if it would prelude her entry into public life. Sure enough, on 21 April 1942 – her sixteenth birthday – she reviewed the Grenadier Guards during a special birthday parade at Windsor Castle. After reaching the royal dais with her parents and sister, Colonel J. A. Prescott marched up, saluted and then announced, 'The first or Grenadier Regiment of Foot Guards are ready for inspection by Her Royal Highness the Colonel.' This was a mammoth task for a teenager, and while reporters on-site wrote that she 'showed no sign of nervousness', it is more likely that Princess Elizabeth was just good at hiding it.

Four days later – with the approval of her father – the Princess went to a labour exchange in order to register for the government's Youth Service Scheme. Accompanied by her mother, she wore her Girl Guides uniform, and borrowed a pen from an official in order to fill out the registration card. The Princess had been keen to sign up since many of her friends were doing the same, and had a keen interest in service thanks partly to her ongoing association with the Girl Guides.

The Princess's need to do something practical in the war effort led to something of a disagreement between herself and her father. While he respected her ideas, the King was far more concerned with training the Princess to take part in royal activities and duties. The Princess was interested in both, but did not back down regarding her wish to be involved in the services. Her parents finally granted her permission to join the Auxiliary Territorial Service, though her admission was stalled for a couple of weeks due to a bout of mumps.

Finally, on 24 February 1945, Princess Elizabeth was given the number 230873, and then on 5 March 1945, an official announcement came from Buckingham Palace. It read: 'The King has granted to Her Royal Highness the Princess Elizabeth a commission with the honorary rank of second subaltern in the Auxiliary Territorial Service.'

At the time of the announcement, the Princess was already attending a course at a driving centre in the south of England, with a strict order from the King that she be treated no differently to any other student. There she learned how to drive and maintain a host of vehicles, including cars and lorries. Wearing overalls, the Princess was filmed working under the bonnet of one vehicle, while being watched by her parents and sister, who were visiting at the time.

On 15 April 1945, Princess Elizabeth completed her driving course and passed out as a fully qualified driver. The Princess later used her driving experience to teach Princess Margaret how to drive, too. Family and friends predicted that it would be a disaster and the two young women would end up arguing, but they never did. Princess Margaret later described Elizabeth as patient, before adding that she was a very good driver, and she was proud of her.

However, while Margaret may have been in awe of her sister, that didn't mean that she wasn't prone to jealousy. On first hearing the news that Princess Elizabeth would be joining the ATS, Princess Margaret desperately wanted to join, too. She later admitted to being frightfully annoyed that Elizabeth was allowed to join, while she herself was too young. 'I couldn't understand why the armed services didn't want the services of a girl of twelve,' she laughed. (She was actually fourteen years old at the time her sister joined the ATS, but the result was the same.)

When the time came for Princess Elizabeth to celebrate her nineteenth birthday on 21 April 1945, there was little fanfare due to the ongoing war. However, her popularity in the services was confirmed when she received telegrams and cards not only from the young women on her Auxiliary Territorial Service course, but also from the Grenadier Guards and the Girl Guides.

18

Conga at the Palace

On 8 May 1945, victory was declared in Europe, and the people of the United Kingdom took to the streets to celebrate. It had been a long six years of war, heartache, fear, despair and bravery, but now it was coming to an end, and the public came out in their millions, cheering, dancing, singing, shouting, climbing statues and balancing on moving vehicles. The war was not yet completely over – victory over Japan would not come until August – but for now, the war had ended in Europe, and everyone hoped that life could finally get back to some kind of normality, slowly but surely.

While Princess Elizabeth and Princess Margaret Rose had been living in Windsor during the war, now they returned to Buckingham Palace, where they – and thousands of bystanders – waited for Prime Minister Winston Churchill to give the broadcast to confirm that VE Day (Victory in Europe Day) had arrived. After what seemed like a lifetime, everyone got their wish, and Churchill addressed the nation to confirm that hostilities would officially end one minute after midnight, but that a ceasefire was already in place. 'Our gratitude to our splendid Allies goes forth,' he said, 'from all our hearts in this island and throughout the British Empire.'

CONGA AT THE PALACE

Loudspeakers broadcast the news to the thousands standing outside Buckingham Palace, and then the royal family, together with Winston Churchill, took to the balcony. There, they waved to the ecstatic crowds, and after Churchill had left, they continued to go in and out for about six hours. Later, Margaret remembered a tremendous relief that VE Day had arrived, while Elizabeth recalled that the joy they felt was profound. So, profound, in fact, that both princesses wanted desperately to go outside and party with the folk on the street. This wish grew when it became dark and the bright floodlights were turned on, shining into their eyes and preventing them from seeing exactly what was going on outside.

Allowing the princesses to leave the palace would not have been a decision that came easily to the protective King and Queen, but Princess Margaret later remembered it as being their idea in the first place. When they did run downstairs and out of the gates, they were so terrified of being recognised that Princess Elizabeth pulled the brim of her ATS cap down low, and Margaret dressed incognito and kept at the back, for fear of looking out of place in the crowd of uniformed friends. Princess Elizabeth, however, soon straightened her cap when one of their friends 'refused to be seen in the company of another officer improperly dressed'.

Together with their pals, the princesses cheered heartily with everyone around them when the King and Queen made another appearance on the balcony. Nobody recognised Elizabeth and Margaret or, if they did, they were too excited by the evening to give them much thought. The two princesses sang their way all over the West End, linked arms with others in Whitehall, danced the conga in the Ritz, marched through Green Park and then back to the palace, where they joined forces with the crowd to shout for the King and Queen to come back out on to the balcony. When patience got the better of them, they sent word that they were waiting outside, and the couple appeared and waved down at everyone – including their daughters.

The group even managed to get into trouble at one point, when the princesses' uncle, David Bowes-Lyon, tipped the helmets off the policemen patrolling London that night. 'He was quite naughty,' Princess Margaret recalled, but admitted that the young man did manage to run around and pop their helmets back on before any real harm was done.

VE Day may have been the first time the princesses had gone out partying, but it wasn't the last. The next evening it was raining, but Elizabeth and Margaret headed back out of the palace, and this time found themselves on the Embankment and in Piccadilly, before doing the conga into Buckingham Palace and singing until 2 a.m. The celebrations continued, and so did the outings, up to the Victory over Japan Day, in August 1945.

In 2020, on the seventy-fifth anniversary of VE Day, the streets were quiet due to the Covid pandemic. However, the Queen recorded a speech – just as her father had done in 1945. In the message, Her Majesty reflected on the King's tribute to the men and women who had sacrificed so much during the war. She then spoke about the impact it had on everyone, and while it all seemed bleak at the time, they kept hope in their hearts. 'Never give up, never despair,' she said. 'That was the message of VE Day.'

19

Joy and Good Fortune in Northern Ireland

On 18 March 1946, Princess Elizabeth boarded HMS *Superb*, and – escorted by two destroyers – sailed off to Northern Ireland. Her journey had begun the evening before, when she left Euston Station in London and headed overnight to Glasgow, before travelling on to Greenock to meet the ship. As she sailed along the Clyde, the Princess climbed up to the bridge and, despite the rain, sat back and gazed out over her surroundings.

This was the first time Princess Elizabeth had left the mainland without her parents, and the first time her standard flag had flown on a ship. There was, therefore, a great deal of excitement as she approached Belfast. For weeks, towns around Northern Ireland had been decorating the streets to welcome the Princess, and some even put pen to paper and wrote poems about her, which were published in the local newspapers.

When the Princess disembarked at 5.30 that evening, she was met by Governor Granville (William Leveson-Gower, 4th Earl Granville), his wife Lady Rose (who also happened to be Princess Elizabeth's aunt), the prime minister, the minister of home affairs, a host of dignitaries and officials, and a guard of honour. The governor was then tasked with accompanying Princess Elizabeth to Government House, where she was to stay during her trip.

On the day after she arrived, the Princess was driven to Harland & Wolff's shipyard where she once again inspected a guard of honour, and then launched aircraft carrier HMS *Eagle* with a bottle of Empire wine. After the boat slid down the launching platform and into the Musgrave Channel, the Princess smiled, while the chairman of Harland & Wolff took off his bowler hat and waved it in the air. It was, agreed everyone, a perfect launch.

Princess Elizabeth then received a gigantic bouquet from seventeen-year-old James Christian, the youngest apprentice at the company, and then went for a tour of the shipyard. During lunch, she gave a speech about the launch of the *Eagle*.

'I would like to wish happiness to those who built her,' she said, 'and joy and good fortune to those who sail in her, and especially to those men of the Fleet Air Arm . . .' The Princess then drove to Comber, County Down, where she attended the christening of her goddaughter, Elizabeth, the daughter of Lieutenant-Commander James King and his wife, Patricia (née Elizabeth Patricia White), one of the Princess's childhood friends.

Next there came a reception, given by the lord mayor of Belfast, during which the Princess met representatives of the Ulster Girl Guide Association and the British Legion. The mayor later received a letter from the governor, thanking him for his hospitality. 'This was of great assistance to me,' he wrote, 'as it enabled the Princess to meet representatives of the organisations in which she takes a particular interest.'

The trip was short but busy, with tree planting, a dance in her honour, and then a two-hundred-mile tour on Wednesday, which took in Dromore, Lurgan, Portadown, Dungannon, Ballygawley, Enniskillen and various other towns, all decorated in Union Jack flags. In Dungannon, the Princess met representatives at the High School for

Girls, and then in Enniskillen, she had lunch at the town hall, before heading to Armagh for more tea and more presentations.

The trip ended the next day, and the Princess once again climbed aboard HMS *Superb* and headed back to Scotland. She took an overnight train back to London, where she emerged wearing a diamond brooch in the shape of an eagle – a gift from those she met on HMS *Eagle*. On her arrival in London, a smiling Princess Elizabeth told officials of the London, Midland and Scottish Railway that she had loved the trip, had been delighted with her reception, and had enjoyed every moment.

20

The Princess Meets a Prince

On 29 November 1934, Princess Marina of Greece and Denmark married Princess Elizabeth's uncle, Prince George. As with all royal weddings, it was a lavish affair, with people camping out overnight just to catch a glimpse of the bride, groom and other royals, including the King, Queen and their daughters. It was a historical event, mainly because it was here that eight-year-old Princess Elizabeth first met the boy who would later become the love of her life.

Prince Philip of Greece and Denmark was five years older than the Princess, and had attended the wedding as cousin of the bride. At that age, there was nothing between the two, other than being guests at a relative's wedding, but five years later their paths crossed again, when the King, Queen, Princess Elizabeth and Princess Margaret were visiting the Royal Naval College in Dartmouth.

By this time, Philip was a cadet in the Royal Navy, and thirteen-year-old Elizabeth was still a schoolgirl. Her governess, Marion 'Crawfie' Crawford, believed him to be something of a show-off, but that part of his personality appealed to the Princess, and despite their age difference, she developed something of a schoolgirl crush.

The two kept in touch sporadically, and by 1945 rumours surfaced in Athens that they were a couple. When the stories hit the UK press,

THE PRINCESS MEETS A PRINCE

journalists telephoned Buckingham Palace, only to be told that they hadn't heard anything about any kind of romance, and firmly denied that there was a possibility that the still-teenage Princess might soon be married.

Then, in 1946, when Princess Elizabeth was twenty and Philip twenty-five, the couple began courting seriously, albeit quietly, so as to try and avoid any more attention from the press. Prince Philip – now a naval officer – had recently returned to the country after the war and was working at an officer training college in Wiltshire. Whenever he could get away from work, he'd hop into his sports car and dash off to London to visit the Princess at Buckingham Palace. There, they were often chaperoned by Crawfie – and gate-crashed by Princess Margaret – but sometimes they'd be able to get away on their own, too. 'We both love dancing,' the Princess told journalist Betty Shew. 'We have danced at Circo's and Quaglino's, as well as at parties.'

As their relationship deepened, the Princess's parents and courtiers became rather sceptical about the possible success of a long-term romance. Despite being a prince, Greek-born Philip was considered rather a poor chap by the royal family's standards, especially when he sometimes showed up to the palace in clothes that had seen better days. He was also known to drive somewhat recklessly, crashing his car on at least one occasion, and everyone worried that he wasn't an appropriate chauffeur for the Princess.

Added to that, the King and Queen were concerned that Princess Elizabeth was falling for the first man to show her any real attention – and their feelings were made no better when they realised that as a twenty-five-year-old man, he had experienced more than his share of attentive women. However, while the royals may have been a little wary, the Prince's family were positively excited about the prospect of him marrying into the British royal family, and the romance was urged on by Philip's cousin, Marina, and his uncle, Louis Mountbatten.

During a long trip to Balmoral in the latter half of 1946, the relationship between Prince Philip and Princess Elizabeth gained pace and, by the end of the year, he had asked her to marry him. Despite any concerns they may have had initially, the King and Queen Elizabeth had warmed somewhat to the Prince, and gave their permission for the marriage. However, it came with a stipulation – they must wait until Princess Elizabeth had come home from a family trip to South Africa before any official announcement was made. This way they could see if the affair really was as serious as the couple insisted it was, the Princess would be twenty-one, and they'd all be able to get on with the trip without the media attention that an engagement would bring.

This delay did not deter the rumours, however, and in some ways, it even helped them along. By the end of 1946, newspapers were full of talk about a possible impending engagement, particularly when Prince Philip was seen helping Princess Elizabeth into her coat, and then the revelation that he was to become a naturalised British subject within the next six months. Once again, reporters bombarded Buckingham Palace with requests for the truth, but there was no news forthcoming, apart from a firm and definite denial. 'Princess Elizabeth is not engaged to be married,' said Sir Alan Lascelles, private secretary to the King. 'The report published is inaccurate.'

No matter how much the British public – and the media – wanted it, there would be no official announcement yet. For now, everyone would have to make do with articles about Prince Philip's Greek background, his naval career, his prospects and his looks. 'He is a blond Greek Apollo,' said one reporter. 'As handsome as any film star.'

21

'I Declare Before You All...'

Turning twenty-one is a milestone for every young adult. It is a time for growth, for independence, for decision making, for opportunity, and often for reflection. For Princess Elizabeth, however, it was a time to dedicate herself to her role as the future queen, and to give inspiration to the millions of people around the Commonwealth.

Her twenty-first birthday arrived when the family were in the midst of a mammoth tour of South Africa, which had begun almost three months before. The tour had been a hard one at times, mainly because the Princess was fretting about being away from her (as yet unannounced) fiancé, Prince Philip. However, as the sun rose above Cape Town on 21 April 1947, her spirits must surely have been raised, when over five hundred birthday cards and telegrams arrived at Government House. She also received a trove of gifts, including several diamond brooches, diamond earrings and a grenade badge from the Grenadier Guards.

The day was a busy one, and Cape Town was turned into one huge festival in honour of the Princess. Bunting hung from many buildings, and HMS *Vanguard* – waiting to take the family back to Britain – was decked out for the occasion. Sitting next to it, three South African frigates gave a twenty-one-gun salute at midday.

The family had intended to ascend Table Mountain by cable car, but weather postponed the trip. Events that did go ahead, however, included a review and march-past of over seven thousand servicemen and veterans. The family then travelled to the Rosebank Show Grounds, where the Princess – wearing a stone-coloured dress and hat – was met by a thousand children, all singing 'Happy Birthday' and cheering.

Perhaps the most important part of the day, however, was when Princess Elizabeth made a speech that would become one of her most famous. Talking about the hardships left over by the Second World War, and the opportunities coming in the years ahead, the Princess (with help from speechwriter and journalist Dermot Morrah) encouraged listeners to move forward together in faith, courage and heart. To accomplish this, she said, everyone in the Commonwealth must give 'nothing less than the whole of ourselves', and to serve others: 'I declare before you all that my whole life, whether it be long or short, shall be devoted to your service and the service of our great Imperial family, to which we all belong.' The Princess then invited everyone to join in with her dedication to service. 'I know that your support will be unfailingly given,' she said.

The Princess's speech was a historic event, so much so that in the USA, broadcaster NBC cancelled all of its programmes in order to play it. This move was normally reserved only for presidential speeches and monumental international issues. In England, an eighteen-gun salute rang out along the Long Walk at Windsor Castle, while Queen Mary wept at the thoughtfulness of her granddaughter's words. Meanwhile, the Girl Guides announced that half a million girls had donated a penny to buy the Princess a specially designed brooch, and Prime Minister Clement Attlee sent a telegram to South Africa. 'Your Royal Highness has lived through some of the hardest yet noblest years of these islands' long history,' he said. 'The simple dignity and wise understanding which your Royal Highness has shown have endeared you to all classes at home.'

Back in Cape Town, the Princess rounded out her twenty-first birthday by changing into an evening gown of white tulle, watching an elaborate firework display, and then dancing at a large ball at City Hall. There, the mayor, Mr A. Bloomberg, gave a speech. 'Cape Town is the most envied city in the Empire, having you here for this historic day,' he said.

After the City Hall event, the Princess and her family went to Government House, where she blew out the candles on her cake and danced until after midnight. At one point, a gold key and a diamond necklace were presented to her. 'We have learned to admire her and love her,' exclaimed representative Field-Marshal Jan Smuts. 'And our hearts go out to her on this unique occasion of her 21st birthday spent among us.'

'I am deeply grateful for this token of goodwill from the citizens of Cape Town,' the Princess said, 'which will always remind me of the very happy birthday I have spent among you all.'

The family would soon leave South Africa, but before they did, Princess Elizabeth sent a telegraph to the lord mayor of London: 'Please convey to the citizens of the City of London my grateful thanks for their congratulations and good wishes sent to me for my birthday.'

22

Wedding Plans at Buckingham Palace

While rumours swirled for a long time about whether or not Princess Elizabeth and Prince Philip would be married, the palace denied all knowledge of any kind of engagement. However, there was only a certain amount of time that this could go on for, and so on 9 July 1947, the engagement was officially announced.

'It is with the greatest pleasure that the King and Queen announce the betrothal of their dearly beloved daughter, the Princess Elizabeth, to Lieut. Philip Mountbatten,' the statement read, before going on to say that the King had gladly given his consent to the union. On 31 July, His Majesty repeated this consent at a special Privy Council meeting, held at Buckingham Palace, though no wedding date was announced. All the media and public knew was that it would be before spring 1948, but still, that didn't stop people asking.

During a tour of Scotland with members of the royal family, the couple were shown around the premises of the Argyle and Sutherland Association Club, where the wife of the chairman was cheeky enough to ask Prince Philip if he could reveal a date. 'Soon,' he said, which was misheard to such a degree that by the time the couple left the building, visitors were repeating all kinds of 'official' dates – all of which were wrong.

WEDDING PLANS AT BUCKINGHAM PALACE

In the end, the date was announced as 20 November 1947. The couple would be married at Westminster, and in preparation, Prince Philip was given the title the Duke of Edinburgh, along with two others: the Earl of Merioneth, and Baron Greenwich of Greenwich in the County of London.

After the long, dark years of the Second World War, the people of the United Kingdom relished the idea of a royal wedding, and gifts were sent in from all over the country. There were cards, letters, small keepsakes, and even poems sent from individuals and families, and then there were more elaborate presents, organised by local councils and covered by donations from constituents.

In Ross-shire, a meeting was held to discuss what kind of gift should be given from the people of the county. It was decided that a gold brooch set would be made, complete with pearls from local rivers. Another Scottish council asked the Princess to choose a gift herself, but that caused problems when Elizabeth decided on something made with antique Scottish glass. Staff searched in vain for such items, only to find that there were little to none around. They settled on an assortment of dishes in Waterford glass, instead. Many other councils donated money, the total of which – over £13,000 – was ultimately gifted to charity.

The couple eventually received over one thousand wedding gifts from around the world. These included books, glasses, tablecloths, tweeds, rugs, furniture, a grand piano, a sewing machine, pictures, tableware, and a picnic basket from Princess Margaret Rose – all of which went on display at St James's Palace in the time leading up to the wedding.

James Jackson was a seventeen-year-old messenger boy at Buckingham Palace when the royal couple were making wedding plans. Of his time with the family, his daughter Sandie remembers: 'He got into trouble once for being in the wrong part of the palace! He was scurrying along a corridor and heard a cough, only to find the King and Queen walking down the staircase. The King coughed to alert my dad, but it was too late and so Dad got into a lot of trouble from his superiors!'

James may not have been very popular on the day he was reprimanded, but when he and his young colleagues bought Princess Elizabeth a wedding gift of a flower-patterned china dessert service, she was more than grateful. On 26 November 1947, James received a letter from the Princess, thanking him for the present, and revealing that both she and Philip were enchanted with it. 'This is a present which we shall use constantly, and whenever we do, we shall think of the kindness and good wishes for our happiness which it represents.'

The Princess also mentioned the extra money that the staff had tucked into the card, which she assured them would come in useful for buying something that they would need in the future.

While gifts are a part of every wedding, so too are the preparations. For the royal family, this includes a guest list of far more people than an average couple. In Princess Elizabeth's case, two thousand were invited from around the world, including royalty, foreign ambassadors, ministers, members of parliament and high commissioners. There was also the choosing of the hymns, colour schemes and outfits, all the while being aware that the country was still recovering from the effects of the Second World War. Princess Elizabeth made herself available for hours of preparations every day, while staff at St James's Palace cancelled holidays in order to keep up with all the demands of a royal wedding.

Of course, the most important decision for most brides is what kind of dress she will wear. In this regard, the Princess was presented with several designs by Norman Hartnell, and in August 1947, Buckingham Palace announced that she had chosen the one she would like. There were to be no details released until the day, but a spokesperson did reveal that the Princess would not be having a trousseau – a set of clothes and items collected for a wedding – so that she would be following the example of other post-war brides. 'The Princess,' the spokesperson said, 'was all the better able to dispense with a big trousseau in view of the fact that she had a fairly large wardrobe for the Royal visit to South Africa.' In the end, however, a small trousseau was prepared, using material found in Buckingham Palace and gifts from overseas.

23

An Ivory Gown and Nine-Foot Wedding Cake

On 20 November 1947, bunting and flags flew from almost every building around the country to celebrate the marriage of Princess Elizabeth and Prince Philip. From Buckingham Palace to Westminster Abbey, the streets were lined with well-wishers, some of whom had camped out overnight in order to get a better view, while others had been lucky enough to book hotel rooms overlooking the route. Many others had arrived by coach from around the United Kingdom, after companies laid on special trips, such was the demand from those who wanted to see the family in person.

The day before the wedding, a rehearsal was performed; food, outfits and the wedding dress itself were delivered to Buckingham Palace; and the Princess spent most of the day quietly, in order to ready herself for her big day. When she woke on the twentieth, she did so to a spectacular sight. According to Marion 'Crawfie' Crawford, she found the Princess peeping out of the window in her dressing gown, unbelieving of everything going on outside her window. Everywhere was awash with colour. Household Cavalry were in full ceremonial uniform, there were mounted guards of honour, marching bands,

AN IVORY GOWN AND NINE-FOOT WEDDING CAKE

soldiers, and the colourful outfits of those who had come out in their thousands to wish the couple the very best of luck.

The Princess had one last breakfast with her parents and sister, and then she prepared herself for the day ahead. When everyone was ready, the Glass Coach left the palace, carrying Queen Elizabeth and Princess Margaret, and then came the Irish State Coach, carrying the King and Princess Elizabeth. The Princess waved, the crowds cheered and waved back, and the fashion-conscious among them strained against the barriers for a first look at the Princess's dress.

The crowds en route may have only seen the top of the gown, but on her arrival at the abbey, the full dress was revealed. The Norman Hartnell ivory satin design comprised a fitted bodice, long sleeves, pointed waistline and a long, full skirt, bought by using clothing ration coupons, since rationing was still in place after the war. It was decorated with seed pearls and crystals, and behind it was a long, embroidered train, which was carried by two pages. Following behind the bride and her father were eight bridesmaids, including Princess Margaret Rose, and together they all walked slowly down the aisle, towards the waiting Prince.

The wedding – conducted by the Archbishop of Canterbury – was broadcast via radio to families around the country. Some huddled in their living rooms, listening to every word, while others packed into local cinemas, wearing their best 'posh clothes'. Cinemagoers took the celebrations seriously, and every time the national anthem played, they got to their feet, and then bowed their heads when it was time to pray.

After the ceremony, the bride and groom signed the register, and then climbed into the Glass Coach, which took them to Buckingham Palace, where dinner was served for selected guests. Afterwards, the nine-foot, four-tier cake was cut, and the couple appeared on the balcony, waving at the excited crowds below.

When the celebrations were done, the Princess changed into a blue going-away outfit, and then the couple headed to Waterloo

Station, where they travelled to Broadlands for the first part of their honeymoon. After a quick return to Buckingham Palace several days later, the couple left for Birkhall, on the Balmoral estate in Scotland, where they expressed their wish to be left completely alone. Before they departed London, however, Princess Elizabeth and her new husband released a statement, thanking well-wishers for the love shared on their wedding day. 'We can find no words to express what we feel,' they said, 'but we can at least offer our grateful thanks to the millions who have given us this unforgettable send-off in our married life.'

As the bride and groom headed off for their honeymoon, it was as though the country was a brighter place – at least for a day or two. One columnist for the *North Star* newspaper wrote that it was nice that the country's thoughts had been taken up with news outside the norm. 'And,' he said, 'we knew contentment, and shared in the happiness brought to a young and dearly loved Royal bride and bridegroom.'

24

Parties in Paris

In May 1948, Princess Elizabeth and the Duke of Edinburgh headed to Paris to spend the Whitsun holiday at the British Embassy. This was to be the Princess's first trip to Paris, and apart from the South African tour a year earlier, it was her first independent trip abroad.

In a timetable published before the trip, it was revealed that on Friday 14 May, the royal couple would visit the president of France, Vincent Auriol, and then open an exhibition, before dining with the president. Saturday would be a private sightseeing trip to Versailles, followed by a dinner in the evening, Sunday would include a church service and then a trip to Longchamps races, and then on the day before they headed back to London, the couple would attend the ballet.

Before arriving in the city, Princess Elizabeth had requested that, for the sightseeing at least, there should be little security surrounding her. Unfortunately, this low-key plan was thwarted when police uncovered a possible murder plot against the couple. Meetings were called, and a spokesperson told reporters, 'We are taking exhaustive precautions to see that they are guarded during every minute they are in public.' This included treating everyone in the crowd as though they were a would-be anarchist or gunman – something for which the Parisian crowds did not particularly care. In fact, some even fought their way through the barriers for a better look at the Princess, and a crowd of twenty thousand pushed their way down a narrow street to watch her disembark from a boat.

During the first official event – the opening of a British exhibition at the Galliera Museum – Princess Elizabeth gave a speech in French. 'The warmth of your welcome has moved us deeply,' she said. 'To us this journey is an exciting and most enjoyable event.'

On presenting the Princess with the Grand Cross of the Legion of Honour, President Auriol made everyone laugh when he rejected the idea of giving the Princess a kiss – something that was traditional for anyone receiving a reward. 'According to the protocol, I should give you the accolade,' he smiled, 'but I delegate my powers to your gracious spouse.'

Afterwards, while laying a wreath on the Tomb of the Unknown Soldier, Princess Elizabeth caused concern by looking somewhat strained, and had to be helped by the Duke of Edinburgh. She was then seen crying, as she waved to the crowds lining the Champs-Élysées – some of whom had climbed on to rooftops for a better view. Newspapers put the Princess's emotions down to fatigue after the journey to Paris, or even excitement, but the real reason was that she was secretly pregnant.

Before the couple had arrived in the city, many shopkeepers proclaimed the trip to be a wonderful start to the summer tourist season. An official made the disclosure that, 'We will welcome her in the warmest manner possible,' and he was not wrong. In the couple's honour it was arranged for the Place de la Concorde, the Champs-Élysées, the Arc de Triomphe, and various other streets and buildings to be floodlit for their journey back from the trip to the opera. There were personal gifts, too, including hats and books. In the seventeenth-century Hôtel de Lauzun, the Princess received a gold vanity set, inlaid with rubies and sapphires, with a powder box, a lipstick container, a cigarette case and a comb nestled inside. Because of security issues, however, all of these gifts were quickly and discreetly whisked off to the British Embassy, where they were carefully X-rayed and examined.

When the couple returned to England, it was reported that not only had they attended a race meeting on Whit Sunday, but they had also been seen in a theatre and the Chez Carrère nightclub, dancing until 2 a.m. Religious organisations protested loudly at the very idea of a princess behaving in such a way. The Imperial Alliance for the Defence of Sunday was one such complainer. In a letter to the prime minister, the organisation protested that it was 'with much dismay' that they had heard of the visit.

Rev. R. Nevil Lyons went further and made it a point to disparage the couple during one of his sermons. Telling parishioners that he was speaking for himself, his church and his congregation, he disclosed his surprise and disappointment that the Princess had chosen Whit Sunday to make such an appearance. He went on to say, 'We were profoundly shocked to learn that the daughter of our King and Queen should be found in such places and in such company . . .'

But while the religious men seethed, Downing Street was deluged with letters defending the couple, and some female reporters came to the Princess's defence. In the 'She' column of the *Sunday Pictorial*, a rundown of Princess Elizabeth's Sunday outings was listed. These included two trips to church, a little flutter at the races, an appearance at a theatre and a nightclub. In the latter, Princess Elizabeth watched a fashion show, did a little dancing, and sipped on soda water, not champagne. Labelling the complainers as 'a handful of misery-mongers' the article went on to say that few would call the events exotic, declared the entire affair to be nonsense, and praised the young couple for their work: 'The sort of work we would like to see entrusted to them far more often,' it said.

25

A Baby at Buckingham Palace

In early 1948, Princess Elizabeth learned that she was expecting her first child. As with other royal pregnancies, this was a delicate and private affair, and the Princess continued her duties as normal. However, when it was announced that the Princess had been forced to cancel several appointments due to ill health, rumours swirled that there was something seriously wrong.

Unwilling to announce that she was actually pregnant, the palace was happy to let unnamed correspondents report that she had a severe cold. 'Her Royal Highness is taking life more leisurely at the moment, and is still at Windsor,' wrote one correspondent, before adding that the doctors had advised her not to go out, else she contract another virus.

On 6 May Princess Elizabeth was back at work, and opened the *Health of the People* exhibition in London. There she met Godfrey, an eight-foot-tall robot, who was unable to bow to her, so winked instead. 'I hope that my gesture will not be misunderstood by your Royal Highness,' Godfrey said, to much amusement from the Princess and those around her. She then gave a speech about children's health, heralding the United Kingdom as one of 'the leaders in medical knowledge and research'.

A BABY AT BUCKINGHAM PALACE

After the much-publicised trip to Paris, Buckingham Palace released a statement that the Princess would not undertake any official duties after the end of June, which was their way of announcing the pregnancy. Some national newspapers were hesitant to talk about the subject, but did tell readers in a roundabout way. 'In Court circles,' it said, 'it is understood that an event of interest and importance to the country will take place in the middle of October.'

Other newspapers were bolder, and as soon as the palace put out the statement, reporters flew to their typewriters. They were excited because, 'No previous Royal announcement of this kind has been couched in these terms,' and disclosed that the cancellations were surely because the Princess was expecting.

Some newspapers discussed where in the line of succession the new baby would fall, while others pondered where the Princess would give birth, since the couple's official residence – Clarence House – was still being renovated. All decided that it was the Princess's insistence that she keep on working which had prompted the announcement in the first place.

She kept as busy as she could, but by summer, the Princess was at Balmoral, where she was said to be in excellent health, walking each day with her mother or Princess Margaret. After that it was back to London, where she kept a relatively low profile in Buckingham Palace, walking in the garden, consulting with her doctors, and watching the changing of the guard from a second-floor window.

On 14 November 1948, Princess Elizabeth gave birth to a baby boy, in Buckingham Palace. There were rumours all day that something was happening, especially when several doctors were seen going in by a side entrance. Once the baby was born, the Duke of Edinburgh was taken to see his wife, before he and the King and Queen Elizabeth went to the nursery to meet the new arrival. Meanwhile, news filtered through to Queen Mary, who threw a white fur wrap over her evening gown and ordered her driver to take her to Buckingham Palace. When she left just before midnight, her car was stopped by the crowds, and some convinced themselves that they could see the tears of joy in her eyes . . .

Shortly after the birth, Buckingham Palace made an announcement. 'Her Royal Highness and her son are both doing well,' it said. A copy was pasted on to the palace gates, where hundreds of royalists whooped and cheered, and sang 'For He's a Jolly Good Fellow'. Bells rang out across the country, gun salutes were heard, and flags were flown to celebrate the new arrival. Soon after, telegrams, cards and packages began arriving from around the world, and reporters rushed to obtain statements from anyone remotely associated with the royal family. The *Aberdeen Press and Journal* were thrilled to be the ones who broke the news to the staff at Balmoral and Birkhall. According to them, a maid at Balmoral declared it to be lovely, while Miss Mackenzie, housekeeper at Birkhall, responded, 'Oh, my word, what splendid news.'

It would take some time for the public to hear that the baby had been given the name of Charles Philip Arthur George but, in the meantime, they were placated with the news that a court-circle source had described him as 'a lovely boy, a really splendid baby'.

26

A 'Normal' Life in Malta

In 1949, while serving as an officer in the Royal Navy, the Duke of Edinburgh was stationed on the island of Malta, and Princess Elizabeth often lived with him. This gave the royal couple the opportunity to enjoy something of a normal life, living in Villa Guardamangia, a home owned by Philip's uncle, Louis Mountbatten.

After leaving Prince Charles in London, the Princess arrived in Malta on 20 November 1949, which also happened to be the couple's second wedding anniversary. As the plane came to a stop at the airport, the Princess could be seen peeking out of the window, as the Duke hurried up the steps to meet her. Wearing a brown coat and a small hat with feathers, she was introduced to various officials, including the prime minister of Malta and the archbishop. The welcome received in the airport was continued when the couple arrived at Villa Guardamangia, where locals – including nuns from a local convent – came out to see them.

In the weeks before her flight, the Princess had consulted with her dressmakers, and made finishing touches to a brand-new wardrobe. This included suits of red and beige, a brown and yellow checked dress, and a yellow overcoat. The introduction of yellow caused raised eyebrows in London, where fashion experts decided that the Princess must surely be experimenting with a new style.

While the trip was mainly a private affair, Princess Elizabeth still fulfilled various official engagements during her time in Malta. One such event happened on 7 December 1949, when she and Countess Mountbatten visited hospitals, and then on 8 December the Princess unveiled four commemorative tablets at the base of the Malta War Memorial at Floriana. However, eyebrows were raised when it was announced that Princess Elizabeth planned to spend Christmas with her husband in Malta, rather than at home with her son, Charles. The one-year-old was recovering from tonsilitis at the time, and it was decided that he'd be better spending the festive season with the King and Queen Elizabeth in Sandringham. When the Princess arrived in London on 28 December, it was expected that she'd go straight to Sandringham but, instead, she dealt with business matters at Clarence House, and then headed to Norfolk just in time to see in the New Year.

There were frequent visits to Malta during the time that the Duke of Edinburgh was stationed there, and was likely the place where the couple conceived their second child, Princess Anne. The couple were back in London on 15 August 1950 for the baby's birth, however, which was to become the first royal birth to take place at Clarence House. The news came in the way of a statement: 'Her Royal Highness Princess Elizabeth, Duchess of Edinburgh, was safely delivered of a Princess at 11.50 a.m. today.' The bulletin concluded that both were doing well.

Back on the island, Princess Elizabeth enjoyed a quiet existence, and was happy being able to do 'normal' things like shopping and wandering around the town where the couple lived. Sadly, their time there came to an end when the King fell into bad health, and the couple needed to spend more time in the United Kingdom, taking on official duties.

A 'NORMAL' LIFE IN MALTA

As queen, Elizabeth never forgot her time on the island, and the royal couple always referred to their stay as a happy time. Mrs Dorothy Gwinnutt from Derby had a special place in her heart for it, too. She had lost her husband, Lance-Serjeant Charles Gwinnutt, when he was serving in Malta during the war, and on hearing that the Princess would be travelling there, the woman sat down and wrote her a letter. The ninth anniversary of her husband's death was coming up on 27 April 1951, and the widow wondered if Princess Elizabeth might be able to place flowers on his grave. Shortly afterwards, Mrs Gwinnutt received a letter from Buckingham Palace, promising that the Princess would arrange a delivery. Sure enough, on 14 May, a package arrived at Mrs Gwinnutt's house, from the Imperial War Graves Commission. Inside, there were three photographs of the decorated grave of Lance-Serjeant Gwinnutt, and a letter explaining that Princess Elizabeth had asked them to forward the photographs to her. 'Words cannot express my gratitude to Princess Elizabeth,' Mrs Gwinnutt said.

27

How Do You Clean a Kettle?

On 5 May 1949, Queen Elizabeth, Queen Mary, Princess Elizabeth and the Duke of Edinburgh headed to Olympia to tour the British Industries Fair. Greeted by the president of the Board of Trade – and future prime minister – Harold Wilson, the foursome looked at a model of the exhibition, and Queen Elizabeth sampled a new perfume called By Candlelight. She did not buy any of it, but Queen Mary was intrigued enough to order some for herself.

Princess Elizabeth, meanwhile, received a portable typewriter from Mrs S. S. Elliott – apparently the only female large-scale exhibition organiser in the United Kingdom – who was in charge of the 'Business Efficiency' part of the exhibition. What made the gift so special? First of all, the item was small enough to fit into a large handbag, but secondly – and for the Princess only – the keys and striking arms were all made of eighteen-carat gold.

Needless to say, Princess Elizabeth was delighted with the gift, and so was the West Bromwich firm B. T. L. Office Equipment Distributors Ltd, which was carrying the item in the Castle Bromwich branch of the fair. On receiving a photograph of Mrs Elliott with the Princess and her typewriter, proprietor Mr W. N. R. Moore framed it and hung it above his exhibition stall, where it received a lot of attention from reporters and visitors.

While business at Olympia was described as fairly steady, footfall at the Castle Bromwich branch was rather slow. Although exhibitors reported that things seemed brisker than they had days ago, there were still no huge orders taking place. However, things turned brighter on 10 May 1949, when Princess Elizabeth and the Duke of Edinburgh arrived at Castle Bromwich, Solihull, in order to visit the fair.

Excited by the royal visit, Lord Mayor Alderman J. C. Burman arranged for all of Birmingham's schoolchildren to have half a day off. In the days before the visit, one group of kids caused chaos when they were seen waving flags and cheering as a young friend rode past them on his flag-covered bicycle. When passersby asked what on earth was going on, the children told them that they were rehearsing meeting the Princess and the Duke.

As security was an issue, all police leave was cancelled, and off-duty firemen were brought in to help. The whole area was abuzz, and as soon as the couple left Stechford Station, they were cheered and waved along the route to the fair. So much so that the car had to go at a walking pace, so that everyone could catch a glimpse of the royal couple. When they arrived at the fair, the Princess inspected the guard of honour, and then during the tour, some of the exhibitors gathered around a small television and watched the proceedings as they happened, excited that this was apparently the first time the couple had ever appeared on Birmingham television.

Organisers went to great lengths to make sure that the Princess had something sweet to smell during her tour. They installed thousands of flowers around the arena, and over a thousand exhibitors created small gardens in and around their stands. The flower theme didn't stop there, however, and organisers even hired workmen to hide behind the scenery, quietly spraying perfume wherever the Princess walked.

Whether or not she even noticed the scent is debatable, and certainly, the newlywed Princess had more on her mind when she toured the homeware stands. She commented that a pressure cooker on display was the same as one used at Buckingham Palace, and then the Duke of Edinburgh became so enthralled with a shaving mirror that he ordered one to be sent to him.

When she reached the stall of W. A. McLellan, who was showcasing a new design of kettle, Princess Elizabeth smiled and said, 'Can you help me? My father wants to know – and so do I – how can you clean the inside of a kettle properly?' The man looked baffled, admitted that he didn't quite know, and the Princess moved on.

'I could only tell the Princess that all kettles do fur up at times,' he said, though later he came to the conclusion that if the King's kettle did need cleaning, perhaps he should just throw it away.

Other stallholders were impressed by the Princess's knowledge of kitchens. 'She certainly knows what she is talking about as far as kitchen work is concerned,' said Duncan Campbell, manager of the London Aluminium Co., though passersby wondered if this was something of an exaggeration.

28

Cheering Crowds, Tea and a Gold-mounted Riding Crop

After touring the British Industries Fair at Castle Bromwich, Princess Elizabeth and the Duke of Edinburgh headed to the Council House, Birmingham, which was an hour-long journey, thanks to the cheering crowds on the way and twenty thousand others who greeted them outside the Council House. Once inside, the couple lunched with, among others, the lord mayor and lady mayoress.

Princess Elizabeth, wearing a royal blue suit, matching hat, bag and ankle-strap shoes, was presented with a gold-mounted riding crop for Prince Charles. Meanwhile, Philip thanked the city for a silver tea service that had been given to the couple as a wedding present, and assured lunch attendees that they used it regularly. He also thanked the mayor for Prince Charles's riding crop. 'It is perhaps a little premature,' he said, 'but I assure you that it will come in very handy someday.'

Outside, young office assistants took to the street and chanted, 'We want Philip! We want Philip!' It was not known whether the couple heard the shouts from inside, but when they appeared briefly on the balcony, the women in the crowd roared their approval. Some fans were left disappointed, however, because the car in which the royals travelled was not open-topped.

Many mothers were heard complaining that they and their children had only been able to catch a glimpse, while an older lady bemoaned that all she got to see was the car and a couple of vague figures. The most disappointed of all, however, were some sales assistants who worked in Lewis's department store. 'From where we were on the second floor of the building,' one said, 'all we saw was a pretty flag and a nice shiny roof of a car.'

The roofed-car situation caused such a scandal that disappointed fans flooded the newspapers with complaints. Reporters phoned Buckingham Palace, where they were told that it had nothing to do with them, since the car was provided by the authorities. Meanwhile, the Daimler Motor Company, which had supplied the vehicle, was adamant that it was asked to send a closed car, and that is exactly what it did.

After lunch the couple travelled on to Selly Oak Hospital, where eight-year-old former patient Helen Turner waited excitedly. The girl had been in hospital during 1948, after being hit by a bus and losing the lower part of one leg. Despite all she had been through, however, she was all smiles on seeing Princess Elizabeth, and moved forward clutching a bouquet in one hand and her crutches under her arms. 'I am eight and a half, your Royal Highness,' Helen said, 'and I want to be an author when I grow up.'

. The Princess was so touched to see the child that the two spoke together for a couple of minutes, before it was time to tour the wards. There, the couple met and spoke to several young soldiers, and then a baby who had just been operated on. 'How dreadful to think a child of that age should have to undergo an operation,' Princess Elizabeth said.

Another patient who was thrilled to meet the couple was a lady called Marie, who had spent her thirtieth birthday in surgery. When the Princess asked her how she was, the young woman replied that it was a great honour to meet her. 'Not at all,' Princess Elizabeth said. 'I'm only too pleased to be able to come.' The Duke of Edinburgh, meanwhile, made the woman laugh when he expressed how cosy it looked in the corner where she lay. 'I could do with a week or two there myself,' he said.

After tea in the Nurses' Home, the day was over, and the royal couple headed back to the station. En route, they encountered students complete with mortarboards and gowns, chanting and singing about the baby Prince Charles. They were thrilled to catch a glimpse of Princess Elizabeth, but someone not so lucky was George Light, whose job it was to stand behind a huge picture of a ship that the Princess was to inspect on her way to the train.

The man's boss, stationmaster Mr W. H. Price, had thought it a magnificent idea for George to stand behind the picture, making it sway so that the boat looked as though it were sailing. While the Princess seemed to enjoy the effect, poor George did not get to see her at all, as when he popped back out from behind the picture, she had already headed off to the platform.

29

The Scandal of Marion 'Crawfie' Crawford

For seventeen years, Marion 'Crawfie' Crawford was the governess of Princess Elizabeth and Princess Margaret. She taught them all subjects, including English and maths, gave them homework and set them tests. She was a popular figure around Buckingham Palace, and – it seemed at the time – completely dedicated to her job. So much so, in fact, that she did not marry her partner, banker George Buthlay, until September 1947, just over a year before her retirement at the beginning of 1949.

Throughout her time with the royal family, Crawfie kept a diary, and sometimes little snippets would appear in the newspapers, detailing what the princesses did in the schoolroom, what subjects they enjoyed, and how they spent their spare time. Sometimes they even included Crawfie's name, but if anyone suspected that she had contributed to the articles, they didn't seem to mind.

When she retired from her position at the palace, the family held her in such high regard that she was given a grace-and-favour home – Nottingham Cottage – in the grounds of Kensington Palace, as well as a comfortable pension. Her popularity was further confirmed when, in January 1949, Queen Elizabeth wrote to Crawfie, thanking the woman for always being by the princesses' side. Then, on 10 March 1949,

Crawford was invested by the King with the insignia of a Commander of the Royal Victorian Order.

It was around this time that Crawfie received an offer from US magazine *Ladies' Home Journal* to publish her memories of palace life. Queen Elizabeth wrote to the former governess in April 1949, stressing her opinion that while it might be OK for Crawfie to provide assistance to authors, she should resist monetary offers and always keep her name out of the articles themselves. She also emphasised that should Crawfie pen any stories about the family, they'd never feel confidence in anyone again. 'You would lose all your friends,' Queen Elizabeth wrote, adding that nothing of that nature had ever been contemplated by servants before.

Whether or not the governess took on board any of the Queen's advice is debatable, and legend has it that Crawfie was actively encouraged by her husband to take up the offer, as he had previously encouraged her to write her memoirs. She certainly signed a contract with the *Ladies' Home Journal* that stated she would be quoted under her own name, and that the articles could be written without the Queen's consent. This was fine with Crawfie, as she was so confident in her writing that she believed Queen Elizabeth might even write a preface.

Unsurprisingly, when a copy of the manuscript from which the articles would be taken was sent to Buckingham Palace, the Queen was appalled with the insider knowledge it contained. She immediately asked for certain details to be edited out, which only added to all the confusion, since Crawfie now (mistakenly) believed that Queen Elizabeth was actively helping with the memoir.

As if publication in the *Ladies' Home Journal* wasn't bad enough, in March 1950, the UK's *Woman's Own* magazine began printing the memoir, too. Full-page adverts were taken out in many newspapers, claiming that, 'Every British family should read this warm and intimate account of the lives of our Princesses . . . This is more than a fascinating memoir of Palace life – this is history.'

Needless to say, the public flew to the newsagents and bought up any available copies of *Woman's Own*. 'The demand is colossal,' said an advert in the *Sunday Pictorial*. 'If your newsagent has sold out, ask him to add your name to his waiting list.' Anyone not able to find a copy of the magazine, however, need not worry, as highlights from the articles were widely covered in newspapers around the country.

They were also compiled into a book entitled *The Little Princesses*, and published by Harcourt, Brace and Company in the States, and Cassell & Co. in the UK. The contents were tame and affectionate compared to modern standards, and at least one bookseller described the book as a 'charming volume . . . Many magnificent portraits of our Princesses at work and at play complete a record which will find a place in the hearts of all who respect our way of life.' The royal family did not see it that way at all, however, and the book caused outrage within the walls of Buckingham Palace.

On 19 November 1950, the *Sunday Express* columnist Ephraim Hardcastle revealed that Crawfie and her retired-banker husband had left their Kensington Palace home and returned to Aberdeen. Hardcastle wrote that the former governess could retire safe in the knowledge that her book, 'has done the finest service to our much-loved Royal Family of any book on palace life written in this generation'. He may have been sarcastic in his observation, since by then it was publicly gossiped about that the family were not happy, and publication of the memoir most certainly contributed to Crawfie's swift move out of her London home. 'She must have gone off her head,' wrote the Queen in a letter to her friend, Lady Astor.

But the drama did not stop there. The woman was interviewed on television, and on the occasion of Princess Elizabeth becoming queen, Crawford's book was reissued. She then went on to put her name to books about Queen Mary, Queen Elizabeth II and Princess Margaret, and wrote a popular column in *Woman's Own*. The latter proved to be her downfall when, in 1955, she wrote an article in advance, vividly describing that year's Trooping of the Colour and Ascot. The story appeared, but since both of the events had been cancelled due to a national rail strike, it raised questions over her authenticity.

In 1977, Crawford's husband passed away, and the *Sunday Express* ran a story on whatever happened to the disgraced governess. 'I have no comment to make on anything,' she snapped when a reporter telephoned her for an interview. There then followed a series of depressive episodes, as well as at least one suicide attempt.

The royal family never spoke to the woman again. Indeed, when she passed away in 1988, none of the family sent flowers, and they did not attend her funeral. 'The Queen certainly knows about her death,' a Buckingham Palace spokesman told reporters. 'I don't know if she sent any message.'

While the governess may not have had any further contact with the family, she did, however, leave a treasured shoebox full of letters and photos to her former charge, Princess Elizabeth (by then the Queen). She in turn, decided to keep it in the royal archives. 'She was not bitter,' Crawfie's lawyer Bruce Smith said, 'more a sense of deep frustration mixed with sadness and regret.'

30

'An Extremely Strenuous Tour Awaits'

The King's health had been a worrying issue for a number of years, with ongoing lung problems, surgery, inflammation, obstruction to the circulation of his right leg, a continuous cough and bouts of influenza. Princess Elizabeth and Princess Margaret had stepped in to cover some of his official trips, while other visits were cancelled altogether.

The King's illness was played down as much as possible by Buckingham Palace – both to the public and to the King himself – but the truth of the matter was that a tumour had been found in his lung and, worse still, it was malignant.

Doctors felt that there was no choice but to remove the King's left lung; a surgery which was performed in an adapted room in Buckingham Palace, on 23 September 1951. The surgery was successful in the fact that the King survived and did his best to rally afterwards, but it wasn't a permanent fix. While His Majesty hoped to be able to take a convalescence cruise in spring 1952, he still had cancer, and behind the scenes, MPs and various advisors prepared for the worst.

On the advice of doctors, the King's 1951 Christmas speech was prerecorded instead of broadcast live, as he now had difficulty in speaking more than a couple of words at a time. 'The King's voice has not yet completely regained its normal strength,' a spokesperson said, 'and is still liable to be a little uncertain.'

At 3 p.m. on Christmas Day, after the royal family had returned from church to Sandringham House, they all sat down together to hear the King's words. He spoke about troubles happening in Korea and Malaya, his regret at having to postpone a trip to Australia and New Zealand, and the importance of friendship and kindness, especially when things appeared hard and cruel. Many people expected the King to talk about his health, which he did by thanking his doctors and nurses for enabling him to come through his illness. 'I have learned once again,' he said, 'that it is in bad times that we value most highly the support and sympathy of our friends.'

After the speech, some listeners were concerned about the King's voice, claiming it to be huskier than usual. A doctor who listened in tried to calm any worries by claiming that the only thing he'd noticed was 'a huskiness of the lower notes, to which we were not accustomed in the earlier days'. He put this down to the King's operation, but assured everyone that, overall, there did seem to be a satisfactory amount of air volume in His Majesty's lung.

The editor of the *Lytham Times* was especially moved by the speech. He expressed his view that everyone who heard it must surely have appreciated the effort it took to produce it. 'Through it could be sensed the tremendous strain,' he wrote, 'but the task was accomplished and fulfilment of duty has always ruled His Majesty's life.'

As 1951 ended and 1952 began, spirits were raised when it was disclosed that the King planned to begin holding investitures again on 27 February, and then would embark on a cruise to South Africa on 11 March. In the meantime, Princess Elizabeth and her husband the Duke of Edinburgh readied themselves for a tour of the Commonwealth, stopping first in Kenya, before moving on to Ceylon, Australia and New Zealand.

On 30 January, the family – including the King, Queen Elizabeth, Princess Margaret, Princess Elizabeth and the Duke of Edinburgh – went to the Theatre Royal, Drury Lane, to watch a production of *South Pacific*. It was the first theatre outing for them since the King's illness, and as they entered the royal box, the audience gave them a standing ovation. Waving their programmes and handkerchiefs, the public whooped their delight in seeing the family – especially the King, who was wearing a casual tweed overcoat over a heated waistcoat.

During an interval chat with a member of the cast, Queen Elizabeth revealed that she couldn't think of a better way of spending a last evening with Princess Elizabeth before she and the Duke of Edinburgh headed off on their tour. The King was in a particularly jovial mood, and onlookers commented on his joyous spirits, rocking back and forth with laughter when a funny scene was played out in front of him. 'I have never seen a man enjoy it more,' said one member of the theatre staff.

The next day, the King, Queen Elizabeth and Princess Margaret travelled to the airport to wave off Princess Elizabeth and the Duke. It was a misty day, and onlookers were concerned that His Majesty was not wearing his hat, preferring instead to hold it in his hand. However, most were also relieved to see him looking so fit, as he – and the rest of the family – headed into the plane to say a final goodbye. That done, the royal party headed for the VIP lounge, and as the plane taxied down the runway, the Queen and Princess Margaret waved their hands, while the King waved his bowler hat in the air. He seemed reluctant to leave.

'An extremely strenuous tour awaits,' said a reporter for the *Yorkshire Post*. Little did he know just how prophetic these words would shortly become.

31

The King Is Dead

When Princess Elizabeth and Philip arrived in Kenya, all seemed well. They were greeted by the governor, Sir Philip Euen Mitchell, along with officers and chiefs from several tribes. She then went straight into a tour of Pumwani African Maternity Hospital, where she was introduced to some of the mothers and babies there, before heading for the European quarter of Nairobi, where she attended a garden party of almost three thousand guests. There, the Princess was presented with a key to Royal Lodge, a wedding present from the people of Kenya.

During a visit to Nairobi's National Park, Princess Elizabeth was able to take photographs of a lioness and her four young cubs. In the days before the visit, rangers had tried to lure the lions to specific spots so that the Princess could see them, 'but the lions would not play,' the ranger said. 'The lioness and cubs were a surprise even to me.' It was a happy visit, and the couple were so intrigued by the abundance of giraffes, zebras and wildebeest that the drive ran late, such was the enthusiasm.

Meanwhile, in England, the King, Queen Elizabeth, Princess Margaret, Prince Charles and Princess Anne travelled to Sandringham, Norfolk, where the family had been staying before their return to

London to say goodbye to Princess Elizabeth. In the days following, the King went shooting and seemed to be in a happy mood. He told his friend, Lord Fermoy, that he would see him again later in the week. 'I have had a thoroughly enjoyable day,' he said. 'I will look forward to Thursday.' Fermoy told reporters that the King had appeared to be in good health, certainly better than he had been since his surgery. Meanwhile, the Queen and Princess Margaret were cruising on the Norfolk Broads, laughing and seemingly worry free.

While the King's health had been at the front of everybody's minds for a long time, now everyone seemed to be relaxing. Indeed, nobody had any idea that when he went to bed on 5 February 1952, he would not wake up. The King's heart stopped beating in the early hours of 6 February, the result of a blood clot.

After the King's valet found him lifeless in the morning, 'Hyde Park Corner' – the codeword for plans relating to the King's death – was put into action, and court officials all rushed to the bedroom to confirm the news. When the news was broken to the Queen and Princess Margaret, both women rushed to the King's bedside, and understandably took his death hard. The Queen had been determined that there was a chance that her husband was getting better. He was only fifty-six, after all, and he had seemed so happy and full of plans in the days leading up to his death.

'Such sorrow is a very strange experience,' she wrote to a friend several months later. Prince Charles, kept upstairs in the nursery with his sister, Anne, was concerned when he noticed that everyone seemed to be crying, and the bad news was broken to him by his nanny. Staff at Sandringham arrived for work only to be told what had occurred overnight. They rushed back to their families, their heads low.

In London, Prime Minister Winston Churchill was informed, as was the King's mother, Queen Mary. She took the news calmly, as though she was prepared for it, but her heart never truly recovered from the shock of losing her son. In Kenya, Elizabeth went on safari

THE KING IS DEAD

as a princess, unaware that she would come back as a queen. At Royal Lodge, the news was broken to the Duke of Edinburgh, who told his wife privately. Staff reported that Elizabeth threw her hands to her face and cried, before stoically planning her return to England. Her first duty as queen would come at London Airport, when she would be obliged to hold her first audience in the cabin of the plane. She would then join her mother and sister at Sandringham, where they would be obliged to curtsy to her.

As the news of the King's death travelled around the globe, the general sense was one of shock. Men, women and children were seen huddled around newspaper stands, some wiping away tears, while others shook their heads in disbelief. Some recalled the King and Queen's support for the nation during the Second World War, while others had memories of their successful tours not only around the country, but the world. Wherever you were, flags flew at half-mast, and the sadness and pain felt by the King's many admirers were everywhere apparent.

Cards, letters and telegrams poured into Buckingham Palace, Sandringham, Balmoral and Windsor. The French premier, Edgar Faure, announced his sadness at the loss of the King, calling him 'a model of dignity'. Former US first lady, Eleanor Roosevelt, was said to be devastated, as she'd always had a special fondness for the King and Queen. 'The responsibilities of Queen have come very soon to Princess Elizabeth,' she said, 'and she has my greatest sympathy.'

Mrs Roosevelt was correct, Princess Elizabeth – now the Queen – would need much support going forward in her new role. A young wife and mother, both she and Philip had believed that they would have many more years of being a family before she would have to step into the role of monarch. This was not to be the case. Now, the whole family would have to adjust to new surroundings, and new jobs – including Philip, who reluctantly gave up his naval career in order to support the new queen.

The King's body was transported to London on 11 February, where it lay in state before being moved to Windsor for the funeral, which was held on 15 February. During this time of mourning, it was as though the whole country stood silent. Many businesses closed, cars were garaged, silent crowds doffed their caps and bowed their heads in quiet contemplation, and memorial services were held throughout the country for those unable to travel to Windsor. And in the middle of it all, the new queen, her mother – now the Queen Mother – and her sister, Princess Margaret, stood in black, their heads veiled, their sorrow on show for all to see.

'Now,' one columnist wrote, 'the country goes forward with a young Queen at the head, to meet whatever may befall and all will wish her a happy and peaceful reign.'

32

Gold Lace and Diamonds at the Opening of Parliament

On 3 November 1952, the Queen and the Duke of Edinburgh slipped out of Buckingham Palace and drove to the House of Lords to rehearse what would be Her Majesty's first State Opening of Parliament. Quietly, the couple entered the building, and spent the next thirty-five minutes going over the speech, talking with high officers of state, walking the route that would be taken during the ceremony, looking through the notes, and sitting on the golden throne. Once the couple had left, loudspeakers were tested, and final adjustments made in anticipation of the important day ahead.

The fourth of November came and once again the Queen travelled to Westminster, but not in a car. This time she was in the State Coach, and wearing not the grey suit she had worn to rehearsals, but a full-skirted, honey-coloured dress with gold lace over the top, white gloves, an ermine coat, and diamonds around her neck and on her head.

Moments before the ceremony, the mistress of the robes and the women of the bedchamber laid Queen Victoria's scarlet, gold and ermine robes across the Queen's shoulders, and then it was time to enter the House. With two pages holding her train, and the Duke of

Edinburgh holding her hand, the Queen walked towards the throne, followed by and under the watchful gaze of ministers, including Prime Minister Winston Churchill. The room was full of colour from the peers' robes, the ambassadors' ribbons, and the sparkles from the tiaras and evening gowns of the peeresses. With the wigs of the judges and the court dress of officials, the whole place was alive with pomp and ceremony.

Once Her Majesty reached the throne, she sat down carefully, the crown heavy on her head. Prince Philip sat nearby on the Chair of State, once occupied by Queen Victoria's husband, Albert. After Albert's death, the unoccupied chair was always placed in the same position when Queen Victoria opened parliament.

After a minor malfunction with the huge, heavy robe, the Queen spoke calmly, with no nervousness detected at all.

Critics had expected the young woman to stumble on her words, or show some kind of discomfort with the powers recently thrust upon her, but as she spoke about the economy, on improving social services and the standard of living, even the harshest of critics had to admit that she delivered her words with dignity, confidence and respect. Her Majesty ended her speech with the words traditionally recited during the State Opening of Parliament: 'I pray that the blessing of Almighty God will rest upon your counsels.'

Princess Margaret watched proceedings from the benches, wearing a silver and white satin gown, and a tiara. As the Queen passed her, the Princess leaned forward and the two women smiled broadly at each other. However, one person conspicuous by her absence was the Queen Mother. She had been seen watching the coach procession from a Buckingham Palace balcony with the children, but her non-attendance at parliament raised eyebrows with at least one Fleet Street reporter.

The inquisitive man rang the Palace of Westminster to enquire as to why the Queen Mother was not there, and was told that perhaps the Lord Great Chamberlain's Office could let him know. Not so, said an official there. 'It is entirely a Court Circular affair.' After getting a House of Lords librarian to search etiquette books for an answer, the journalist finally came to the decision that it must have been a family custom, and left it at that.

On going home to Buckingham Palace, the Queen and the Duke of Edinburgh posed for photographs in the Throne Room, and then they and their children, Charles and Anne, walked out on to the balcony and waved to a crowd of twenty thousand people cheering outside. Philip picked up the children in turn so that they could see over the balcony, and then when the family went back into Buckingham Palace, Prince Charles ran out for one more wave, much to the delight of the crowd. Her Majesty's first State Opening of Parliament had been a success, and even the hardest of Fleet Street reporters couldn't help but declare the day to be a moving experience.

33

The Death of Queen Mary

Just months before the 1953 coronation, Queen Mary passed away. Her health had been faltering since the death of her son, and understandably she had taken his loss hard. George VI was the third of her children to pass away, and afterwards it was as if she had given up on life. By the time of her death, she had been confined to bed for a month, and the public were said to be concerned. During that time, there were frequent updates on her condition, which was dismissed as a lingering gastric illness. In later years, however, some biographers have claimed that her death was caused by lung cancer, and others by a hardening of the arteries.

Whatever the cause, before she did pass away, Queen Mary was adamant that whatever happened, it should not interfere with the coronation of the new queen. She got her wish, and aside from a short period of mourning, the country – and the royal family – soon got back to preparations.

Queen Mary's death, however, spelled a new era for the royals. She had been a fixture of British life for many years, and the public had admired her during her own time as queen, and then as the King's mother. Many of the older generation were devastated by her passing, and some even expressed themselves via poetry, and sent their creations to local newspapers. Towns around the country flew their flags at half-mast, letters and telegrams flooded into Buckingham Palace by the sackful, and courts, businesses, public buildings and organisations announced moments of silent reflection.

Newspaper columnists and reporters, meanwhile, went all out in disclosing their own feelings of loss. 'Queen Mary never faltered from the path of duty,' said the *Inverness Courier*, 'nor did she ever fail to play her part as counsellor and friend, as well as Queen to her husband during his 25 years' reign.'

The *Bucks Advertiser* expressed their sorrow thus: 'Her passing strikes deep home to us all. For here was a Royal Lady so close to the hearts of us all . . . Watching over her family and the family of nations.' The *Banbury Advertiser*, meanwhile, wrote that 'Her very appearance was symbolic of all that is meant in this country by Royalty.'

But while the country mourned, one family member was not particularly hurt by Queen Mary's death. Princess Margaret had always hated the way her grandmother commented on her appearance, or criticised her love of dance, and felt that their relationship was one of indifference. While the two did occasionally exchange letters, Margaret went on to call the old lady an ogre, and told her friends that she did not care for her grandmother at all.

Queen Mary's funeral was held on 31 March 1953, and she was interred beside King George V in St George's Chapel, Windsor. That day, planes were banned from flying below a mile above Windsor, wreaths were spread out on the triangular lawn of the castle, and the only flag flying at full-mast was the Royal Standard, to signify that the Queen was in residence. A service was held in the chapel, in front of 1,500 people, and included Queen Mary's favourite hymns, 'Abide with Me' and 'Glorious Things of Thee are Spoken'.

Towards the end of the service, the Queen rose from her seat, and was handed a silver bowl containing earth from Frogmore – the former royal home. The coffin disappeared into the ground, and as the Archbishop of Canterbury said the famous words, 'Earth to Earth, Ashes to Ashes, Dust to Dust', Queen Mary's granddaughter sprinkled earth on to the coffin.

With the coronation looming, the British people had the new queen on their minds. Not only had she lost her father, but now her grandmother had passed, too. The *London Evening News* passed along their sympathies. She was, they said, 'Queen Mary's dearly loved grandchild, who carries the burdens of decision and responsibility which are implicit in the traditions of the British Crown.'

34

'I Name this Ship *Britannia*'

In 1952, just days before the King's death, the John Brown & Co. shipyard, on Clydeside, was commissioned to build a large, luxurious ship, capable of ferrying the royal family around the world. It took over a year to build, and when it was done, security teams were put on round-the-clock shifts not only to make sure that no trespassers could go onboard, but also to ensure that the timbers supporting the ship did not give out.

On 16 April 1953, the Queen – wearing a black fitted coat and a matching straw hat – and the Duke of Edinburgh travelled to the shipyard for the much-awaited ceremony. Dock workers turned out in their thousands, and the Queen smiled and waved, and walked to a special transparent cabin, which was built to house the launch ceremony. The name of the ship was a closely guarded secret, and despite the thousands of people in attendance, everyone was completely silent, anxiously waiting to hear what she would be called.

'I name this ship *Britannia*,' the Queen said, and cheers and whoops of delight echoed around the yard. 'I wish success to her, and to all who sail in her.' She then pressed a button, which released a bottle of Empire wine, and *Britannia* slid into the water through a steady mist of rain, and to the sound of 'Rule Britannia' playing in the background.

The boat's name was the idea of the late king, and after launching it successfully, Her Majesty went to the shipyard's model room and spoke about her father. 'Had he been here today,' she said, 'he would have been as delighted as I am to see the fine ship our yacht promises to be.'

The Admiralty announced shortly afterwards that the boat would be officially commissioned in January 1954. The statement also detailed the number of staff on board. It would have, 'a full crew of 22 officers and 225 ratings, including Royal Marines', though additional crew would be employed as necessary during long tours.

Although the building of the new yacht was justified by saying that during times of war it would be able to turn into a hospital ship, complete with helicopter landing pad, it was widely criticised by MPs. The problem stemmed from how much it had cost to build, since this had been estimated to be £1,800,000, but MPs worried that this could rise much further. When Commander Allan Noble, parliamentary and financial secretary to the Admiralty, spoke at Westminster, he addressed the costs involved with the building of the ship, as well as what it would cost to convert it into a hospital. He estimated that it would be between £160,000 and £200,000, although this was never an issue, since in all her years at sea, *Britannia* was never called upon to become a hospital.

'This yacht is to enable Her Majesty to travel vast distances to visit the Commonwealth and Empire,' Noble told MPs, 'and I think that she should have a yacht that is in accordance with our tradition as a maritime nation.'

While the House of Commons cheered after Noble gave his speech, by 1954, MPs complained again when the cost of *Britannia* rose to £2,139,000, because of extra costs and substantial changes to furnishings and fittings. The subject was given considerable discussion in the House of Parliament, during which time it was decided that no justification could be made for any charges related to the alterations. It was also discovered that a considerable amount of overtime was paid in order to get the ship ready to sail to Tobruk, Libya, in May 1954, to bring the Queen and the Duke home after their Commonwealth tour.

The subject of the Royal Yacht *Britannia* was not a popular one, but in the end, it may have proved its worth. The ship was used considerably by the Queen and her family, sailing around the world on a regular basis for over forty years, until its decommission in 1997.

35

Bunting, Tea Parties, Crowns and Complaints

While the country was mourning the death of the King, it was also happy to welcome and support the new queen. Nineteen fifty-three was to be her coronation year, and in respect of that, there was a definite buzz in the air. Schoolchildren were presented with special celebratory books, and always looking for a good royal connection, businesses made sure that they had a plentiful supply of banners, bunting, streamers and anything Union Jack-related.

Photographers got in on the excitement, too, and offered their picture services for coronation teas, parties and functions of any kind . . . 'All supplied in Coronation Souvenir Covers at no extra cost.' Committees were created, and fundraising events such as dances and whist drives organised in order to raise money for souvenirs and programmes, all to be given out to households and local schools.

The enthusiasm for the upcoming event gave some citizens pause for thought. One ex-sergeant wrote to his local newspaper, explaining that he was on duty at the coronation of the Queen's grandfather, George V. 'It was a wonderful and never-to-be-forgotten sight,' he said, before wondering if any other soldiers were still around from that time. 'Forty-two years seems a long time,' he added wistfully.

BUNTING, TEA PARTIES, CROWNS AND COMPLAINTS

While many respected the religious aspect of the coronation, others thought that it should be purely a civil and legal event – or indeed, no event at all. One reader of the *Barnoldswick & Earby Times* was so incensed that they penned a mammoth letter, explaining how they would plan the coronation if they were in charge. Calling themselves Loyal But Sane, they described how there would be no 'Toy Town' soldiers, no dukes, earls, page boys or cushion carriers. Instead, there would be a selection of working-class folk at the ceremony, and demonstrations would take place around the country. 'I wonder how many workers' houses, nurseries, old folk's rest homes, could have been built by the money spent on all the London decoration?' they pondered.

A kinder view was put across by the mayor of Hampstead, Harold G. Judd, who wrote to his newspaper to ask if anyone who owned a television might consider lending it to hospitals or care homes, or inviting others into their homes, so that those less fortunate could watch the ceremony. 'I should be most grateful if they could follow the example which some have given,' he wrote.

While most cities, towns and villages were excited to plan coronation festivities, at least one felt that the money would be better spent elsewhere. In early 1953, the east coast of England was hit with mammoth floods, and was still recovering as the coronation drew closer. In a parish meeting in the village of Hameringham, it was decided that the money that would normally be spent on celebrating should be better off donated to the flood relief fund. It was agreed that the best – free – way of celebrating would be to say a prayer for the Queen in the local church, but that all the children of the village should be given a small souvenir to remember the day.

On Coronation Day itself, the plan for millions around the country was to dress in their Sunday best, attend one of the many ceremonies of thanksgiving, then gather together to enjoy a broadcast of the main event. While many children fidgeted at the very thought of sitting through hours of sermon, the villages of Sibford Ferris and Sibford

Gower knew what to do to keep them occupied. After the broadcast, they decided, the day would be dedicated to fun. In that regard, there were fancy-dress parades, maypole dancing, fancy-dress sports, cricket, tea parties, crowns, a whist drive and other entertainments in the school hall. As well as that, everyone over the age of sixty-five would be presented with caddies of tea. 'There will be something for everybody,' a committee member said, 'from the youngest baby to the oldest inhabitant.'

But no matter how hard committees and councils tried, there were always going to be complaints, and these came in the form of letters to local newspapers after the Coronation Day had come and gone. While some people were enraged by the cost of the celebrations, others were incensed that not enough money had been spent. One letter writer from Nottingham was absolutely furious that the decorations in the city were taken down a week after the coronation. Writing under the pseudonym of Very Disappointed, they noted that while some could visit the centre every day, therefore seeing the decorations, others were not so lucky. 'Owing to various duties,' they wrote, 'many haven't had the pleasure of viewing these displays, which are seen perhaps only once in a lifetime.'

36

'I Shall Strive to Be Worthy of Your Trust'

The coronation of twenty-seven-year-old Queen Elizabeth II took place on 2 June 1953. According to Her Majesty, her rocky ride from Buckingham Palace to Westminster Abbey was 'horrible' as the carriage was not really designed for travel, having only been sprung on leather. As well as that, it took a long time to reach its destination due to the fact that the horses could go no faster than walking pace. But away from how uncomfortable it all was, the procession was spectacular, a glittering array of colour and sound.

As with her father, and the numerous kings and queens before her, the ceremony included the recognition, whereby the Queen's Scholars of Westminster School chanted 'Vivat Regina Elizabetha! Vivat! Vivat! Vivat!' as the Queen made her way to the Chair of State. The oath was next, and Her Majesty promised to govern the people of the United Kingdom and other countries in the Commonwealth. Then it was time for the anointing of the holy oil, while the choir sang 'Zadok the Priest', before the delivery of the Orb, the Ring and the Sceptre, all leading up to the crowning itself.

The crown used in the coronation was – and still is – St Edward's Crown, made with solid gold and set with 444 precious stones. It was placed on the Queen's head, while she was sitting on King Edward's Chair, signifying that she has been given worldly power. However, this would be the only time the Queen would wear that particular crown. The more familiar crown was the diamond-encrusted Imperial Crown, which would be worn at the end of the coronation, and then to most of the State Openings of Parliament during her reign.

In 2018, the Queen sat down with BBC commentator Alastair Bruce to describe how it felt to wear the Imperial Crown. She described how she had to remember to lift her speech notes up, rather than look down to read them. 'Because if you did, your neck would break,' she smiled. Thus was the weight of the crown.

After she was presented with a bible and she moved to her throne, archbishops, bishops, the princes of the blood and the peers of the realm stood before her and swore their fealty. When each person had touched the crown and kissed the Queen's hand, the trumpets played.

'God Save Queen Elizabeth!' the people in the abbey shouted. 'Long live Queen Elizabeth! May the Queen live forever!'

At the end of the ceremony, Her Majesty left Westminster and headed back to Buckingham Palace, where almost-three-year-old Princess Anne was waiting for her. The toddler was furious when her parents and brother had left her behind to attend the abbey. However, when her family, the pages and the maids of honour took to the balcony, she was included, and waved enthusiastically to the roaring crowds below.

It wasn't the only balcony appearance by the Queen that day. By evening, it was raining in London, but the crowds remained in the Mall, huddled under newspapers and umbrellas. They were rewarded just before 10 p.m., when the waving and smiling Queen and the Duke of Edinburgh stepped out once again. The floodlights were then switched on, and the crowd gasped in awe as the lights created a fairytale scene down the Mall, towards Admiralty Arch. When the couple went back into the palace, the crowds began to disperse, but those determined to stay were rewarded once more at 10.40, when they appeared again, and for a final time around midnight.

That evening, the Queen broadcast a message to her people, thanking them for their loyalty and affection, and pledging always to strive to be worthy of their trust. 'I thank you from a full heart,' she said. 'God bless you all.'

37

The Princess and the Equerry

In 1944, twenty-nine-year-old former RAF Captain (and married man) Peter Townsend became equerry to King George VI. It was in this capacity that he met fourteen-year-old Princess Margaret, and while he didn't think anything of it at the time, the association with the Princess would ultimately lead to great heartache on both sides.

In 1952, shortly after her father died, Princess Margaret fell in love with the much older man. By this time, she was twenty-one and Townsend thirty-seven, but still, the love was reciprocated, and the two became a couple, albeit a secret one due to the age difference and the fact that Captain Townsend was soon to be a divorced man. The Queen urged the Princess to be discreet about the relationship, but it wasn't long before whispers gathered pace around the palace, and eventually, the news reached the reporters of Fleet Street.

By this time Captain Townsend had moved to Clarence House to look after the Queen Mother, and he and Princess Margaret discussed marriage. Newspapers were suspicious enough about the relationship to casually mention that the equerry had been seen accompanying Princess Margeret to official royal functions. However, since that was part of his job, the public didn't think anything of it. That all changed when the coronation came along, and Princess Margaret was seen picking a piece of fluff from his jacket outside Westminster Abbey. From that moment on, there was no stopping journalists from wondering if there was something more than a professional connection between the pair, and when the foreign press began printing the rumours, the UK followed suit.

On 14 June 1953, the *People* printed an article entitled 'Princess Margaret: Scandalous stories of her romance'. In the piece, the unnamed reporter demanded that the public be made aware of the rumours of an affair between the Princess and the equerry. They repeated the stories published in New York and France that claimed that the Princess was in love either with Peter Townsend or publisher and politician Mark Bonham Carter. According to the report, the Queen Mother favoured Townsend, and the Queen had been in discussions with the Archbishop of Canterbury as to the consequences of the Princess marrying a divorcee with children. One outcome, it was discovered, was that if the marriage did go ahead, the Princess would have to renounce her royal titles, just as her uncle Edward VIII had done in 1936.

Interestingly, the *People* journalist was firm in his belief that stories of a marriage proposal were untrue, and questioned why someone who was third in line to the throne would even contemplate marrying a divorced man. He also demanded that an official denial should come. 'Let the truth be made known,' he wrote. 'That is the way to stop the scandalous rumours.'

The article caused controversy with the British people, who began writing in to the newspaper with their views. One woman assured the editor that the only thing that was important was Princess Margaret's happiness, and that neither church nor state must stand in the way of that. Another reader browbeat the newspaper for repeating the stories in the first place. 'If she is having a romance that is her own private affair,' wrote another. A representative of the French newspaper quoted in the article even demanded (and received) an apology because part of the original story had been mistranslated.

By July, the whole country was abuzz as to whether or not Princess Margaret should marry Peter Townsend. It was the subject discussed by mothers watching over their children in the playground, it was read in newspapers over breakfast, and it was deliberated on by teenagers on their way to and from school. Who would ever want to be a princess, they asked themselves, if they were kept from marrying the man they loved?

While the British public were obsessed with the subject, behind the scenes the Queen found herself in a difficult position. While she supported her sister as much as she could, Her Majesty had to give permission for her to marry, since Margaret was under the age of twenty-five. This made things complicated because, as head of the Church of England, the Queen knew that the church would not support a marriage between the Princess and a divorced father of two. It had been Townsend's wife who had initiated their separation, but even so, Prime Minister Winston Churchill did not approve of the marriage between Townsend and the Princess, and was sure that his parliament would feel the same way.

By July, the *Daily Mirror* ran a poll, asking the British public if the Princess should marry Townsend. They responded in their thousands, not only in Britain, but from all around the world. Out of the 72,277 people who voted, only 2,305 said 'No', and the supporters wrote in in their droves to relay their opinions that Princess Margaret should be supported if she decided to marry.

The *Sunday Pictorial* columnist Rex North also became involved, when he asked in his column if the clergy would marry them, and if they had any advice for the couple. 'Princess Margaret is a credit to our Royal household,' he wrote. 'Peter Townsend, a war hero, was the innocent party in his divorce.'

Around the same time, Doctor Donald Soper, president of the Methodist Conference in Birmingham, gave a speech which attacked the *Daily Mirror* poll. He described the article as an 'unwarrantable and disgusting intrusion into the affairs of that Royal personage ... I make that protest as strongly as I can, and I believe this conference will support me in it.'

But regardless of what newspaper columnists and the results of a poll said, there was no hope of Princess Margaret and Peter Townsend marrying while she needed permission from the Queen. Instead, the equerry was sent to work for the British Embassy in Brussels, and Princess Margaret was left on her own.

38

A Surge of Crowds in Scotland

The twenty-third of June 1953 was a grey, misty day, as the royal train pulled into Princess Street Station, Edinburgh. This was to be Elizabeth's first trip to Scotland since becoming queen, and it was a formal affair. The trip was much anticipated by the people of Scotland, though in the days leading up to the trip there were rumblings that some activists would try to stage a demonstration to argue that Queen Elizabeth was coming to visit as 'Queen of Scotland', instead of sovereign of the United Kingdom of Great Britain and Northern Ireland.

The *Inverness Courier* took umbrage at what they called 'the hotheads', declaring that they were 'loth to believe that any genuine Scots would so demean themselves as to bring discredit on their own country by any word or deed which could be taken as an affront to the Queen'.

Seemingly oblivious to the political rumblings, the Queen stepped on to the platform with her husband, Philip, as a twenty-one-gun salute rang out from Edinburgh Castle, and the lord provost of Edinburgh, St James Miller, stepped forward to present her with the keys to the city. With him were a variety of officials, magistrates in their traditional robes and the guard of honour. The Queen accepted the keys, and returned them to the provost. 'I return you these keys being perfectly convinced that they cannot be placed in better hands,' she said. She then inspected the guard of honour, and left for Holyroodhouse, which was to be her residence for the trip.

Outside, the huge crowd roared. This was the first time many of them had seen Elizabeth, and certainly the first time since she became monarch. The men, women and children who lined the route had been waiting there for hours. Some had even been there all night, either trying to rest on benches or huddled under blankets on the cold, hard cobbles. They didn't seem to mind, however, and as the royal party passed by, they enthusiastically waved hats, hands and handkerchiefs.

The Queen — wearing a powder-blue suit and tiny white hat — waved to them from her horse-drawn coach. While the weather may not have disturbed the fans too much, it did destroy the chances of a planned fly-past in an E formation. The event was deemed too dangerous to perform in the present weather, and hastily called off.

Arriving at Holyroodhouse, the Queen was welcomed by Argyll and Sutherland Highlanders, but while she chatted to some, it was the regiment's resident pony to which she gave most of her attention. Clutching a large bouquet of flowers, she patted the pony and spoke to his groom, before heading to lunch.

The next day, the Queen and the Duke attended a ceremony of national thanksgiving at St Giles' Cathedral, in front of a 1,700-strong congregation. The service was full of pomp and ceremony, and included Her Majesty being blessed and the national anthem sung. The Queen was then 'offered' the honours of Scotland, which included the sword of state, and the Scottish crown on a cushion. There was a tense moment when the Queen seemed to falter slightly as the heavy crown was placed in her arms, but she recovered and handed it successfully to the Earl of Angus. Later that afternoon, there was an elaborate garden party at Holyroodhouse. Nine thousand guests were invited, and all wanted to catch a glimpse of the Queen, wearing a cotton summer dress and wide-brimmed hat.

Her first state visit to Scotland as queen was a huge success, with further trips to a youth rally and an ex-servicemen's housing estate. However, a visit to Glasgow City Chambers on 25 June ended in something of a disaster. Temperatures were approaching 80 °F by the time the Queen arrived in George Square, and she was met by a crowd of thousands. Despite a mounted police presence, the excitement led to a surge, which saw many people crushed or collapsed, including children and a seventy-eight-year-old woman, who was rushed to hospital. As the affected children were passed through the crowds to safety, police linked arms in an attempt to control the throng, who were now chanting, 'We want the Queen!' Her Majesty managed to take everything in her stride, and eventually went into the building, before appearing shortly after on the balcony.

The Queen's train arrived back at Euston Station, London, on the morning of 30 June 1953. Wearing a slate-grey coat and a green feathered hat, she was greeted by various officials. '[We've had a] very nice journey,' she told them, before heading home to Buckingham Palace.

39

Aureole, a Difficult Horse

As a keen horsewoman since childhood, Queen Elizabeth was the owner of many horses over the course of her life, including those she enjoyed riding and those bred purely as racing horses. In her study, she kept books about the different pedigrees, and also a racing ledger, where she would record the meets and results of every horse she owned, as well as deciding which races they would train for, and which horses should be bred.

'The Queen has an encyclopaedic knowledge of pedigrees and breeding records,' Brigadier Stanley Clark OBE wrote in 1957, adding that at the beginning of each season, she would always sit down and work out her plans.

In 2021, *Horse & Hound* magazine asked the Queen to name her favourites, and one of those listed was Aureole, a chestnut stallion that had been bred by her father, King George VI. The horse was born in 1950, and had not been entered into any races by the time the King passed away. He was inherited by Queen Elizabeth, and although known for his temperamental nature, went on to have a successful career from 1952 to 1954.

On 6 June 1953, Aureole ran in the Derby at Epsom, and despite a busy schedule during coronation week, the Queen – dressed in a blue hat and coat – was excited to attend the race. During a conversation with jockey Gordon Richards, she predicted that his horse, Pinza, and another, Pink Horse, would be the ones that Aureole would need to look out for. She was proved correct, when Pinza won, followed by Aureole, and then Pink Horse.

The race had been a tense one, not only for the Queen, as the Queen Mother, the Duke of Edinburgh and Princess Margaret all looked stern in the royal enclosure. But as disappointed as she was, the Queen was not a poor loser, and congratulated both Richards (who had finally won the Derby on his twenty-eighth attempt), and Pinza's owner, Sir Victor Sassoon. 'The Queen has many Derby years before her,' Sassoon told reporters. 'Will she worry about not winning this time when she has already won something infinitely more valuable – the hearts of all her subjects?'

Aureole was a magnificent-looking horse, but there was no denying that he had a spiky temperament. He would often 'play up' at the beginning of his races, unseating his rider and displaying agitated behaviour. Because of his personality, the horse was written off by many, but the Queen insisted that he be given the chance to prove his worth. That he did, in 1954, when he won several races, including the Coronation Cup, the King George VI and Queen Elizabeth Stakes, and the Hardwicke Stakes.

Before the latter, the Queen and the Duke of Edinburgh almost had an accident while riding horses around the course, when they narrowly missed a telephone cord that was strung between the grandstand and the number board. Ducking to pass under the wire, the Queen and Duke went on their way, while Princess Margaret was seen holding it up in order to get underneath. The story caused a bit of a ruckus in the press, but clerk of the course, Major J. C. Bulteel, was quick to dismiss it. 'There was a little bit of wire on the course,' he said, 'but it was of no danger to anyone at any time.'

AUREOLE, A DIFFICULT HORSE

Aureole was retired after his 1954 wins, and later became a champion sire. Years later, Princess Anne spoke about her memories of him. The Princess explained that, as a child, she would often accompany her mother around the Sandringham stables. Aureole would be there, but his behaviour made it clear that he was not looking for friends. 'He was a difficult horse,' she said.

40

Princess Margaret Decides Between Love and Duty

Princess Margaret's former boyfriend, Peter Townsend, returned to the United Kingdom in 1955. The Princess was now over the age of twenty-five, did not need permission from her sister to marry, and stubborn Winston Churchill was no longer prime minister. However, issues were still complicated, when this time Prime Minister Anthony Eden – himself a divorcee – told the Queen that he objected to the idea of the marriage, and so did his ministers.

It was not known if the wedding would even go ahead, since Princess Margaret had not yet made up her mind, but still, the prime minister sent word that if she was to marry Townsend, she would have to give up her place in the line of succession, as well as her civil list income.

This decision put the Princess into a dilemma. Should she give up her royal privilege to marry the person she loved, or should she continue living without Townsend, as she had done for the past two years? Was the spark of their early relationship still there, or had it dulled with the passing of time? The Queen Mother pretended that the situation wasn't happening, while the Queen had many discussions with the Princess, and was said to have been sympathetic to her situation. However, there were whispers that she would much rather her sister not marry Townsend, though she knew that, ultimately, it was a decision only Princess Margaret could make for herself.

While the Princess pondered her future, once again the newspapers and the public were enthralled by the whole situation, and further polls were conducted around the world. When Clarence House released a statement to say that no decision would be announced regarding her future, this just succeeded in making everyone even more obsessed. Crowds gathered not only at Clarence House, but also in Lowndes Place, where Townsend was staying. Reporters rang the doorbell and put their pencils to their notebooks, but all they could get was the agitated housekeeper telling them that the captain would not be coming out, that he would be having lunch in his home. When he finally did make an appearance, Townsend refused to tell them anything concrete. 'I am sorry,' he said, 'I can't yet. I am going away for the weekend. I cannot say where I am going.'

Of course, it didn't matter if he could say where he was going, since Townsend and Princess Margaret were tailed wherever they went. When they were seen arriving separately at a friend's house in Binfield, near to Windsor Castle, villagers could do nothing else than gather around the gates in the hope of seeing the couple together, and journalists grilled them about what they had seen and what cars the couple were driving.

Everyone had an opinion on whether or not the couple should be free to marry without any interruption, but despite the meetings, the discussions and the anxiety, in the end, the possible repercussions were just too much. On 31 October 1955, Princess Margaret released a statement. 'I would like it to be known that I have decided not to marry Group Captain Peter Townsend,' she said. She went on to say that while she was aware that she might be able to go into a civil marriage, provided she renounce her rights of succession, she had decided not to, because of her belief in the Church and her duty to the Commonwealth. 'I have reached this decision entirely alone,' she said, before thanking Townsend for his support and devotion.

Reporters rushed to speak to Townsend, but were told that he was in no fit state to speak to anyone. 'He is a man of dignity,' wrote Keith Waterhouse for the *Daily Mirror*. 'He has behaved throughout this whole affair with tact, restraint and above all, humility.'

When all the gossip and intrigue died down, Peter Townsend moved back to Belgium, where he married an heiress and had more children. Princess Margaret went on to marry photographer Antony Armstrong-Jones in 1960, and had two children of her own, but the marriage was not a happy one and ended in 1978. She and her former love met briefly one last time in 1993, though their love was not rekindled. The captain passed away in 1995, and was buried in France, where he had lived for some time. Princess Margaret did not attend the funeral.

41

Rain, No Umbrellas and a Dirty Red Carpet

It was a cold, drizzly November day in 1955 when the Queen made her first trip to Birmingham since her coronation, but despite the weather, everyone was in a bright mood. In the days before the visit, residents had dragged out their ladders and carefully fastened bunting to their roofs, fielding it all the way down to the garden gates. Flags were attached to porches and fences, and balconies were decorated with anything remotely red, white and blue-related.

In the new estate of Shard's End, a group of female fans – supported by donations from local shopkeepers and companies – had painstakingly painted a huge banner, welcoming the Queen to their area, and fastened it to poles. By the time 3 November rolled around, however, the rain had washed most of the words away, and all that was left was pale red ink smudged into the fabric. Other decorations fared better, including a 'Long May She Reign' sign, festooned in red, white and blue streamers.

Now, the decorating was finished, and the main concern was being able to see the royal couple on their journey from the station. The police urged people to leave their umbrellas at home, because, 'It will be difficult for the crowds to see the Royal visitors if there is a forest of umbrellas in front of them.' Now, the Queen – wearing a light green coat with black collar and cuffs, and a matching hat – waved to those who were soaked through from standing in the downpour. Most had been there for hours, perched on stools and folding chairs brought from home. One woman was heard telling another that she didn't care how wet it was, as long as she got to see the Queen. As the crowds pushed forward, and some complained about the lack of space, another woman laughed and told her friends that it would all be worth it in the end.

The topic of pushing and shoving had been a worrying one for the Birmingham police force. So much so that just days before the visit, Chief Constable E. J. Dodd made an appeal during a press conference. 'Don't surge across the road when the Queen's car comes into view,' he said. 'Not only could it be dangerous for the children who may be at the forefront of the waiting crowds, but it would also mean that fewer people would get a view.'

After visiting King Edward's School, receiving a box of chocolates from outside the Cadbury factory, visiting the Joseph Lucas factory, and inaugurating new buildings to house the Colleges of Technology, Commerce and Art, the Queen and the Duke of Edinburgh headed to the Council House for lunch. There, thousands of flowers had been installed, 'to give the impression of sunshine and warmth on a November day'. Whether or not that was achieved during the downpour was up for debate.

Also at the Council House, a special landline had been laid so that amateur radio enthusiasts could cover the visit for the local hospital. The idea was that the team would follow the couple all over the city, and had already asked patients what they wanted to hear during the broadcast. One of the most popular subjects was the Queen's clothes, and the woman in charge of dissecting them was the secretary of the local radio association, Freda Cocks. 'I used to be a buyer for a fashion shop,' she said, 'so I think I know something about clothes.' When the Queen got out of the car in front of the Council House, Freda perched on a makeshift stand and spoke into her microphone, recalling in great detail exactly what Her Majesty was wearing.

After lunch, the Queen and the Duke of Edinburgh drove to the newly built All Saints' Church for a five-minute visit with the Bishop of Aston, the architect of the building and various church representatives. Outside, an adventurous ice-cream man allowed youngsters to stand on the roof of his van, and they cheered as the Duke helped his wife out of the car. Once into the church, the couple studied the photographs of the church's construction, before signing the visitors' book. 'Her Majesty said that she thought the church was beautiful,' said the Rev. C. L. Martineau. 'She was very interested in its beginnings, and I was able to tell her a little about the church life here and the community life.'

Back at the station, a red carpet was laid out for the royal couple to walk upon on the way to their train. Unknown to those who had rolled it out, however, was the fact that a fast train to London was due to speed through the station at any moment. When it did, the whoosh began pulling the carpet under the carriages, until a dozen quick-thinking police officers jumped on it, and pulled it back into place. By this time, the carpet was covered in footprints, and was made no better when the station's cleaner casually pulled his trolley down the middle of it. A hasty cleaning was performed, and then the Queen and the Duke arrived to catch their train.

The visit had only been five hours long, but the Queen left a lasting impression. 'As she passed by, with her Consort at her side, young and old alike caught the excitement and the promise of the new Elizabethan Age,' wrote one columnist.

The feeling was mutual, and just days after the visit, the lord mayor of Birmingham received a letter from Major Edward Ford, the Queen's assistant private secretary. In it, Ford thanked him for the enthusiastic welcome given to the couple. 'The Queen and Duke of Edinburgh very much enjoyed their visit to Birmingham,' Ford wrote. '[They] were deeply touched by the warm reception which they received from its citizens.'

42

When the Queen Met Marilyn

The evening of 29 October 1956 was a chilly one, though the crowds outside London's Empire Theatre were grateful that at least it wasn't raining. It was the night of the Royal Command Performance, where a showing of *The Battle of the River Plate* was to take place in front of not only Her Majesty, but some of the biggest stars in the world. These included Joan Crawford, Brigitte Bardot, Anthony Quayle, Victor Mature, Norman Wisdom and Peter Finch. However, the star the crowds most wanted to see was Marilyn Monroe.

Marilyn had been in England since July, making *The Sleeping Prince* (later retitled *The Prince and the Showgirl*) with Laurence Olivier. During this time, she became fascinated with the Queen, bombarding her assistant with questions about Her Majesty, and buying souvenirs in places like Floris, Harrods, Simpsons of Piccadilly and Cornelia James. All of the stores had one thing in common – they were favourites of the Queen and her family.

But it didn't stop there. Marilyn wanted desperately to meet her, and hoped that she might even be invited to Buckingham Palace for tea. This seemed a perfectly reasonable request to Marilyn, who wrote it on her PR man's to-do list. Co-star Laurence Olivier, however, thought the whole idea was preposterous. He had decided early on that he did not like Marilyn, and so scrubbed off her requests every time. Fortunately for the actress, officials at Buckingham Palace did not feel the same way as Olivier.

While a trip to the palace may not have been a possibility, a Command Performance was. And so it was that on 29 October, Marilyn stood in the long line-up, excitedly chatting to Victor Mature and nervously licking her lips, while she waited her turn to finally meet the Queen.

When Her Majesty arrived at the theatre with Princess Margaret, she was wearing a beautiful black, full-skirted gown and a diamond-and-emerald tiara. There she was greeted by Charles Penley, the Empire's general manager, and introduced to various people inside the foyer. That done, she made her way upstairs, where the celebrities were waiting, walked along the line and finally reached Marilyn.

Shortly before the Command Performance, a notice had gone out that the actresses should be dressed conservatively, but Marilyn had rebuffed this request and chose to wear a gold, low-cut gown, with spaghetti straps. The Queen gave the actress a quick look up and down, took her hand, and then Marilyn descended into a deep curtsy. During the moments that followed, the two women talked about being neighbours, and Windsor Park.

'She asked how I liked living in Windsor,' Marilyn told reporters afterwards, 'and I said, "What?!" and she said that as I lived in Englefield Green, near to Windsor, we were neighbours. So, I told her that [my husband] Arthur and I went on bicycle rides in the park.'

After talking with Marilyn for a short time, the Queen moved down the line, and then accepted a bouquet from six-year-old Nicholas Douglas Morris. When Princess Margaret reached Marilyn, the two had a brief conversation about the making of *The Sleeping Prince*, and then the actress encouraged the Princess to see the new play by Marilyn's husband, Arthur Miller.

'The Princess laughed and said she might,' Marilyn said. True to her word, the Princess did go to see the play, A *View from the Bridge*, shortly after.

While their meeting was quick, it would seem that Marilyn left quite an impression on the Queen. Years later, an unnamed friend revealed that, afterwards, Queen Elizabeth watched all of Marilyn's films. 'I thought Miss Monroe was a very sweet person,' she said. 'But I felt sorry for her, because she was so nervous that she had licked all her lipstick off.'

43

Scandal on *Britannia*, and a Trip to Portugal

The sixteenth of February 1957 was a cold bright morning, but in spite of the chilliness, the Queen – wearing a navy-blue wool dress, a half-length fur coat and red hat – couldn't stop smiling as she climbed the plane steps at London Airport. She was on her way to Portugal for a state visit, but it can be safe to say that the smiles were probably on account of who she would see there – her husband, the Duke of Edinburgh.

For the past four months, Philip had been on a colossal forty-thousand-mile solo world tour on board the Royal Yacht *Britannia*. He had visited Melbourne to open the Olympic Games, Antarctica, and a host of countries, but had missed various family dates at home, such as Prince Charles's birthday, his wedding anniversary, Christmas and New Year.

The tour was seen as something of a diplomatic mission, but the separation had been hard, and certain corners of the media took the opportunity to throw shade on the royal marriage. There were whispers as to why the Duke had gone off on his own for four months, and some prophesied that he had insisted on going in order to find some kind of purpose outside his marriage. Matters were made worse when, shortly before the end of the tour, it was announced that the marriage of Philip's private secretary, Michael Parker – who was on *Britannia* with the Duke – had come to an end, and he had resigned from the royal household.

Some believed that this story was a smokescreen to hide issues in the royal marriage, and there was an abundance of media interest. In the end, Parker's solicitor, Eric R. Summer, released a statement, confirming that the man had separated from his wife, and announcing that he had chosen to resign. 'He has told me that with all the worry in the present circumstances of his marriage, he feels he cannot give of his best in his appointment,' Summer told reporters.

Now, the *Britannia* had arrived at Setúbal with the Duke on board, and preparations were under way for him and the Queen to reunite before the tour of Portugal began shortly after. This involved extra police being drafted in not only to protect the royal couple, but also to deter any tourists that might decide to follow them. This decision may have seemed extreme, but in the weeks leading up to the royal visit, excitement had been bubbling over just about everywhere. Workmen were employed to clear any litter along the royal route, bunting and flags were everywhere, photos of the Queen and the Duke were on display in neighbourhood windows, and some hotels were even renting out their windows for a better look. Dress shops even sold out of formalwear, such was the rush to buy something fancy to wear on the procession route.

While people have speculated on, and even dramatised, what the royal couple's reunion consisted of, it is impossible to know the truth. What is known, however, is that when the couple began their tour of Portugal, they were all smiles, and the country gave them a spectacular welcome. There were parades, there were banquets, there were gun salutes, there were half a million flag-waving fans lining the streets, and there were even thousands of doves released just in time to fly over the Queen while she unveiled a memorial tablet dedicated to her great-grandfather, King Edward VII.

In addition to that, there were also one hundred students who were desperate to throw their black cloaks on the ground for the Queen, just as Sir Walter Raleigh had done for Queen Elizabeth I. Police cancelled that particular adventure, but failed to stop several young boys from wading through the Tagus River in order to climb up on to a pavilion where the Queen and Duke were being greeted by the president of Portugal, General Francisco Craveiro Lopes. Mud and water dripping from their trousers, they succeeded in mingling with the dignitaries, until security finally spotted them.

When it was time for the couple to leave Lisbon, a massive crowd lined the streets, and children from a British school sang the national anthem. Once at the airport, little girls curtsied and presented the Queen with bouquets of tulips, while Portuguese officials kissed her hand. 'Thank you for a wonderful time,' she said, before climbing the steps to the plane. As it taxied down the runway, many fans wiped tears from their eyes, while the Queen waved and smiled from the window.

The mood remained just as high when the couple arrived for a short visit to Porto, where they rode through the city on an open-topped bus, while fans waved, laughed and snapped photographs. They then left for England, the trip a massive success, and the rumours of an unhappy marriage put behind them.

'Elizabeth conquered Lisbon both as a woman and Queen,' one reporter decided.

44

Opening Parliament in Canada

There was one word that was repeated over and over again when the Queen and the Duke of Edinburgh embarked on a trip to Canada in October 1957 . . . confidence. Her Majesty seemed happier than ever, smiling and completely at ease during each and every occasion.

The trip was just four days long, but included eighteen official engagements, most of them the kind of events usually seen on a royal tour: banquets, a wreath-laying service and meetings. However, there were some out-of-the-norm occasions too, such as when the Queen opened the Canadian parliament, the first time a reigning sovereign had done so. The occasion was a success, though the blistering temperature of the room, caused by television lights, made one woman faint and many more complain about the heat.

Her Majesty, wearing a long gown and diamond tiara, seemed undisturbed by the heat, however, and perfectly recited a speech as the Queen of Canada, in both English and French. During it, she expressed, 'my gratitude and that of my husband for the warmth of the loyalty and affection with which we have been welcomed here in Canada'.

Then there was a ceremony to mark the beginning of work on the Trans-Canada Highway, which caused everyone – including the royal couple – to jump in shock, when the Queen pressed a button and ignited a gigantic bang, just yards from where they stood. A light moment came when they were presented with a 350lb stuffed sturgeon, which had been caught off the coast of Nova Scotia. The fish was given to the couple because of an old law declaring that all sturgeon were owned by the royals. The presentation was a light-hearted one, and the Queen and Duke laughed accordingly. Afterwards, the Duke offered it to the National Museum, but they assured him that they had enough trouble finding room for the one they already owned.

Although there were some grumbles that the trip to Canada had been predominantly spent in Ottawa, it was hailed a success by most of those who witnessed it. The general consensus was that Her Majesty had come across as very human, motherly and caring. On the evening before they left for the United States, the royal couple met 1,300 guests at a government reception, and shook hands with every person there. They also spent a great deal of time with the Government House staff who had looked after them during their stay, and the Queen became engrossed in talking to some of the older people who remembered her father.

Perhaps the highlight of the visit for the Canadian people was when they got to see the Queen on live television. Twenty-seven-year-old Michael Hind-Smith was the producer for the event, and declared it to be, 'the most exciting broadcast I've ever done'. During a ninety-minute rehearsal, the Queen went through her speech several times, and then had tea with Hind-Smith. 'We didn't talk to her about television at all,' he said. 'We tried to make her comfortable and at ease.'

Using a script as well as a teleprompter, Her Majesty seemed relaxed during her ten-minute broadcast to Canada and the USA, which included passages in fluent French, too. 'It has been lovely,' the

Queen told viewers. 'We look forward all the more keenly to 1959, when we hope to be with you again.'

While the trip and the broadcast brought forth a light, human side to Her Majesty, back in the UK grumbles were felt from certain quarters. These complaints included an annoyance that Britain had never had a televised speech, and wondered why the playful side of her personality was not apparent at home.

In a column for the *Shields Daily News*, one critic thought that it was time the Queen was given the opportunity, 'to emerge in Britain as the regal but essentially human person she becomes on her overseas visits'.

On 16 October, the couple bade farewell to Canada and boarded a flight to Virginia, USA, before heading to Washington as guests of President Dwight Eisenhower and the first lady.

45

The Queen Meets the President

After the spectacular reception in Canada, the Queen and the Duke of Edinburgh flew to the United States. First, they stopped briefly in Virginia, and then the couple arrived in Washington on 17 October 1957 to meet President Eisenhower.

There they were given a twenty-one-gun salute, the keys to the city and a rendition of the British national anthem. While President Eisenhower gave a rousing speech about the special relationship between the UK and the USA, the Queen clutched notes for her own speech. Afterwards, she thanked the president for his kind welcome. 'As Queen of Canada, I bring you the warm greetings of a friendly neighbour and a staunch ally,' she said.

On the way from the airport to the White House, there were so many people lining the streets that the couple's driver likened it to the president's Inauguration Day, and British officials compared it to the 1953 coronation. There were people waving, marching bands, motorbikes, secret service agents hanging on to cars and, in the midst of it all, the Queen, Eisenhower and the Duke of Edinburgh waving to everyone, exchanging words and smiling broadly.

By the time the couple arrived at the White House, the president's grandchildren were pressed against the windows for a better look,

THE QUEEN MEETS THE PRESIDENT

while Mrs Eisenhower smiled as the Queen and the Duke climbed the steps towards her. After the greetings, there was a private lunch, they were shown to their rooms and, later that day, attended a state banquet, where they were served food on plates decorated with the presidential gold seal.

The visit to the White House was a happy one, and before she left the president told the Queen that if there was anything he could do for her, to let him know. She smiled and nodded, and asked Eisenhower to come to England for a visit.

On 21 October, the royal couple arrived in New York – their final destination before flying home to England. As their train pulled into Stapleton Station, Staten Island, crowds gathered outside. Some of the youngest were teenagers, who had played truant from school in order to try and see the couple. Others were housewives who had travelled into the city, and hundreds more were uniformed and undercover officers, making sure that nobody got closer than they should. All seemed excited to see the Queen, and some were overheard commenting on how beautiful she was, and how handsome the Duke appeared in real life.

The couple were greeted by Richard Patterson – a representative of Mayor Robert Wagner – and State Governor W. Averell Harriman. On the request of the Queen, they were then driven close to a hospital where some of the wounded had been transferred during the war, before being taken into the city. On a ferry trip across the Hudson, a replica of the *Mayflower* ship – complete with seventeenth-century costumed crew – was towed into view. When the ferry reached the Statue of Liberty, the Queen couldn't believe how big it was.

Despite the fact that she was there for just fifteen hours, there were ten engagements fitted into the visit to New York. These included a parade, complete with confetti and torn paper raining down on to the street, a gun salute vibrating the windows of the nearby skyscrapers, a trip to the United Nations Headquarters (during which she became the first British monarch to address the UN Assembly), and a trip to the top of the Empire State Building, where the couple's liftman was Edward Aloysius Quinn, a former London policeman.

While dozens of security personnel manned the doors, and helicopters hovered overhead, the Queen was presented with a gold-plated model of the building. Later, it was discovered that security had been increased because a would-be assassin had made phone calls, threatening to kill the Queen.

Security threats aside, Her Majesty seemed to enjoy a lunch with Mayor Robert Wagner and former president Herbert Hoover. There she was presented with a medal of honour, and gave a speech, thanking everyone for their hospitality, and commenting on how big the United States was. She also gave special mention to a festival she had been able to see in Jamestown, Williamsburg, and a football game in Maryland. 'I cannot leave without saying that I wish I could stay longer and see more of your great country, the Middle West and the West Coast,' she said.

46

Happy Christmas from Sandringham

Christmas Day 1957 was a historic moment for the UK. For the past twenty-five years, families had gathered around the radio to listen to the annual royal festive speech, but this time was different. For the first time ever, many families would not only hear the Queen's words, but would be able to see her, too, thanks to a relatively new wonder – television.

The year 1957 had not been an easy one for the Queen, and she had found herself on the receiving end of criticism by Conservative peer John Grigg, Baron Altrincham. The man had described Elizabeth as like 'a priggish schoolgirl' when giving speeches, as well as prim, a pain in the neck and even aloof. The venom of Altrincham sent shockwaves around the United Kingdom, and when it was disclosed that Buckingham Palace was not pleased with the insults, the man doubled down and took a swipe at the Queen's employees, too. The Altrincham affair was inconvenient and embarrassing, but it wasn't the first time the Queen had been criticised as having a somewhat awkward tone while speaking. Indeed, during 1957, unfair criticism had also been levelled about her appearance.

With this in mind, when the Queen was approached to read her annual speech on live television, she was not only hesitant, but actively against the idea. When she eventually agreed, she made an effort to practise for weeks beforehand. These rehearsals not only included going over the words of the carefully prepared speech, but also the way she would deliver them. With all the criticism thrown at her during the year, the Queen was determined to appear more approachable to everyone who tuned in.

As families (including her own) gathered around their televisions, the programme began. The first frames were of the exterior of Sandringham, where the Queen and her extended family were in residence. The sound of a choir singing the national anthem then led to the appearance of Her Majesty, wearing an elegant gold gown, and sitting behind a desk in the Long Library. Her first choice – the study – was deemed too small for the amount of equipment needed to televise the speech. On the desk in front of her, photographs of Prince Charles and Princess Anne were perched, while an array of Christmas cards was displayed in the background.

Taking a glance at her notes, the understandably nervous Queen wished her public a Happy Christmas, and told viewers that it had been twenty-five years since her grandfather had broadcast the first Christmas message. Now, watching the speech on television would be another landmark event. 'I very much hope that this new medium will make my Christmas message more personal and direct,' she said, and then – perhaps as a dig to the Altrincham affair – she added that it was inevitable that she might be seen as a remote figure to many. 'Now, at least for a few minutes, I welcome you to the peace of my own home,' she exclaimed.

The increasing use of television, and the quickening pace of the world, had been a worry to some people, and the Queen urged everyone not to throw away ageless ideals, but to have courage moving forward. She urged watchers and listeners not to be afraid of the future. 'I can give you my heart and my devotion to these old islands, and to all the people of our brotherhood of nations.' She then urged everyone

When Princess Elizabeth was born, the country became obsessed with everything she did. The princess was soon dubbed 'the most popular baby in the land'.
(Classic Image/Alamy)

Elizabeth and Margaret were close to their parents, and the couple tried their hardest to give the girls something of a 'normal' childhood.
(Bettmann/Getty Images)

(above) Princess Elizabeth was determined to do her part for the war effort. In 1945 she joined the Auxiliary Territorial Service (ATS). On VE Day she danced through the streets in her uniform.
(Shutterstock)

(left) When Princess Elizabeth married Prince Philip on 20 November 1947, the country celebrated with street parties and lots of bunting.
(Hulton Archive/Getty Images)

Prince Charles was born in November 1948, a year after Princess Elizabeth married Prince Philip. Princess Anne arrived several years later, in August 1950. *(Lisa Sherridan/Studio Lisa/Hulton Archive/Getty Images)*

Although in ill health, the death of King George VI was a great shock to his family and the country, and propelled Princess Elizabeth into the role of queen, long before she expected to become one. *(Paul Popper/Popperfoto via Getty Images)*

The coronation of Queen Elizabeth II was a happy occasion, enjoyed by her family, friends and the nation as a whole. *(Sipa/Shutterstock)*

The young Queen visits Glasgow during her 1953 trip to Scotland. *(Topical Press Agency/Hulton Archive/Getty Images)*

Wherever the Queen went, there were always flowers to collect and guards to inspect.
(Smith Archive/Alamy)

In 1953, Elizabeth toured Scotland for the first time since becoming queen. There she visited Edinburgh, where she met dignitaries and was presented with the keys to the city.
(Smith Archive/Alamy)

The relationship between the Prince and Princess of Wales was hardly harmonious, but there were lighter moments, such as this one during the 1982 Braemar Highland Games. *(Kent Gavin/Mirrorpix/Getty Images)*

The Queen loved her time aboard the Royal Yacht *Britannia*. She is seen here waving to crowds during a 1979 tour of Kuwait. *(Tim Graham/Getty Images)*

The Queen visits the Isle of Arran in August 1997. Just weeks later, she would be forced to defend her reluctance to return to London, after the death of Diana, Princess of Wales. *(Tim Graham/Getty Images)*

The Queen loved horse racing and was thrilled when her horse Estimate won Royal Ascot's Gold Cup in 2013. *(Maureen McLean/Alamy)*

The Queen and Prince Philip were married for seventy-three years, until his death in 2021. She once described him as 'my strength and stay'.
(Tim Graham/Getty Images)

to come together to set an example to the world.

After gazing several times at Philip, seated off-camera, the Queen ended the speech by quoting from *The Pilgrim's Progress* by John Bunyan. 'Though with great difficulty I am got hither, yet now I do not repent me of all the trouble I have been at to arrive where I am . . .' That done, the camera panned in for a close-up of the Queen and, with a smile, she wished everyone a Happy Christmas, and a prosperous New Year.

The first ever televised Christmas speech had gone well, and even American journalists praised Her Majesty, calling her 'serene'. They then applauded her more natural and casual approach, as a welcome change.

Interestingly, in the weeks preceding the broadcast, there was concern that the power lines around Sandringham might break down and spoil the event. The Eastern Electricity Board quelled fears of this by installing high-voltage power lines, as well as duplicate links for television and sound. Still, while radio listeners received a 'very good to excellent' reception, residents of Kent were perturbed to discover that during the televised broadcast, voices with an American accent were heard popping in and out of the speech. A bizarre theory was put forward that the interference was caused by police cars in Florida, which were sharing a waveband with the UK television network. This created a fun anecdote in the newspapers, though nobody could say if it were true.

47

Thunder, Umbrellas and the Magna Carta in Lincoln

When it was announced in 1958 that the Queen and the Duke of Edinburgh were to visit Lincoln, during a tour of both the east coast of England and Scotland, the city was buzzing. Thirty-one years before, the Duke of Windsor (then the Prince of Wales) had opened the Usher Art Gallery, and now the Queen would be visiting the establishment herself. The whole day was mapped out to include a folk-dancing display at the Sincil Bank football ground, the opening of the Pelham Bridge, a trip to the cathedral, and then on to the castle. What nobody could plan, however, was the weather.

When 27 June finally arrived, the summer weather was – as is often the case in the UK – atrocious. When the Queen disembarked from the royal train, she was already wearing a gold-coloured mackintosh over her blue woollen dress, but was quick to put up her umbrella. The Duke, on the other hand, didn't seem prepared at all, and left the train without a coat. The thunderous rain that greeted him forced him to rethink, and a mackintosh was quickly thrown over his grey suit. With puddles forming around the forecourt of the station and wind howling around the building, the Queen was welcomed by the mayor and the lord lieutenant. A sword presented to the city by Richard II was then tendered to the Queen and, as per tradition, she touched it and then handed it back to the mayor.

As they left the station for their first stop on the Lincoln tour, the royal couple passed crowds six deep, many of whom had been waiting for hours despite the weather. Cries of 'Move your umbrella,' and 'Aww, what a shame,' rang out, and sadly, many didn't catch a glimpse of the couple at all. The thousands of coloured umbrellas, and headscarves carefully covering hairdos, and of course the rain, put paid to that. Earlier, as the Queen inspected a guard of honour outside the station, one man was heard to mutter, 'I'm going to see them even if it does mean I get pneumonia.'

At the Usher Art Gallery, both the Queen and the Duke were presented to councillors and aldermen, and then signed the visitors' book and autographed photographs of themselves. The Duke mentioned that he had visited Lincoln in the past, and then the couple both agreed that the gallery was superb. When someone mentioned the weather, the Queen's reaction was to express regret and disappointment with the downpour. She was relieved, however, to be told that the children she was about to see at the football ground would mainly be under cover.

When they did reach the ground, the couple were driven around in an open Land Rover, and the Queen clutched on to her umbrella as the rain poured down. Still, the weather didn't seem to dull the crowd, and they cheered, shouted and waved hands, hats and handkerchiefs. In photos of the event, it is hard to spot anyone who isn't smiling or laughing, despite the incessant downpour.

The eleven thousand relatively dry children gave the couple a huge welcome from the undercover stand, but the schoolchildren who had rehearsed their morris-dancing display for weeks and weeks were less lucky. The ground was far too soggy to even think about dancing, so some singing was performed, instead.

It was still lashing down by the time the royal couple arrived to officially open Pelham Bridge, and as the Queen shivered under her umbrella, everyone else – including the Duke, the dignitaries and the crowd, stood out in the rain. After unveiling the tablet commemorating the bridge opening, the Queen gave a speech. She spoke about the history of Lincoln, and then congratulated everyone who had helped to design and build the new bridge, adding that she hoped it would help travellers to navigate their way around the city easily.

At the cathedral, the Queen visited the Airmen's Chapel, where she unveiled a window dedicated to those from Flying Training Command units who had lost their lives during the war. She was then shown a copy of the Magna Carta, and sat in a chair that had been once occupied by Edward I in 1301. That done, it was on to the castle, where the couple signed photographs before finally leaving the city, on their way to the equally rainy seaside town of Scunthorpe. On her way on to the train, the Queen turned to the mayor. 'I hope you will say what a wonderful welcome we have had,' she said. 'We have been very touched.'

In spite of the weather, the Lincoln visit was a talking point for the city for weeks to come. So much so, that staff at the *Lincolnshire Echo* were inundated with visitors, all seeking out photographs of the visit. Such was the popularity that the newspaper had to release a statement asking people to bring cut-outs of the photographs with them for reference. 'This will greatly simplify the work of the Photo Sales Dept,' they said, 'as 80 photographs in all were taken.'

48

The Queen Meets the Kennedys

On 4 June 1961, US President John F. Kennedy and his wife Jacqueline arrived at London Airport for a brief but busy visit to London. They arrived under spectacular fanfare, with Prime Minister Harold Macmillan, a selection of officials and dozens of news crews all there to greet them. However, this was quiet in comparison to the welcome they received from the five hundred thousand excited individuals who lined their route from the airport to the home of Jacqueline's sister, where the couple were to stay.

The crowds had been there for hours, and some had even lugged their picnic baskets down to the streets, sipping on tea and eating sandwiches on the grass verges lining the route. By the time the Kennedys left London Airport, the crowds were simply beside themselves with excitement, especially when Mr Kennedy stood up in his open-topped car and gave everyone a wave.

The London trip centred on a meeting with Prime Minister Macmillan, and the christening of Jacqueline's niece, Anna Christina. On arriving in England, the president joked that, 'Tomorrow, I am about to assume my most sombre responsibility – which is to become the godfather of a new English citizen.'

While the christening garnered a lot of attention, the meeting that most intrigued the British public took place on the evening of 5 June, when the first couple travelled to Buckingham Palace in order to meet the Queen and the Duke of Edinburgh. Their journey there was an eventful one, and the swarm of tourists and fans outside their residence was loud and vocal.

'We want Jackie!' they screamed, and then, 'Good old Jack!'

When they finally left the premises, President Kennedy gave an impromptu interview to the BBC, and then they headed for the palace, where mounted policemen and officers struggled to hold back the crowds. Once inside, they sat down for dinner with a group of fifty, which included the Queen, wearing a full-skirted gown and a sapphire and diamond necklace. There then followed a four-course meal of cold cream of pea soup, sole, lamb and a soufflé. It was, said the Queen's press secretary, 'a good old English dinner'. President Kennedy left England later that evening, leaving Jackie to spend more time with her sister, Princess Caroline Lee Radziwill. He left under a fanfare of car horns, traffic jams, fans running in front of his vehicle, and even fireworks popping off over the London sky.

Writer Gore Vidal later told Princess Margaret that during the Buckingham Palace meeting, Jacqueline had found the Queen to be heavy going. 'But that's what she's there for,' the Princess replied. The Netflix series, *The Crown*, dramatised the meeting, and portrayed Mrs Kennedy as a fairly rude and aloof guest, uninterested in a tour of the palace. We do not know the realities of what Jacqueline really thought about the Queen but rumours abound that, shortly after the meeting, she criticised the palace décor, and Her Majesty's fashion sense.

When the *Daily Express* wrote that the Queen 'stole the scene' from Mrs Kennedy, they received a quick slap from reader David Cuthbert, who wrote to them all the way from New Orleans, USA. 'How dare you,' he said, before giving his view that nobody 'could ever steal the scene from the superlative wife of the US President.'

THE QUEEN MEETS THE KENNEDYS

In 1962, the Queen and Mrs Kennedy reunited, and apparently warmed – slightly – towards each other, while sharing stories of their love of horses. A more sombre meeting came in 1965, when Jacqueline had become a widowed mother to two children, Caroline and John. The family flew to England to be presented with one acre of land in memoriam to the assassinated President Kennedy, and once again, the streets were lined with people, but this time the welcome was reserved and tinged with sadness. At a hillside in Runnymede – the location of the memorial – the Duke held John's hand, and the Queen spoke briefly to each of the children, as well as their mother.

As the breeze blew the trees, Mrs Kennedy sat stoically, as Prime Minister Harold Wilson gave his regret that President Kennedy's life had ended 'in the deep purple of martyrdom'.

The Queen then gave a heartfelt speech about the late president. 'My people shared his triumphs, grieved at his reverses and wept at his death,' she said.

49

Trees, Tea and Soapy Suds in Corby

On the evening of 19 June 1961, the Queen and Prince Philip left Windsor on the royal train, heading for Northamptonshire. They were to visit Corby, a new town with the steelworks at the heart of it. After staying overnight on the train, the royal couple arrived in Corby on the morning of 20 June and, after a short ceremony at the station, were greeted by thousands of residents, including many from local schools.

Six-year-old Annette Finn lined up on the roadside with her fellow schoolfriends, all waving tiny flags. 'The royal car came into view,' she remembers. 'It was black and shiny, passed in a flash, and I only got a short glimpse of a smiling lady in a big hat. I thought our Queen would be wearing a crown, so I was a little disappointed, and didn't believe that she was the lady we were all waiting for. The thing was, I always thought that our headmistress, Miss Smith, looked like the Queen, so when I saw the lady driving past, I wondered why Miss Smith was in the car, instead of Her Majesty!'

Another child who was confused by the royal visitor, was Bernadette Noble, who saw the Queen's white tulle and flowered hat as she exited her car. 'Look, Mummy,' she exclaimed. 'The Queen must have just washed her hair!' Mrs Noble did a double-take and had to admit that the style of the hat made it look as though it were a pile of soapy suds on top of the Queen's head. The woman was so amused by her child's comment that she wrote to the *Daily Mirror*, where the editor of the letters page had to admit that the white 'snowball' hat did look rather frothy.

The Queen and the Duke were given a rapturous welcome in the town's Market Square, where they were both presented with flowers (a bouquet for the Queen, a buttonhole for the Duke) before signing the visitors' book and several photographs. They then headed to the foundations of a nearby church, spoke to church officials and planted two trees, before a quick stop in the town's library to look at a detailed plan of Corby.

The highlight of the day for the Buchan family was when the Queen called into their home on the newest estate, Beanfield. Knowing in advance that they would have royal visitors, Mrs Buchan nipped out to buy a new tea set, some tea leaves and some oatcakes, and as the Queen toured the home, she happily accepted them. 'She did not sit down at all while she was in the house,' Mrs Buchan said afterwards. 'She said she did not have time.'

After asking the Buchan family about their taste in decorating, the cost of their rent and showing interest in their son's guitar, it was time to leave. The Queen handed back her cup, and the royal couple got back into their car, ready for a visit to the British Steel plant. There was a great turnout of steel men when they arrived to watch 140 tonnes of molten steel being poured from an open-hearth furnace. They then left on the royal train, headed for their next stop – Stamford in Leicestershire.

The Queen visited Corby several times in the coming years, including in 1982, when she was given a tour of the new secondary school, named after the Queen Mother. Disaster struck moments before Her Majesty arrived, when a pupil unleashed a stink bomb in the hallway and staff had to run around opening doors and windows.

If the Queen noticed, however, she certainly didn't say. Instead, she was given a tour of the building, where she met a variety of students, including thirteen-year-old art student, Richard Morgan.

'We all stood there wearing our plastic aprons and our name tags,' Richard remembered. 'And when the Queen came in, she noticed a mural that we'd made, depicting a building site. On the picture, there was a worker that – for some reason – had his head cut off. "Oh!" the Queen exclaimed. "This gentleman has had an unfortunate accident!"' The children were happy to see a lighter side of Her Majesty, and after staring at the mural for a moment, she carried on with the tour.

50

Sympathy and Kindness at Addenbrookes

On 28 May 1962, the Queen opened the first stage of the new Addenbrookes Hospital in Cambridge. Wearing a primrose-coloured coat with a matching straw hat, Her Majesty unveiled a plaque, and expressed her belief that there would never be a shortage of doctors and nurses willing to work in such a large, modern hospital. 'The professions of medicine and nursing not only enjoy as high a respect as any but also, I believe, give those engaged in them the satisfaction equalled in few other callings,' she said.

While the visit was officially to open the hospital, unofficially, the Queen wanted to visit a five-year-old patient, called Michael, who was currently in intensive care. Just days before, the child had been playing outside his home, close to the Sandringham estate, when he was accidentally hit by the Queen's driver, Francis Murray. The driver had been travelling to the RAF station at Marham to pick up the Queen and take her to Sandringham, when he had been unable to avoid the little boy. Michael had suffered a fractured skull in the accident, and underwent surgery in King's Lynn Hospital, before being transferred to Addenbrookes, where he was said to be 'slightly improved . . . but remains serious'.

The Queen was notified of the accident, and asked the local police superintendent to call the boy's foster mother to express her sorrow and concern. 'She said she would be keeping in touch with the hospital,' said the woman. Her Majesty's schedule was then changed so that she could personally pop in and see the unconscious child. Once in the room, the Queen stood for several moments in quiet reflection.

'The decision was the Queen's alone,' wrote one columnist. 'And in making it she demonstrated once again that fund of sympathy and kindness which endears her to her subjects.'

After the tour of Addenbrookes had been completed, the Queen went to Cambridge University and had lunch at Trinity College. Later, she inspected Peter Paul Rubens's *Adoration of the Magi* at King's College Chapel, which she described as 'A most wonderful piece of work.' After some time at the chapel, she moved on to Papworth Village Settlement, which had originally been founded during the First World War for those suffering from tuberculosis. There, she planted a tree, and looked around a leather shop attached to the complex, which was currently renovating her personal trunk with the words 'The Queen' emblazoned on the front.

In late June, the little boy injured by the royal car was discharged from hospital, and headed home. There his foster mother told reporters that he had made a remarkable recovery. '[He is] in good health and spirits,' she said.

Shortly after, royal driver Francis Murray resigned from his job. He had been at the palace for ten years, first as a car washer and then as a driver, and the loss of his job would also mean giving up his flat, too. When word spread that the man was leaving his position, reporters were sure it was because of the accident, and bombarded him with calls. He assured them that while he felt regret that it had happened, he was not responsible for it, and that was not the reason why he was moving away from London. 'It may seem strange that I have decided to leave after all these years,' he said. 'But I want more time to spend with my wife.'

51

Prince Charles and the Cherry Brandy

In June 1963, Frances Thornton, a reporter for the *Stornoway Gazette*, was shocked to see fourteen-year-old Prince Charles sitting in the bar of the Crown Hotel in Stornoway, nursing a glass of cherry brandy. The teenager was currently studying at Gordonstoun boarding school, was obviously underage, and the sight of him drinking alcohol was sure to create a scandal. Thornton mentally logged the sighting, though when Prince Charles's personal detective appeared, he asked what the Prince was doing there and escorted him out. Thornton went home and wrote her story, but when it was published, Buckingham Palace put out a firm denial and said that the article was simply untrue.

'It made life very difficult for me,' Thornton said. 'I was questioned by police and people began to talk.' However, she was determined to prove that her words were correct, and thankfully for her reputation, questions were asked, and after speaking with the Prince's detective once again, the truth was revealed. Buckingham Palace then retracted their denial and a statement was prepared, in agreement with the headmaster of Gordonstoun.

The Queen's press secretary revealed that Her Majesty wanted it to be known that the palace had been misinformed about the visit to the Crown Hotel, and that they regretted denying the story. 'It does now appear that the prince did in fact, have a drink,' a spokesman later added. An investigation was then carried out to discover why they were given the wrong information in the first place.

While the incident created much fuss in the media, the general public didn't seem to think much of it all, and some even wrote to the newspapers. 'To read some reports of the incident,' wrote Miss J. Parris, 'one would think the prince and his pals were out on a drinking spree.' Another reader predicted that the Duke of Edinburgh was sure to have found the whole thing entertaining, while another wondered if the truth would have ever come out, had Frances Thornton not been so adamant that she was telling the truth.

Prince Charles had his chance to tell his side of the story during an interview in 1969. Asked about the affair, the Prince explained that he thought 'it was the end of the earth' when the scandal came out, and that he'd have to move to 'Siberia or wherever'. He explained that he had been on a cruise from school at the time, and ended up in the Stornoway hotel, where they were to have a meal. He was disappointed to see that people were staring at him through the window, so went into the more private bar area – which he said was his first time in a bar – and ordered a drink because it seemed like the proper thing to do. 'And hardly had I taken a sip when the whole world exploded round my ears.'

In 1985, during a trip to Stornoway, reporters joked about the cherry brandy incident, and asked if the Prince would be visiting the Crown Hotel. 'Oh, shut up,' he laughed. 'That was a sign of a misspent youth.' Seven years later, the bar was renamed in the Prince's honour, and on the day of opening, cherry brandies were on the house.

52

One More Baby at Buckingham Palace

In September 1963, during the family's annual Balmoral holiday, it was revealed that the Queen and the Duke of Edinburgh were expecting a baby: 'It is announced from Buckingham Palace that the Queen will undertake no further engagements after Her Majesty leaves Balmoral in October,' the statement said. An addendum to this came from the Queen's press secretary, who added, 'Both the Queen and the Duke of Edinburgh are, of course, very happy about it.'

The Queen's age of thirty-seven was – in 1963 – classed as an advanced age to have a baby, and many had thought that the royal family had stopped growing after the arrival of Prince Andrew in 1960. The news was surprising, and radio stations around the world stopped their programmes to make the announcement, while newspapers held the front page in case of any further information.

Unfortunately for them, nothing was forthcoming, so instead, reporters were left guessing when the baby was due, and created stories based on how far down the child would be in the line of succession. Some even revelled in the fact that there would be a fifteen-year age difference between Prince Charles and the new arrival.

There were few sightings of the Queen after the announcement, though several days later, she did travel back to England to see Princess

Anne settled into her new school in Kent. 'The girls all look so alike in their uniform that I don't know whether I shall be able to pick out Princess Anne when I come next,' the Queen told headmistress, Elizabeth Clarke. After that, Her Majesty kept a fairly low profile, and even opted to give a sound recording of her Christmas speech, instead of appearing on television as she usually did.

March 1964 arrived, and with it a flurry of news reports on the comings and goings at Buckingham Palace. When royal midwife Sister Helen Rowe moved in, rumours swirled that the baby was about to be born. Not so, said a palace spokesman. Instead, the woman had been called in, 'as a normal precaution'.

On the evening of 10 March 1964, it was announced that a baby boy had arrived, weighing 5 pounds, 7 ounces. As hopeful crowds gathered around Buckingham Palace, a sign was posted on the railings. 'The Queen has had a comfortable night,' it said. 'Her Majesty and the baby are both well.' What it didn't say, however, is that for the first time, Philip was present at the birth – a certain sign that the attitude towards pregnancy and birth was shifting. This change was demonstrated by the Queen herself, as after the birth of Edward, she revelled in managing the balance between her job and her family, and would spend far more time with her younger children than her older ones at the same age.

Across London, people celebrated the birth of the latest royal baby. Flags were flown and gun salutes were fired, though a planned twelve-plane RAF flypast was told to veer away from Buckingham Palace to avoid disturbing the Queen and her new baby.

On a chilly, rainy 4 April, the Queen left the palace and headed to Windsor, giving the country a first glimpse of the baby in his mother's arms. However, it would take until 20 April before registrar William Prince drove to Windsor to officially register the birth, and only then did the country get to hear that the baby's name was to be Edward Antony Richard Louis.

ONE MORE BABY AT BUCKINGHAM PALACE

On 1 May 1964, another addition to the family arrived, when Princess Margaret's daughter Sarah was born. The baby's father, Lord Snowdon, told reporters, 'She looks a super baby.' Shortly afterwards, the Queen arrived for a visit, and the next day Prince Edward was christened in the private chapel at Windsor Castle.

53

When the Beatles Met the Queen

On the morning of 26 October 1965, thousands of screaming teenagers gathered on the road outside Buckingham Palace. They weren't there to see any of the royal family, however. Instead, they were waiting for the arrival of the world's biggest boyband – the Beatles. Paul McCartney, John Lennon, George Harrison and Ringo Starr were to receive MBEs from the Queen, and youngsters – mainly girls – had travelled from around the country just to catch a glimpse of them.

It was an exciting time for all involved, and in the days before the visit, the Beatles ordered new suits and had their hair cut specially. 'If you want a detailed description of my suit,' said George Harrison, 'it is dark blue, with a label inside saying, "Another Beatles original".' The fans, meanwhile, created hats with the band members' faces on them, wrote their names all over their shirts, and bought autograph books, just in case.

By the time the band arrived at the palace, Beatlemania was in full swing. Mounted and linked-arm policemen strained to hold the crowds back, chants and screams could be heard across the Mall, and many fans climbed on to the Victoria Memorial for a better look. One small boy managed to scramble over the gates, and was shown a quick exit by security, while a teenage girl – her shirt covered in messages for the Beatles – reached the top before she was persuaded down by coppers and hauled away.

One older officer was overheard complaining about the entire event. 'I've never seen anything like it at an investiture before,' he grumbled. In the end, the band's Rolls-Royce went past so quickly that the frenzied fans barely caught a glimpse of the young men inside. That didn't stop the crowd surging forward, however, and many officers lost their helmets as they struggled to close the gates.

As the teenage crowd screamed, 'We want the Beatles! We want the Beatles,' inside the palace the band rehearsed what was about to happen, and – according to Ringo, were 'drilled by the guards', as they marched towards the room. Then it was time for the investiture to begin. All four band members approached the Queen together, and bowed. Her Majesty – wearing a dress of gold silk – presented the MBEs and asked several questions about their career. When she enquired as to how long they had been together, Ringo joked that it had been forty years, and laughter rang out around the room.

Someone else receiving an award that day was Alderman Ernest Gardner, who was thrilled to meet the Beatles as they all waited to be presented to the Queen. 'They were the life and soul of the party,' he said. 'I thought they were very sound young men – knowledgeable and interesting to talk to.'

After the ceremony, palace staff asked for the band's autographs, and then as they exited the palace, reporters were there to greet them in the quadrangle. They described the Queen as great. 'She was so very sweet and put us all completely at our ease,' they said. As palace staff waved from the windows, the Beatles were driven back out of the gates and through the still-frenzied fans. 'The Queen was like a mum to us,' Paul said afterwards.

54

Heartache at Aberfan

On 21 October 1966, the children of Aberfan, Wales, kissed their parents goodbye and headed to school. It was the last day of term, and they were excited that in just a few hours, they would be free of school for a week. While teachers called their names for the register, they had no idea of the destruction and heartbreak that was about to befall them.

Situated above the school was a massive colliery spoil tip, which was built on a local spring. It had become so wet from the spring and the rain that at 9.15 a.m. it slid down the hill like an avalanche, destroying everything it came into contact with. The slurry hit and destroyed Pantglas Junior School, as well as part of the secondary school, cottages, a farmhouse and eighteen village houses. It also demolished water mains, and travelled over the railway embankment. Shocked parents and locals all tried to rescue the children and adults trapped in the remains of the school, but while some were brought out alive, most had tragically died. In all, the slide killed 116 children and 28 adults.

In the days following the disaster, Prime Minister Harold Wilson visited the village, as did the Duke of Edinburgh and Princess Margaret's husband, Lord Snowdon. When Lord Robens, the chairman of the National Coal Board, visited the tip, he was sure that the spring had only just been discovered. However, when Lord Justice Edmund Davies – the man in charge of leading the inquiry – visited the village, he was stopped by two miners, who told him that, 'It has always been there. It is not an unknown thing.' There then followed years of fights to remove the remaining spoil tips, and introduce legislation to govern mine and quarry tips, and stop them becoming a danger to the public.

On 29 October 1966, Philip returned, this time with the Queen. There, at the personal request of Her Majesty, they laid a wreath on the communal grave. Philip occasionally pointed out sights he had noticed during his earlier visit, and then the couple went to a chapel, spoke to teachers, rescuers and nurses, looked out on to the slope where the tip had collapsed, and stared at the spot where the school had once stood. Some mourning locals opened their curtains for the first time since the disaster, and silently smiled to the couple. Others opened their front doors and waved, while some approached and talked about their loss. 'Your grief is shared by everyone,' the Queen told one devastated mother.

Thirteen-year-old Colin Jones had lost his sister, Susan, in the disaster. The Queen asked him if he had seen the avalanche happen, and the boy replied, 'It was like thunder.'

When others told her that there was a strange peace before the slide, Her Majesty shook her head. 'I cannot understand the silence before it all happened,' she said.

Sitting in the living room of Aberfan grandmother Beatrice Williams, the Queen sipped tea and nibbled on Welsh cakes. There she discussed the disaster with Beatrice and her husband Councillor Williams, who had lost seven members of his family just days before. Mrs Williams described Her Majesty as being 'very upset. She was the most charming person I have ever met in my life – really down to earth.'

Councillor Williams saw first-hand the grief on Her Majesty's face, and afterwards told reporters, 'I think the visit of the Queen to the village as a mother has been beneficial to the mothers who lost their children.' As she left the Williams's house, Her Majesty was presented with a posy of freesias, from Mrs Williams's three-year-old granddaughter. On it was a card with the words, 'From the remaining children of Aberfan.'

Another local, William Lloyd Evans, who lost his wife and two children, described how the Queen had told him that she was 'deeply grieved'. The Duke of Edinburgh, meanwhile, asked the man why he thought the slurry had descended with such speed. 'I told the Duke that it was no surprise to me or anyone else,' Mr Evans said. Other parents told reporters that the Queen had said she felt thankful she was able to meet them.

When the tour of the village was finished, the couple travelled to the Church Village Hospital where seven surviving children were recovering from their injuries. The Queen told the parents how lucky they were that their children had survived, and afterwards, nurses reported that she had tried so hard to cheer the children up that laughter could be heard coming from the ward. 'There were tears in the Queen's eyes as she talked to us,' said Jean Gough, who lost two children in the disaster. 'She really feels this very deeply.'

It is said that the Queen felt great guilt for not visiting Aberfan as soon as the disaster happened, though many years later, her press secretary Lord Charteris admitted that it was her advisors who had cautioned against going so soon. The people of the village never held her lateness against the Queen, however, and she visited several times over the years, including 9 May 1997, when she met many survivors in the local community centre. 'A gathering like this wouldn't have happened without the Queen,' said former pupil Gareth Jones. 'I think it's nice that she remembers the village after all these years.'

55

A Royal Photo Scandal

In September 1968, an unnamed man walked into the offices of *Paris Match* magazine and presented them with unpublished photographs of the Queen and her family, taken – presumably – by family members. The man did not reveal how they came to be in his possession, but a technician at the magazine surmised that, 'They were almost certainly copies of originals . . . But from the quality of the prints we presumed they had been taken by an amateur on a very ordinary camera.'

Employees at *Paris Match* loved the shots, and decided that they were all in good taste. They went on to publish them on 1 October 1968 and, unsurprisingly, they caused a sensation. The photos showed the Queen shortly after the birth of Prince Edward, in 1964. In one shot she was in bed on her own, fully made-up, and wearing a nightgown, earrings and a necklace. In another, she was holding her newborn son, and the family was around her. Other photographs were just as personal, and none were ever intended to be seen by the public.

A spokesperson at the palace released a statement. 'Since the photographs are of such a personal kind,' they said, 'the Queen would naturally prefer that they had not been published.' The palace told reporters that they would not give permission for further publication, had no idea how the pictures got out of the palace, and that the security breach was an internal matter.

On the day *Paris Match* ran their story, the *Daily Express* wrote a front-page article about the leak, and assured their readers that at the present time, the photos would not be published in Britain. The very next day, one of the photos was on their front page, with the headline 'The Picture That Anne Took'. There were more photos inside, and others appeared in the days after. The angle the newspaper took was that they were being published in many different countries so, 'it is only fitting that the British people should share a picture series that will catch the interest of the world'.

There then followed outrage and questions from various quarters, including broadcaster David Frost, who questioned the right of anyone to publish such private pictures. The *Daily Mirror* hit back at the *Daily Express*, when it was suggested that they had wanted the photographs for themselves. 'The story that the *Daily Mirror* offered large sums of money for the publication of these pictures is an invention,' the chairman of IPC Newspapers Ltd announced.

This reaction wasn't the general consensus of the British public, however, and many enjoyed seeing the royal family in relaxed, personal pictures, instead of stilted, posed shots. One anonymous royalist even wrote to the *Aberdeen Evening Express*, calling the situation, 'A fuss'. She went on to say that 'anyone who saw the pictures of the Queen sitting up in her bed holding her baby . . . surely can't see any harm.'

When the Press Council announced that they would be looking into the circumstances of the photographs, Buckingham Palace told reporters that they had not requested or initiated such a probe. Actually, the investigation came on the authority of chairman Lord Devlin. It took almost two months, but finally on 26 November, the council rejected the complaints, after *Daily Express* editor Derek Marks told them that Buckingham Palace had told him no prohibition was placed on publishing the photos, and that it was a matter within his discretion.

A ROYAL PHOTO SCANDAL

The Queen's press secretary, William Heseltine, released a statement, detailing that Her Majesty had not made any complaint to the Press Council, and had no wish to see it pursued. 'Her Majesty trusts, however, that it will not be allowed to form a precedent for the future publication of private photographs, either of her own family or of those of any of her people.'

56

Prince Charles Comes of Age

In 1969, Prince Charles was the most talked-about member of the royal family. Not only was he going to turn twenty-one that year, but he was also studying at Cambridge, and soon to be invested as Prince of Wales. The Prince was growing up, and while he considered himself to be shy, he had a keen interest in acting and the theatre. As a teenager, he had also played various musical instruments – including the cello and trumpet – acted in school plays and sang in the choir. He was, therefore, a fairly friendly personality, but he was soon to be tested in ways he couldn't quite imagine.

In preparation for his investiture, the Prince was to spend a term at Aberystwyth University, where he was going to learn the Welsh language and history. The Queen was a popular figure in Wales, and during her lifetime, she visited more than three hundred times. As a princess in 1946, she even became an honorary bard during an investiture at the National Eisteddfod of Wales, and fondly remembered the ceremony for the rest of her life.

Prince Charles, however, had a slightly different early experience, when some of the Aberystwyth students, along with Welsh nationalists, did not take kindly to an English prince coming to Wales. During one visit before attending the school, there had been chants for him to go home, and while the Queen's go-to motto was never complain, never explain, Prince Charles tried to talk to the demonstrators. His idea was to see if there was something he could do to change their minds about him, but instead, it seemed to make them more outraged. He persevered, but after asking questions, which he hoped would calm the situation, in the end he had to give up. 'There was no point,' he said.

The experience had made Prince Charles a little apprehensive about going to Aberystwyth University, especially when some were vocal about the interference it would cause, in terms of security, etc. In the weeks leading up to his term at the university, there were demonstrations calling for anarchy not monarchy, and even the principal admitted that Charles might have a hard time with the nationalists in the country. 'This is a comparatively small group of students,' he said. 'Whether they will be able to attract other students one has no means of saying.'

The controversy even created trouble between English and Welsh students, with one side demonstrating and the other side throwing water at them from the balcony of a hall of residence. One student gave up his sea-view room for Charles, moving down the corridor, next to the Prince's personal protection officer. 'If the Prince and his bodyguard want to be friendly then we will be,' he said. Another student – next-door-neighbour Geraint Evans – told reporters that, 'I shall not show any hostility. I just think it would be better if he did not come.'

Some Welsh people were so incensed that they wrote to their local newspapers, causing royalists to reply, telling Prince Charles that he was more than welcome in the country. The media became involved, too, with at least one columnist exploring the idea of whether or not the heir to the throne would be in danger when attending the university. Some students arranged sit-in demonstrations, while others were said to be on hunger strike, such was their disdain for the Prince studying alongside them.

Talking to interviewer Jack de Manio, Charles admitted that there might be more demonstrations when he got there, but he hoped that they wouldn't involve being pelted with eggs or tomatoes. By the time the Prince arrived at the university on 20 April 1969, some were suspicious from afar, while others asked the Prince to visit with them in the evenings. There, they were able to form something of a bond over coffee and discussions. Even his Welsh language tutor, nationalist Edward Millward, was quite impressed with the Prince. 'His pronunciation was very good indeed,' he said after their first class.

However, while he may have been able to change the minds of some of those he met, Charles did not impress college parking attendant Steve Fullerton, who gave the Prince a ticket for leaving his MG car in a no-parking zone. 'I didn't know whose car it was,' Fullerton said. 'But if I had it would have made no difference.' And just to prove his point, he slapped the vice-chancellor's car with a ticket, too.

57

Eggs and Bomb Threats at the Investiture

After settling into Aberystwyth University – and with the investiture just a month away – Prince Charles held a press conference in the office of the college registrar. During the frank interview, he told reporters that he would likely not change anything about his life, that he felt a duty towards the country and the Commonwealth. He would like his investiture to be dignified and colourful, but he wasn't blind to the fact that certain quarters still did not want an English prince to be the Prince of Wales. 'I shall be glad when it's over,' he said, 'because having spent a year in the midst of controversy and talk it's a friction point for many people.'

In the weeks before the 1 July 1969 ceremony, demonstrations and threats reached fever pitch. Fires were started, and cars, bridges, walls and road signs were painted with slogans such as 'Shame over Wales'. There were many bomb scares called in, and then disaster struck when one of the scares came to fruition, with a package exploding at a Cardiff post office. Thankfully, nobody was hurt, but the device did blow a hole in the wall.

In Abergele, two men were killed while trying to blow up local government offices. At first, it was not known if the incident was the result of a protest gone wrong, and some wondered if it had been a robbery attempt. The men's cousin, however, told reporters, 'It was because of the idea of the Investiture of the Prince of Wales. They hated it and decided to do something about it.' He explained that they were not normally prone to violence, but on this occasion they had decided to take the lead from many other demonstrators who wanted to make their feelings known.

On the evening before the investiture, the Queen, Prince Charles, the Duke of Edinburgh and many other members of the royal family travelled overnight in the royal train from London to North Wales. On researching the route that the train would take, demonstrators went all out to disrupt the journey. Several fake explosives were found under bridges, threats were called into stations, and telephone cables were cut. A couple of teenage travellers found themselves in hot water when they hid their rucksacks in undergrowth after departing a train. They were seen by staff of a local prison, who phoned the police. Rushing to the scene expecting to find another fake (or possibly real) explosive, the officers were relieved to discover that the boys were completely innocent. They had merely hidden the luggage so that they could go and have a cup of coffee in peace. The threats and phone calls kept the police working all through the night, and inevitably delayed the royal train's arrival in Caernarvon.

When the party did eventually arrive at the station, they transferred into open-topped carriages, where a demonstrator threw a banana skin at Prince Charles, and another tried to pelt the Queen with an egg as she entered the gates of the castle. The latter caused an almost-riot when the crowd tried to restrain the man, before the police intervened and sent him on his way.

Shortly before the ceremony, a device went off in a field, and a man was hauled off for questioning, but thankfully, during the actual investiture, everything was relatively quiet. There was the usual pomp and pageantry, speeches and marches, and in the midst of it all, the Queen crowned her son Prince of Wales, before he spoke: 'I, Charles Prince of Wales, do become your liegeman of life and limb and of earthly worship. And faith and truth I will bear unto thee, to live and die against all manner of folks.'

While some locals were still vocal about the Prince becoming Prince of Wales, others were kinder. One Welshwoman, Rose Powner, arrived at her place of work on the day of the investiture wearing full Welsh costume. 'Prince Charles is just the right man for Wales,' she said. 'I think these extremists are mad.'

58

A Different Side to the Royal Family

Although she was the head of state, the Queen was more often than not considered an elusive figure. She was a woman frequently seen shaking hands with dignitaries and celebrities, and giving carefully worded speeches, but as for hearing her views or indeed revealing her personality, that was a rare occurrence indeed.

This all changed in 1968, when cameras were invited into the Queen's world. The idea was to follow the monarch and her family for a year, and it was planned as part of the celebration of Prince Charles's investiture as Prince of Wales. Unofficially, however, it was a PR exercise, a way of reviving interest in the royals, and showing that they were a 'normal' family like everyone else. The *Royal Family* documentary would be a joint BBC/ITV project, and there would also be an accompanying book, which President Nixon's press secretary, Ronald Ziegler, later described as 'A fine memento of a memorable film.'

BBC One controller Paul Fox told reporters that the documentary was 'a film which, through the perceptive eyes of its producer, Richard Cawston, enables us all to see the Queen and her family as they have never been seen before'. The Duke of Edinburgh had an active interest in the filming process, and took the role of advisor seriously. Afterwards it was his approval – and that of an advisory committee – that decided which scenes would be allowed into the finished project.

When the documentary aired in the summer of 1969, nearly 40 million Brits gathered around their television sets to watch. This impressive figure was a thrill for the networks, but not so those who had organised events that clashed with the programme being televised. One such occasion was a festival of music held at the De La Warr Pavilion in Bexhill-on-Sea. The attendance numbers were 'disappointing', grumbled one official, who brought the matter up at a local council meeting.

Festivals aside, television viewers were intrigued by the documentary, and thrilled to see the royal family taking part in official duties, such as state banquets, garden parties and meetings. However, the most entertaining scenes were those showing the family in private situations. At one point, the Queen is seen wearing a green dress and pearls, with a corgi at her feet, while she goes through dress designs and jewellery suitable for upcoming events. She wonders if one wool-coated design would be a good choice for a May trip to Austria, and then pulls a sapphire tiara out of a red box, and asks the dresser if they can find a way of wearing it. A ruby necklace is next, and the Queen joyfully talks about the history of the piece, including the fact that it was gifted to her great-great-grandmother, Queen Victoria.

Perhaps the most precious part of the documentary is when the Queen goes to her summer home – Balmoral – with her family. As a piper plays outside her window, the Duke of Edinburgh and Prince Edward sail off on a small rowing boat. 'Get in!' shouts the young royal, when his father takes too long to embark. The Queen is seen walking her dogs, and then attends to paperwork, before she and Prince Edward head to a newsagent, where they buy an ice lolly and bullseye sweets. Despite the frequent assumption that the Queen never carried cash, she hands over some coins, gives the change to Edward, and then they head back to the car. 'Disgusting that this gooey mess is going to be in the car,' she chuckles, as Edward tucks into his treat.

During another informal Balmoral scene, the family head out for a barbecue. The Queen and Princess Anne gather and crumple newspapers to start a fire (which Anne decides will be a guaranteed failure), while Prince Charles enthusiastically mixes up some salad dressing. Philip watches over the food, complains that it isn't cooking quickly enough, and then fields questions from an inquisitive Prince Edward. Princess Anne shows her proud big sister side by telling the boy that he has the prettiest face she's ever seen. Meanwhile, the Queen inspects Prince Charles's salad dressing. 'What do you think of that?' he asks. 'Oily,' she replies.

After watching the documentary, the public response was immediate and, for the most part, positive. One journalist wrote in the *Hartlepool Northern Daily Mail*: 'It has had the effect, perhaps, of permitting us to know our Queen as no other generation of Britons has known its sovereign.' It was this attitude that dismayed some royal advisors, who realised that opening up the Queen's world in such a public way destroyed any mystique she once had.

They also worried that the influx of royal television coverage during 1969 would create a case of over-exposure for the family. 'Her Majesty has therefore decided this year to break with the normal pattern and deliver her Christmas greetings in the form of a written message,' Buckingham Palace announced in October.

The unique *Royal Family* programme has not been broadcast on UK television since 1977 – the year of the Queen's Silver Jubilee. However, in recent years, modern viewers have been able to watch (and comment on) it for themselves through websites such as YouTube.

59

Walkabouts and Ruined Frocks in Coventry

On 30 June 1970, the Queen visited Coventry in order to open the new general hospital. While there she would also pay a visit to the cathedral and university, as well as a quick stop in the shopping precinct she had opened while still a princess. The visit was to be a historic one, because for the first time in the United Kingdom, she would be doing an official walkabout where, instead of chatting to a select few, the Queen would meet people of all ages lined up in the street. It wasn't new for Her Majesty to stop and talk to the occasional sightseer, but the idea of a proper walkabout had come from a recent trip to New Zealand and Australia, which had been much more informal in tone than usual.

The new format caused concern at the Coventry division of the Warwickshire and Coventry police force, who were concerned about the Queen's security. With this in mind, they closed off bridges in the Precinct where the walkabout was to take place, engaged two hundred police officers to handle the crowds, and erected barriers. However, when reporters brought up the problem of security with the Queen's press officer, William Heseltine, he was unperturbed.

'The biggest problem is not security,' he said, 'but to ensure that you have enough space around the Queen. If she is going to walk about, space must be reserved around her so that people can see her.'

While the police stressed about security, shopkeepers went about decorating their stores just in case the Queen should drive past. One of these was Mr Davison, boss of Davison's Footwear Ltd, who spent hours with his staff tying red, white and blue bunting outside his shop. Unfortunately for him, vandals arrived that evening, stood on each other's backs and tore the lot down, leaving Mr Davison furious. When it was pointed out that the Queen would not see the bunting anyway, since she would not be going down that road, Davison – who was busy redecorating – retorted, 'I know she will not be passing my shop, but I think it is a good idea for all shopkeepers to do something for a royal visit. We will have a Union Jack flying all day.'

By the time the Queen arrived in the city, excitement had reached fever pitch, and thousands of fans crowded around the cathedral and the Precinct in the hope of catching a glimpse of her. Her first stop was to Walsgrave Hospital, where she opened the building and gave a speech. She then spoke to nurses and patients.

'She is so natural,' said student nurse Helen Ogilvie, 'it takes your breath away. Everybody tells you this, but you can't believe it.'

So natural, in fact, that when the Queen spoke to Matron Catherine Madden, the woman was somewhat taken aback when Her Majesty asked if anyone had been lost in the hospital. The matron assumed that she meant passed away, until another member of staff pointed out that the Queen actually meant had anyone got lost trying to find their way around.

The visit to Walsgrave Hospital was so successful that by the time the Queen reached the new cathedral, she was running twenty-five minutes late. The crowds did not mind, however. As the Queen got out of the car, wearing a yellow dress with matching coat, the sun shone, the public waved their flags and cheered, and Her Majesty

WALKABOUTS AND RUINED FROCKS IN COVENTRY

waved back, before entering the cathedral. The excitement of those inside was muted compared to those on the street, but even so, the visit caused great joy for two Swedish students, who were unexpectedly introduced to the Queen while working in the ruins of the former cathedral, situated close to the new one.

They were thrilled to meet Her Majesty but, outside, Danish teacher Taral Hoyle-Hansen was disappointed. He was on holiday in Leamington, and had visited Coventry that day purely to see the cathedral. 'When I arrived,' he said, 'I found that I couldn't go into the cathedral because of the Royal visit. I shall have to come back now.' When the Queen exited the building, Taral accepted his disappointment, lifted his camera, and snapped a few photos of her.

Another person left saddened that day was seventeen-year-old Gail Finch. Gail worked as a Saturday girl at the cathedral, and had been looking forward to the Queen's visit for weeks. Instead, however, she found herself in hospital (and not the one that Her Majesty was visiting) with a blood infection. 'She was really looking forward to dressing up and possibly being spoken to by the Queen,' her father told reporters.

When Her Majesty reached the Precinct, she spoke animatedly with the men, women and children lined up behind the barriers. There were conversations about the new hospital, which the Queen thought looked like a hotel, and even a moment where a woman leaned over the barriers to show the monarch a snapshot from her family album. In fact, most of the crowd leaned over or against the barriers at one point, and while all seemed well at the time, when the Queen left it revealed a huge problem.

For reasons unknown, somebody had decided that the barriers should be painted in preparation for the royal visit. Unfortunately, while they had weeks to take care of such matters, they were only painted a day or two before being needed. The result of this was that everyone who had leaned on them went away with paint stripes all over their clothes and handbags. Some of the women involved with the destruction were so furious that they headed first to the local newspaper and then on to the council, where they intended to make a formal complaint.

'It is disgusting that this should happen,' said Mrs Beatrice Hewins. 'My new coat is ruined. I am in a right mess and it won't come off.'

60

The Princess Anne Kidnap Attempt

On the evening of 20 March 1974, Princess Anne and her husband Captain Mark Phillips were travelling down the Mall, on their way back from a charity film screening. As they drove towards Buckingham Palace, the car was overtaken by a white Ford Escort, which stopped rather abruptly. Immediately, a man called Ian Ball got out and ran towards Princess Anne's car. Inspector James Beaton, a policeman who was travelling with the royals along with a lady-in-waiting, got out to see what was happening, and noticed that the stranger had a gun. The two quickly exchanged fire, and then a car window was smashed, the chauffeur was shot, the detective was shot, and then . . . his gun jammed.

As the detective struggled to fix it, Ball took the opportunity to open the car door. They then had what Princess Anne described as, 'a discussion about where or where not we were going to go'. While the man was adamant that the Princess was to go with him, she politely assured him that she would be going nowhere with him at all. By this time, passersby had noticed something sinister going on and had alerted a policeman. He tapped Ball on the shoulder, and ended up being shot in the stomach. Added to that, a journalist coming down the Mall in a taxi was also shot when he stopped to help.

While all this was going on, a man wandering down the Mall saw the commotion and headed over the road, gawped into the Princess's car, and then wandered away seemingly without a second thought. A woman walking nearby thought that the car was backfiring, until she saw police arriving from all angles, while another woman went up to the car, and saw Princess Anne on the floor. 'Get down,' the Princess shouted. 'It is a maniac.' Meanwhile, the lady-in-waiting – who had been sent out of the car to safety – saw the kidnapper's abandoned gun on the road. She moved to pick it up and was immediately told off by a lady watching from the sidelines.

The Princess later joked with interviewer Michael Parkinson that the kidnapper's most dangerous moment was when there was a scuffle between him, her and Captain Phillips, which resulted in the back of her dress being torn to pieces. 'I lost my rag at that stage,' she said. A fight then broke out in the back of the car, during which time Princess Anne ended up on the floor, and from there was able to reach the door handle, and did a backwards somersault on to the road. When the kidnapper got out of the other door, she got back in.

Moments later, Ball was finally tackled to the ground by two men, one of whom was a policeman who had heard an emergency message on his radio. In Ball's pocket was a typed ransom note addressed to the Queen, demanding £3 million. 'Your daughter has been kidnapped,' it said. 'The following are conditions to be fulfilled for her release.' The demands included the money in unmarked notes to be taken to a waiting plane, a pardon for his offences, and a lawsuit against the police if his identity was revealed. He also demanded that the Queen come to the plane personally, so that he could question her. Also in Ball's possession were handcuffs – two of which were locked together as leg shackles – and two pistols, along with ammunition.

After the Princess was able to go home and police scoured the area, the prime minister, Harold Wilson, demanded a full report, and Buckingham Palace released a statement detailing what had happened. Princess Anne added that while she and her husband were thankful to be OK, 'we are deeply disturbed and concerned about those who were injured'. She commented on the bravery of her detective, who continued to look after the couple even when injured. 'We are extremely grateful to all those members of the police and the public who tried to help us,' she said.

In all, there were nine shots fired during the kidnap attempt, and the detective, the chauffeur, the policeman and a journalist were all hit and taken to hospital. Thankfully, none of them were killed, though the passing policeman was seriously injured and had to have emergency surgery.

When the case went to court, the courtroom was told how Ball had planned the kidnap in great detail, and had telephoned the Buckingham Palace press office in order to gain information about Princess Anne's public appearances. Ball told the room that he had attempted the kidnap so that he could 'draw attention to the lack of facilities for treating mental illness under the National Health Service'. Several weeks later, he pleaded guilty to attempted murder and kidnapping, and the judge detained him under the Mental Health Act, 'without limit of time'.

Several months later, the Queen opened a new police training complex, and addressed the episode in her speech. 'They do a vital and often dangerous job,' she said, 'as I and my family have recently had a special opportunity to appreciate.'

On 15 August 1974 – Princess Anne's birthday – Buckingham Palace made the announcement that the Queen was to award Princess Anne, Mark Phillips and Anne's lady-in-waiting, Rowena Brassey, with bravery awards. 'The Queen is taking the opportunity of Princess Anne's 24th birthday to show her appreciation and to express her admiration of the Princess's calm and brave behaviour throughout the incident in The Mall,' the statement said. Awards were also given to the others involved in foiling the kidnap attempt, including James Beaton, who received the George Cross.

Many years later, Princess Anne said that she had thought about the possibility of being kidnapped before the actual attempt. 'One thing about horses and sport is that you have to prepare for the unexpected,' she said.

61

A Most Boring Dresser in the USA

On 3 July 1976, the Queen and the Duke of Edinburgh flew to Bermuda, where they met the Royal Yacht *Britannia*. They then sailed to the United States to celebrate the bicentennial – the 200th anniversary of independence. After arriving in Philadelphia on 6 July, the couple were met by Mayor Frank Rizzo, before heading to City Hall, where the Queen was presented with a royal proclamation. It was then onwards to the Independence National Historical Park, where Her Majesty touched the Liberty Bell, and dedicated a new 6-ton bell, gifted to the people of the United States from the people of the UK.

Unfortunately, not everyone was happy with the presentation, and a group of protestors carried placards and demanded that the Queen take the bell back to England. The religious group apparently took offence because unlike the original, the new bell was not inscribed with the phrase, 'Proclaim liberty throughout all the land.'

Philadelphia toured, it was then time for a two-day visit to Washington, DC, where President Gerald and Mrs Betty Ford, along with Secretary of State Henry Kissinger, greeted the couple in a lavish reception at the White House. The celebrations included marches, speeches from the president and the Queen, a state dinner, a wreath-laying ceremony and, of course, the ever-familiar twenty-one-gun salute.

New York was a spectacular, and the Queen and the Duke of Edinburgh arrived on the Royal Yacht *Britannia*, as it sailed up the Hudson River, in full view of the Statue of Liberty. There were millions of fans waiting to greet them, and as with previous trips, the couple were showered with confetti and ticker tape as they waved from an open-topped car. The Queen was declared an honorary citizen of New York at Federal Hall, before heading to Bloomingdale's department store.

The next visit was to Charlottesville, Virginia, where the Queen presented the University of Virginia with a certificate from the Royal College of Heralds. She then headed to Monticello, a home that America's third president, Thomas Jefferson, had designed, and which the Queen was particularly keen to visit.

On 11 July – the Queen's last day in the United States – the Royal Yacht *Britannia* sailed into Boston, and was met by a twenty-one-gun salute from the USS *Constitution*, as well as a host of naval boats and pleasure crafts, all there to mark the bicentennial. Once on dry land, Her Majesty rode in an open-topped car with Governor Michael Dukakis, attended a morning church service, and then stood on a dais underneath the balcony of the old State House, where the Declaration of Independence was first read to the Boston people.

There Her Majesty gave a speech, thanking everyone for their warm welcome, and speaking about the history of Independence Day, claiming that if the patriots had known that one day a British monarch would stand under the same balcony, 'Well, I think they would have been extremely surprised. But perhaps they would have also been pleased.'

While on her way to Boston's City Hall, she spoke to a group of locals dressed up as British soldiers. The Queen was happy to converse with this crowd, but not so much with a crowd of demonstrators, who held up banners, shouted anti-royalty comments and protested about British troops stationed in Northern Ireland. As she made her exit after lunch inside City Hall, the demonstrators were still there, standing relatively close and booing loudly. As always, Her Majesty kept her usual calm stance, and instead chose to greet the crowd who were happy to see her.

After climbing aboard the *Constitution* for a presentation, the Queen and the Duke of Edinburgh gave a party on *Britannia*, where she knighted John Moreton, a British diplomat who had organised the trip to the United States. This was believed to be the first time Her Majesty had conducted such an event outside the UK. That done, *Britannia* sailed from Boston and headed to Nova Scotia and Montreal, in Canada, where the Queen was due to open the Olympic Games.

As she sailed out of United States waters, Her Majesty sent a message to President Ford, declaring that she and Philip were moved by the welcome they had received, and that in spite of the troubles in the world, 'it is good to know that the people of the United States are as generous, resolute, and kindly as ever'.

Aside from the few demonstrations, the United States tour was a successful one. However, there was one snipe from Richard Blackwell, compiler of the 'Worst Dressed' women's list, that wasn't particularly welcomed. Describing the Queen as a most boring dresser, the fashion designer exclaimed that Her Majesty's hat looked as though it had been made by actress and keen crocheter, Ali MacGraw, and had shrunk. His comments did not go down well with staff at the offices of the Queen's designer Norman Hartnell.

'Her Majesty is quite aware of what she likes,' said one senior member of staff, while Buckingham Palace expressed that the criticism was tired, and that the Queen had had a number of outfits made in anticipation of her visit. 'These are backed up by clothes she already has,' a spokesperson said.

62

Street Parties and Downpours at the Silver Jubilee

The year 1977 was the Queen's Silver Jubilee, and people from all over the country and the Commonwealth came together to celebrate and commemorate. It was one whole year of celebration, with church services, major royal tours, craft exhibitions, theatre shows, cricket matches, flower festivals and numerous town processions, all marking the twenty-fifth year of the Queen's reign. There were even village-hall showings of the controversial *Royal Family* documentary, with proceeds being donated to charity, as well as lookalike competitions and special events.

However, the biggest excitement was reserved for celebrations in June, when it was hoped that the people of the United Kingdom would take to the streets and hold mammoth get-togethers. The whole country was buzzing at the idea of street parties such as the ones that had been held for the coronation in 1953, and in the months leading up to the Jubilee, councils and individuals came together to make plans and raise funds. There were permits to be signed, roads to be closed, police forces to be advised and, of course, food to be bought.

STREET PARTIES AND DOWNPOURS AT THE SILVER JUBILEE

This was great news for shops and supermarkets, who stocked their shelves in preparation.

One 'cash and carry' store in Walsall was so excited about the street parties that they took an advert out in the local newspaper. Directing attention to club secretaries and party organisers, they offered their services for 'All your bulk requirements in flags, bunting, hats, novelties, balloons, catering disposables, crockery, china and other gifts.'

On 6 June, the Queen lit a beacon on Snow Hill, Windsor Castle, in order to start a chain of bonfires throughout the United Kingdom. The next day, she and Philip headed to St Paul's Cathedral. They were met by cheering crowds (some of whom had camped out the night before), a trumpet fanfare and gun salute, before the royal couple went into the cathedral for a special thanksgiving service. During a walkabout afterwards, the Queen and the Duke of Edinburgh spoke to fans about the Jubilee, and accepted gifts of flowers and homemade cards.

A lunch followed in the Guildhall, and then later Her Majesty gave an impassioned speech. Talking about the time she pledged her life to the service of the people, the Queen said, 'Although that vow was made in my salad days when I was green in judgement, I do not regret nor retract one word of it.' She then thanked everyone in Britain and the Commonwealth for their encouragement during the last twenty-five-years.

As thousands of people lined the Mall to watch the Queen wave from the balcony of Buckingham Palace, adults and children across the country dressed up in their finery and took to the streets. Many towns, villages and cities were decked out in bunting, flags and balloons, all with a common theme – red, white and blue. Neighbours brought out their picnic tables, kitchen tables, and even wallpaper tables, in order to create a gigantic place for everyone to sit, and chairs of every size were carried out into the lanes.

Old ladies brought out their freshly baked scones, young mothers carried sandwiches, and dads searched in the chest freezer for ice cream to go with the jelly. The week before, children in school were presented with a Jubilee coin, and had been busy making their own streamers and decorations. During the street parties, many took part in hat competitions, fancy-dress competitions, dancing, singing and parades. It seemed as though everyone in the country had a role to play in the Jubilee celebrations, and it was hard to find anyone who did not have a smile on their face.

Even the British weather couldn't dampen the spirits of those people who wished to celebrate, and as showers threatened overhead, the parades continued with raincoats and the partying was moved to garages, sheds and porches. 'Everyone was determined to have a good time despite the weather,' the mayor of Lichfield told reporters, and the country had to agree.

63

Stray Dogs and Gigantic Cheese in Chester

When it was announced that the Queen and the Duke of Edinburgh were to visit Chester on 2 November 1979, there was great excitement. This was the first official visit to the city since 1957, when Her Majesty opened the new County Hall and visited the Royal Infirmary. During that particular trip, a visit to Chester Racecourse was interrupted when two stray dogs somehow made their way to the course and ran over to where a march was scheduled. Organisers scrambled to remove the animals, but they needn't have worried. As a big dog fan, the Queen was happy to watch their antics, and she and Philip were seen and heard laughing together at the incident.

This time it was hoped that dogs would not interrupt the visit, though there was a rumbling of grievances before the couple arrived. Local union leaders were said to be outraged by the expense involved in hosting the royal couple, and Chester and District Trades Council even turned down an invitation to be represented at a planned thanksgiving service. 'The Trades Council,' said secretary Graham Nicholls, 'could not accept that whilst the City Council is campaigning to reduce public expenditure, it can justify the extravagant outlay for the Royal visit.'

The council scrambled to say that the cost of the visit would be minimal, and the cost of a gift for the Queen had been raised by fundraising. Some council staff, however, fumed. 'The Queen's visit is a great honour for the city,' said council leader Derek Owens-Kay, 'and I am disappointed at the communistic attitude of the Trades Council . . . I deplore this attitude.'

Trades Council secretary Graham Nicholls was so insulted by the remarks flying around Chester that he wrote in to the *Chester Observer* newspaper, lambasting them for making the unions look anti-royalist. 'Had we been so, we would have said so without hiding behind any other pretence,' he wrote. Mr Nicholls did add, however, that many trade unionists would be standing on the royal route. Why? Because their children had been given a half-day holiday from school, forcing their parents to take time off, too.

Forced to take time off or not, thousands of people seemed ecstatic to meet the Queen and the Duke of Edinburgh as they arrived in Chester to attend a thanksgiving service at the cathedral, commemorating 1,900 years of the city. After the service had ended, there was an informal walk to the Town Hall, where a presentation was to be made. Some of the folk standing in the autumn sunshine had been there since dawn, and some of the children clutched drawings and brass rubbings to give to the Queen.

Wearing a three-quarter-length salmon-pink coat and a matching hat, Her Majesty accepted so many gifts and bouquets that she ended up dropping some. Once at the Town Hall, Philip was in good form as he asked one official how he knew for sure that the city was 1,900 years old. The man told the Duke that he had seen the age on a pipe. 'Did you put it there?' Philip jokingly asked.

While it was a case of too many bouquets in Chester, when the couple reached Grange Farm, Great Mollington, it was dairy products that caused the problems. The Queen and Prince Philip spent almost thirty minutes touring and inspecting the cheesemaking, under the watchful eye of director William Oulton Wade. However, while Her Majesty seemed happy to be presented with a 56lb block of cheese, it created problems for her staff when it wouldn't fit in the boot of the royal car. After much negotiation, it was hauled off in a black limousine accompanying the entourage.

The Duke of Edinburgh was in an especially good mood throughout their visit, and took great interest in a tour of the Ellesmere Port boat museum. There, children were dressed up in nineteenth-century costumes, while the Queen unveiled a plaque. When the tour moved on to Widnes, Prince Philip was seen joking with bystanders and bursting into laughter at various moments. On spotting a group of older ladies watching the proceedings from the comfort of folding chairs, he laughed. 'I should be sitting there, not you,' he said. 'You all look too young.'

When the royal couple went on a walkabout in Warrington, close to the birthplace of children's author Lewis Carroll, they were greeted by ten-year-old Janet Bowden, who was dressed as Alice from *Alice's Adventures in Wonderland*. The child was too shy to speak to Her Majesty, but in all likelihood the Queen would not have heard her speak anyway above the roaring crowd surrounding her. The day was a huge success, and by the time they left, the police were relieved that any sniff of anti-royalty protests was firmly behind them.

64

Prince Charles Finds a Wife

In the United Kingdom and around the world, the romantic life of Prince Charles had always been the subject of gossip, mainly because whoever he chose would possibly go on to produce an heir to the throne. On 26 June 1969, an interview with the Prince was broadcast on BBC and ITV, during which he was asked if he believed that his future wife should be a titled woman.

'Well, I suppose this is awfully difficult,' he said, before going on to say that he had to be mindful of the fact that when he did marry, it would be to someone who might someday be queen. He had given a great deal of thought to the situation, and felt that maybe if he married a princess, or someone linked to a foreign royal family, they would at least know what they were getting into, and how to handle it.

When Lady Diana Spencer was unexpectedly photographed with the Prince in 1980, rumours began in earnest that she was the one he had chosen to become his wife. Lady Diana was the nineteen-year-old daughter of Earl and Countess Spencer. Born on the Sandringham estate, she had known the royal family for her entire life, though did not get to know Prince Charles well until she was sixteen, when he was good friends with her older sister, Sarah. The two met each other properly in a ploughed field, where Diana impressed Charles with her sense of humour and fun. She thought he was pretty amazing, and in the years after, the two became closer. When Lady Diana travelled to Balmoral in 1980, Prince Charles, 'began to realise then that there was something in it'.

The shy, virginal nanny/nursery teacher was twelve years younger than Prince Charles, but deemed by his family to be a perfect choice for a wife, and hopefully mother of the next heir to the throne. Diana told journalist Grania Forbes that she never thought about the age difference, while Prince Charles joked that she would keep him young. What the public didn't know at the time was that behind the scenes it was also felt that Diana would take Prince Charles's mind off Camilla Parker-Bowles. He had been in love with her for many years, but they had been unable to marry due to family disapproval.

The media went into a full-blown frenzy at the idea that Lady Diana and Prince Charles were a couple, and began camping outside her Earl's Court flat, just for a glimpse of the young woman going to work. They would follow her down the street, ask questions about her love life, and even chase after her car as she drove away. It was a frantic time for Diana, particularly as she hadn't been officially proposed to yet, and had no idea what the media intrusion would be like if she ever did marry Charles. It was also a stressful time for the Queen, and relations between her and the press came to a head during the 1980 Christmas holiday, when she was staying at Sandringham.

Many reporters had travelled to the Norfolk estate in the hope of seeing Lady Diana, but were left disappointed when she did not appear to be there. After seeing them peering at her from every corner, the Queen finally had enough and shouted at them to go away, and rumours abound that she had driven her Range Rover within inches of a swarm of paparazzi.

Prince Charles, meanwhile, caused outrage in the newspapers when he was overheard wishing the reporters a Happy New Year, and their Fleet Street editors a less happy one. Finally, the Queen's press secretary, Michael Shea, stepped in. 'The Queen is very angry,' he said, 'at what she considers is an intrusion of her privacy.' She understood the interest in Lady Diana, but felt it unnecessary to invade the family's privacy at Sandringham.

In early February 1981, just days before Lady Diana was to leave England for a trip to Australia, Prince Charles proposed to her in his living room at Buckingham Palace. He had thought she might need the time away to think about the proposal, but Lady Diana was quick to say yes. When she arrived back in England after her holiday, the secret plans were under way, and the couple met with the Queen and the Duke of Edinburgh in order to decide when and where to make the announcement that they were to marry. The Queen also shared the information with Prime Minister Margaret Thatcher, who then notified her senior ministers.

On 24 February 1981, the Queen was performing an investiture at Buckingham Palace, when the lord chamberlain, Lord Maclean, made the announcement that the couple were to marry. 'It is with the greatest pleasure that the Queen and the Duke of Edinburgh announce the betrothal of their beloved son, the Prince of Wales, to the Lady Diana Spencer . . .' The Queen beamed her approval, and then got back to her job. A photo shoot and interview then took place at the palace, where Prince Charles and Lady Diana told of their happiness at the upcoming wedding. The Prince then famously declared, 'whatever in love means', when it was mentioned that the two looked to be perfectly in love.

His good friend Camilla Parker-Bowles, meanwhile, told reporters that she was delighted for the couple, had hoped an engagement would happen, and was sure that they would be very happy together. In the years ahead, it would be revealed that Charles and Diana were anything but happy, and not at all suited. But for now, the country went into a state of madness, and millions celebrated the wedding of the year, which took place five months after the engagement, on 29 July 1981.

65

A Trip to the Cobbles

Coronation Street is the longest-running soap opera in the United Kingdom, with millions of viewers tuning in every week. First shown in December 1960, the programme centres on a cobbled street in the fictional town of Weatherfield, and tells the tales of its residents, friends and family.

When the Queen and the Duke of Edinburgh arrived for a tour of the new *Coronation Street* set on 5 May 1982, the country was in the midst of the Falklands War, and Prince Andrew was serving as a helicopter pilot there. As the couple were introduced to series regulars, one actor – Peter Adamson, who played Len Fairclough – spoke to the Queen about the situation. 'It must be a very worrying time for you and your family,' he said. 'All our hearts are with you, ma'am.' The Queen – never one to complain or explain – thanked him for his kind words.

But it wasn't all melancholy talk on the bunting-clad cobbles that day. Actor Bernard Youens – who played window cleaner Stan Ogden – received a laugh when he offered to clean the windows of Buckingham Palace. The Queen then spoke to him and actress Jean Alexander – who played Stan's wife, Hilda – at some length, asking questions about how long the fictional couple had lived on Coronation Street, and what their relationship was like with their lodger, Eddie, played by Geoffrey Hughes.

When the Duke asked Julie Goodyear (barmaid Bet Lynch) if the Rovers Return was open, she smiled broadly. 'I said I would pull him a pint any time,' she said. 'I would even open specially for him.' One thing the royal couple did not comment on, however, were Goodyear's dangly earrings – one with a photo of Prince Charles, and the other with a picture of Princess Diana. '[The Queen] smiled when she saw the earrings,' Goodyear told reporters, 'and I think the Duke quite enjoyed them.'

While everyone was eager to know if the royal couple watched *Coronation Street* at home, nobody dared ask the actual question. Columnist Janet Buckton added her views in the *Coventry Evening Telegraph*. 'I doubt whether she has the Buck House sets tuned in at 7.30 on a Monday and Wednesday,' Buckton wrote, 'But she can't fail to have heard of the true talents of all that lot who bring pleasure to millions.'

The Queen returned to the cobbles in July 2021, to mark the soap's sixtieth anniversary – a celebration which had been delayed because of the Covid pandemic in 2020. As the royal car pulled into the famous street, Her Majesty received a rapturous welcome from ITV staff, some of whom spoke to her about the difficulties of walking on the cobbles. 'No, I know,' the Queen replied, 'I've been told. Probably better not.'

The cobbles weren't the only difficulty discussed, however. During lockdown, the filming of *Coronation Street* miraculously managed to carry on, despite the issues presented by testing and social distancing. When the Queen met Bill Roache (Ken Barlow), she commented on how marvellous it was that everyone had been able to carry on during the pandemic. Roache replied, 'Well, ma'am, you're the one who has carried on,' no doubt referring not only to the virus, but also the recent passing of the Duke of Edinburgh.

Barbara Knox, who played Rita, thanked the Queen for bringing the good weather with her. 'You're like a ray of sunshine,' she said, 'and you've given us all such a lift.'

66

'It's Always Lovely to Have a New One'

On 5 November 1981, it was announced that Prince Charles and Princess Diana were expecting their first child. This was to be the Queen's third grandchild, and she had been told about it personally in the days before the palace shared the news. She was said to be absolutely delighted with the prospect of adding to the family and, as she gave a luncheon on the day of the announcement, was greeted with many warm congratulations and good wishes.

Just a day later, the Queen headed to Newcastle-upon-Tyne to open the city's new Metro transport system, though the walkabout consisted mainly of well-wishers all asking for news of the Princess. Not one to talk about her personal life to strangers, the Queen smiled and accepted their good wishes, though offered no further information. When four-year-old Helen Davies handed over a pair of knitted booties, the Queen smiled. 'My goodness,' she said, 'you were quick off the mark.' Of course, the booties were not knitted by the child herself, and her aunt Marjorie was quick to step forward and explain that they had been made from a family pattern.

From the outside, it seemed to be a happy time – 'A baby will be marvellous,' Prince Charles said. 'Naturally my wife is overjoyed.' Privately, however, the pregnancy was fraught with ill-health from the beginning. When the Prince attended a dinner alone on 9 November, he spoke to reporters. 'You have all got wives,' he said. 'You know the problems. She is all right, but it is better not to do too many things.'

Shortly after, the Prince and Princess attended carnival day in Chesterfield, where a group of women took the opportunity to ask Princess Diana about her morning sickness. Standing outside the local bakers, she confided that she was feeling better, but the experience hadn't been very nice. 'I told her it would get worse before it got better,' Dorothy McLeish said to waiting reporters.

The media intrusion into the life of the Princess had always been manic, but as soon as the pregnancy arrived, it became overwhelming. Finally, the Queen saw no other option but to invite newspaper and television editors, and the Press Association, to Buckingham Palace. There, Press Secretary Michael Shea discussed the family's concerns, and asked editors to see Diana's private life as private. 'The Princess feels totally beleaguered,' he said.

On 21 June 1982, fans, reporters and onlookers crowded outside St Mary's Hospital, Paddington, while inside, the Princess of Wales was giving birth to her first child – something she later described as a 'very bad labour'. It was an important day for the country, given that the new baby would be an heir to the throne and would likely one day become monarch. People came and went throughout the day, but no news was forthcoming. As night fell, many people remained at the hospital, but hundreds of others gathered around Buckingham Palace since it would be there that they'd see the first official announcement. Sure enough, at 10.25 p.m. an announcement was tied onto the railings, revealing the long-awaited news: 'Her Royal Highness The Princess of Wales was safely delivered of a son at 9.03 p.m. today. Her Royal Highness and her child are both doing well.'

'IT'S ALWAYS LOVELY TO HAVE A NEW ONE'

As the news filtered through to the crowds outside the hospital, there were cheers and songs, and much waving of flags. Some even climbed walls and stood on anything they could in order to get a better view. When Prince Charles exited the hospital, just over thirty minutes after the official announcement, he received a warm and noisy welcome.

One woman rushed forward to kiss his cheek, while reporters gathered around to ask questions of the mother and her newborn. 'It's a rather grown-up thing, I've found,' Charles said, before revealing that the baby had blond hair, but no name so far. With the crowds growing noisier and noisier, the Prince asked reporters to relay his wish that they be quiet for the sake of his sleep-deprived wife, still inside the hospital.

The next day, the crowds remained, and visitors went in and out. One of the most popular was the Queen, wearing a long fuchsia coat. As she entered the hospital, she was seen giving Prince Charles a kiss, before heading up to see her grandson. As she left in the rain, the crowds were desperate to hear her thoughts, but were left disappointed when all they received was a quick wave. On her way to an official engagement, the Queen Mother was asked her feelings on the royal birth. 'It's always lovely to have a new one, isn't it?' she said.

When the Prince and Princess of Wales left the hospital with their son later that day, there was a warm reception for them all. The Prince held the baby in his arms, while the Princess – in a green smock dress – took over at the bottom of the steps. Once again, crowds cheered, waved and asked for a name. Several days later they got their questions answered when it was announced that the baby would be called Prince William Arthur Philip Louis.

67

An Intruder at Buckingham Palace

As the country waited to hear if the Queen's third grandchild would be a boy or a girl, preparations were being made to host US President Ronald Reagan and his wife, Nancy. This was to be the first time an American presidential couple had ever stayed at Windsor Castle, and it was deemed historically significant. It was also logistically difficult, since Windsor was not equipped to host the president's large staff and the host of worldwide reporters that would have their cameras trained on every inch of the castle. In the weeks leading up to the visit, representatives from the USA flew in for meetings with the household, and then finally, on 8 June 1982 – at the tail end of the Falklands War – President and Mrs Reagan arrived.

While the president's security was carefully planned at Windsor, it was actually Buckingham Palace's walls that were compromised. While the Reagans were at the castle, a man called Michael Fagan managed to get into the palace, and went into a room used for storing presents for the upcoming birth of Prince William. He sat on a throne and drank wine, but after pottering around for a while, he apparently grew bored and went home.

A short time later, on the morning of 9 July 1982, Fagan climbed over the wall of Buckingham Palace once more, and again entered the building through an unlocked window. Since the door to that room was locked, he could go no further into the palace, so went back out of the window, climbed a drainpipe and entered another room. This one gave him access to many of the palace's corridors, where he was able to walk completely unnoticed by staff. He wiped the muck from the drainpipe onto a curtain, broke an ashtray and then wandered into the Queen's bedroom, allegedly with the intention of slashing his wrists in front of her, though Fagan later denied this.

On seeing her tiny figure in bed, he opened the curtains, and immediately Her Majesty sat upright, asked what he was doing there, and then told him to leave. Fagan told her that she was a nice woman, and she repeated her request for him to leave and then pressed an alarm bell. This did not bring anyone, since a footman was walking some of the corgis outside, and the corridor policeman had gone off duty. The official story went that the Queen placed a call to the police from her bedside phone. While waiting some time for them to come, she managed to catch sight of a maid and, together with a footman, managed to usher Fagan into a pantry and divert his attention with the promise of a cigarette. The police eventually arrived, and the man was led away.

During the investigation into the affair, it was revealed that there had been a lapse of security at the palace, with some alarms not working correctly, and the button in the Queen's bedroom, linking her to the police control room, not fully installed. One alarm that was triggered happened when Fagan entered the Stamp Room, but that had not been responded to. After the investigation, police patrols were stepped up, and a new committee was created to ensure that the Queen would once again feel safe in Buckingham Palace. Fagan was not charged with trespassing – since it was not a criminal offence – but was admitted to a psychiatric hospital for several months.

Much has been made of the encounter between the Queen and Michael Fagan, with some going so far as to say that they had a full conversation about the royal family. However, a decade after the intrusion, Fagan told Radio 4's *Famous for 15 Minutes* programme that, actually, nothing much happened at all. 'She just said "get out",' he said, 'that was it.' It was also reported that Her Majesty did not stay in the room after phoning the police, and instead hopped out of bed and rushed for the door, leaving Fagan sitting on her bed, his thumb cut from the broken ashtray.

Another intruder story came in 1987 and then again in 1992. During the latter, a man entered Buckingham Palace, but was detained before coming into contact with the Queen. The former story was slightly more disturbing, when it was reported that on 22 January 1987 – while the Queen was in residence at Sandringham – a man broke into the garden and was wrestled to the ground by an officer.

Norfolk police admitted that a man had broken into the grounds, but when a newspaper report surfaced to say that the Queen had seen the intruder while she was walking in the garden, sprinted back to the house and locked herself in, interest piqued. Journalists immediately phoned Buckingham Palace to get the details of the worrying incident, but the palace was keen to play it down. 'The incident was reported fully ten days ago,' said a spokesman. 'We have nothing to add.'

68

Controversy at the Opening of Parliament

On the evening of 1 November 1982, the Queen arrived at Heathrow Airport after a four-week tour of Australia and the South Sea Islands. She could have been forgiven for spending the next few days recovering from jet lag, but instead she went straight back to work, receiving notes and making last-minute preparations for the State Opening of Parliament, to take place on the third.

The Queen was to travel to Westminster in the Irish State Coach, but hours before the event, there was a large security alert at the Royal Mews, where the coaches were parked. The Mews were open to the public for a couple of hours on certain days, but for the most part remained closed. The security situation was triggered when a *Daily Mirror* reporter and photographer had been able to obtain security passes from somebody that they had met in a London pub. The men then travelled to Buckingham Palace out of hours, flashed the passes, parked their cars and were able to wander around the coaches unbothered.

When the newspaper announced what they had done, there was an uproar, and a row broke out between Buckingham Palace and Scotland Yard as to who should take the blame. It was a concerning situation, especially after the recent incident where Michael Fagan had been able not only to enter the palace, but to reach the Queen's bedroom, too. Still, while the Home Office said that lessons would be learned, the trespass was not considered to be serious. 'No member of the royal family was at risk,' a spokesperson said.

It was a cold, misty morning when the royal coach carrying the Queen, Prince Charles and Princess Diana left Buckingham Palace, and security was considered to be the biggest operation since Guy Fawkes threatened to blow up the Houses of Parliament. It was safe to say, however, that none of the cheering crowd had any interest in historical security concerns, and every eye was on a nervous Princess Diana, who smiled and waved as the coach passed by.

The Queen's speech to parliament (which was written as usual by the prime minister) caused a few raised eyebrows. First of all, there was the announcement that a bill would be brought before the House of Commons to privatise British Telecom. Then came another to sell off other assets, such as the electricity network and parts of the British shipbuilding industry. The whole plan seemed to be 'clearing the decks' before a general election, which did eventually happen on 9 June 1983, and gave the Conservative Party, under leader Margaret Thatcher, another win.

The speech was considered by some to be chilling, especially the measures presented to privatise British Telecom, which, it was felt, could leave those in rural areas without a telephone. Donald Stewart, MP for the Western Isles, was particularly concerned, and urged for a divorce between Scotland and England. 'Until that is achieved,' he said, 'the outlook for Scotland, its industry and its people, is terrifyingly bleak.'

While many members of the public heard the Queen's speech on the news and then went about their daily lives, some were still talking about it for days to come. One reader of the *Fife Free Press* even went so far as to write into the letters page with a list of items he would like the Queen to announce. These included the wish that coal prices could be reduced from £6 to £1 a bag, cheap butter to be sold to British consumers and not exported, the incomes of lower-paid workers to be tax-free, and the British people to be involved in major decision making. 'It would be a shot in the arm for the elderly,' he wrote, 'to hear Elizabeth II say: "The royal family will no longer be a charge on the nation."'

69

Faux Pas and 'Dowdy' Clothes in Canada

The Queen and the Duke of Edinburgh's tour to Canada was supposed to take place in July 1984. However, when it was revealed that an election would occur in the country during that time, the Queen headed off on her holidays, and then finally travelled to Canada in September.

The fourteen-day tour was a busy one, with visits to Shediac, the lobster capital of the world, Fredericton (where marijuana was found on the plane that the Queen was about to board), Ottawa and Fort Wellington, among others. While the royal couple were treated to military pageants, flypasts, dancing, singing and all the usual events timetabled for a royal visit, there were also various issues which resulted in the trip being considered rather controversial, and perhaps not as enjoyable as the couple had hoped.

When they arrived in Toronto, it was to great excitement. This was the first time the Queen and The Duke of Edinburgh had visited in over a decade, and people came out in droves. Not content with lining the streets, some climbed trees, clambered up statues and sat on window ledges for a better view. They were rewarded with a wave, before the Queen was treated to a fifty-thousand-spectator-strong military tattoo, which included a gun salute, an inspection of the regiments, bands and marches.

But while the tattoo may have been enjoyable, the remarks from certain corners of the Canadian media were not. One newspaper called the Queen dowdy and matronly, criticised her hairstyle and even her hats, cartoons were published, and reporters decided that the couple not only looked bored, but were boring in themselves. When one newspaper cracked the remark that, 'at 58 [the Queen] looks tired at times. Her powder is a little too heavy. Her legs have visible veins', it was considered an insult too far.

The Canadian prime minister, Brian Mulroney, stepped in to describe the comments from the newspapers as unfair, while the British press banded together to ask fashion designers to give their view of the Queen's dress and style. Of course, everyone said that she looked perfectly fine, and her hat-maker, Freddie Fox, made the point that she was a monarch, not a fashion icon. 'You can't have both,' he said.

Even Buckingham Palace got involved, when reporters phoned the switchboard for a comment. A spokesperson dismissed the 'carping criticism' and refused to refer directly to the episode. Instead, he described the tour as extremely successful. 'She has attracted big crowds wherever she has gone,' he said. Meanwhile, Canadian readers took to writing in to their own newspapers, lambasting their coverage and accusing writers of being 'downright insulting to her Majesty'.

The Queen may have attracted big crowds, but she also attracted the rather unwanted attention of State Transport Minister James Snow. While being guided down a presentation line in Amherstview, Ontario, the man was accused of annoying the Queen by touching her back several times. It is a well-known rule that nobody must touch the Queen, and while she didn't say anything about the incident at the time, it was noted that Her Majesty jumped forward several times, and even glared at the unknowing gentleman.

Newspapers were quick to report on the faux pas, and the embarrassed man was forced to put forward his side of events. 'I did not touch her back,' he exclaimed. 'I may or may not have touched her elbow. I can't say for sure if I did.' Snow went on to say that if he did indeed touch Her Majesty, he did it by accident, and certainly did not intend to create an international incident. 'Nobody told me that it was wrong,' he said. 'I was just trying to be helpful.' An official retorted that they really did expect it to be 'a matter of common sense'.

Tour over, the Duke of Edinburgh flew back to London, while the Queen went on to Kentucky to visit horse breeders. Hearing that she would be arriving at Blue Grass Airport, crowds of people braved the rain and headed there. One of those was Professor Graeme Fairweather, from Scotland. 'The last time I saw the Queen was about 30 years ago,' he said, 'in similar conditions about 4,000 miles away ... It wouldn't matter if it were freezing cold and all icy – I'd still be out here.'

When the Queen finally returned to England on 16 October, it was just days after the Brighton bombing, when the Irish Republican Army (IRA) attempted to kill the prime minister and various members of the government. Security was exceptionally tight at Heathrow Airport for the Queen's arrival, but thankfully Her Majesty was able to return home without any drama.

70

Complaints and Crying Children in Scotland

On 7 August 1985, the royal family, including the Queen, the Duke of Edinburgh, Princess Margaret, the Prince and Princess of Wales and their children, sailed out of Southampton on the Royal Yacht *Britannia*. It was a wet and windy evening, and the weather was not expected to get any better, as they sailed towards Scotland for a cruise around the Western Isles, and then on to their annual holiday in Balmoral.

When *Britannia* – and the royals – reached the Caithness port of Scrabster, on 14 August, the Queen Mother was waiting to greet them. She was on holiday in Scotland already, and the reunion in the port caused great excitement with locals and reporters, who labelled it as one of the biggest royal reunions they'd ever seen. The only disappointment for everyone was the lack of sightings of Prince Charles's sons, Prince William and baby Prince Harry, who had been born eleven months earlier. Diana and Charles had opted to leave the boys on *Britannia*, while they visited the Queen Mother at the Castle of Mey.

A day later, on 15 August 1985, *Britannia* sailed into the Inverness Firth, so that the Queen and Prince Philip could visit the city, open the harbour extension and then the new Raigmore Hospital. *Britannia* anchored off Alturlie Point and the royal couple were ferried into the harbour by barge while the Royal British Legion Pipe Band played. It was forecast rain and the public had been warned to come wearing raincoats, but luckily for everyone, the weather stayed dry, with barely any wind at all.

The Queen and Prince Philip made it to dry land, and were greeted by the lord lieutenant and introduced to various dignitaries. It wasn't long, however, before spectators realised that the Queen's salmon-coloured outfit looked suspiciously like the one she had worn during a 1981 visit to Inverness. Reporters headed to the archives and discovered that, sure enough, it was the same outfit. The discovery caused such a fuss that a Buckingham Palace spokesman had to step in and tell journalists that it wasn't unusual for the Queen to wear outfits more than once, but it had been a complete coincidence that she had worn the same one during both visits to the Highlands.

Children in Scotland had just gone back to school when the royal party rolled in but, as it was classed as a historic event, they were allowed to line the streets to see the Queen. However, there was a moment of worry when it was revealed that teachers demanding pay reviews had got no further forward with their fight, and might not be willing to take their charges from the classrooms. A columnist at the *Inverness Courier* was so concerned that he wrote an entire piece about the importance of making sure the royal couple had a terrific welcome. 'It is essential for teachers' demarcations and disagreements to be pushed into the background for the two to three hours of Thursday's royal visit,' he wrote.

In the end, the teachers were more than happy to take the children down to see the Queen, but this caused problems when they realised that somebody had forgotten to officially invite local schools along. There was much discussion in the staffrooms, and in the end many teachers rang the police and the Raigmore Hospital to request that space be made for them on the street and outside the building. This was done, and the schoolchildren got their wish of seeing the royal car from the street. 'What annoyed us was the fact that we were not invited,' said one teacher. 'It is not every day you get to see the Queen.'

After unveiling a plaque to open the harbour, the royal couple toured the offices and then headed to the Inverness Town House, the district council's headquarters. Before they arrived, however, the couple's car pulled over for a walkabout, where they met many of the locals who had lined the streets. There, they wished one lady a happy birthday, and met a couple who had flown in from Ohio, USA.

One little boy was so devastated that the Queen had missed collecting a bouquet he had brought with him that an equerry helped him over the barrier, and a lady-in-waiting took him to meet Her Majesty. Another child was not so happy when the Duke lifted her over the barrier to go and meet the Queen on the other side of the street. The child screamed, turned her back to him, and had to be returned to her mother.

After signing the visitors' book outside the Town House, the couple headed to Raigmore Hospital, where they were met by patients, nurses, doctors and porters waving from the windows. There, Her Majesty listened to a speech by the chairman of the Highland Health Board, before unveiling a plaque and then making a speech herself. Recalling how her sons had attended nearby Gordonstoun school, 'I am well aware,' she said, 'of the comfort it is to know that the hospital services in Inverness enjoy such an excellent reputation.'

The Queen and the Duke then toured separate parts of the hospital. Her Majesty met various children on her way around, including some that had already been discharged but had come back just to see her, and another who had recently had his appendix removed. Her Majesty assured the youngster that getting rid of an appendix was the best thing to do.

It was a quick but worthwhile visit, with the Queen staying in Inverness for just over two hours, before heading back to *Britannia* en route to Aberdeen, before travelling on to Balmoral. Philip, meanwhile, kissed his wife on the cheek, told her he'd see her later in the week and headed to Inverness Airport, where he flew off to a private engagement. 'The visit went like clockwork,' said a relieved spokesman. 'Even the rain held off.'

71

Eggs and Demonstrations Down Under

On 22 February 1986, the Queen and the Duke of Edinburgh arrived in New Zealand, where they were to visit various towns and cities, including Auckland, Hastings and Wellington. The tour was an eventful one, but not for the reasons they'd hoped it would be. In fact, the overall feeling was one of tension. There were loud protests from anti-monarchists, and one demonstrator even tried to join the royal motorcade, but was stopped by police.

The anti-royal demonstrations seemed unending, and continued when the royal couple attended a garden party in Christchurch at the end of their trip. As they were arriving, four women and a man sprang forward and tried to drop their trousers, but were wrestled to the ground by police. The officers had been looking out for such an event since, days before, a man pledged to give a '21-bum salute' and had dropped his trousers as the Queen and Prince Philip toured Hawke's Bay. The baring of bottoms was a traditional Māori insult, and the use of it during the tour drew a backlash from MPs in the UK. Referring to the act as an 'outrageous insult', one MP called for an urgent look at the Queen's security before she contemplated another visit to New Zealand.

While the Queen possibly did not see the bare-bottomed insults, she was certainly aware of an earlier protest in Auckland, when two women threw raw eggs at her car. One cracked against the windscreen of the open-topped vehicle, while the second splattered on to the Queen's pink outfit, causing her to rub at it in an attempt to get it off. The women were apparently protesting because of the 146-year-old Treaty of Waitangi, when Māori tribes ceded sovereignty to Queen Victoria.

While the Queen was visibly disturbed by the egg throwing, she later made a joke of it in a speech at a state banquet. 'New Zealand,' she said, 'has long been renowned for its dairy produce – though I myself prefer my New Zealand eggs for breakfast.'

When the couple arrived in Canberra, Australia, on 2 March, security was tight because of the demonstrations seen in New Zealand. This leg of the trip would be a historic one, when the Queen signed the Australia Act 1986, giving Australia the right to handle its own legal appeal process. This meant that the country would cut its constitutional links with the United Kingdom, though the Queen would remain the monarch.

The next day, when attending the Royal Humane Society awards, the Queen met eleven-year-old Alfred Collins, who two years prior had saved his father from a rampaging boar. Smiling at the young boy, the Queen gave him Australia's Star of Courage award. 'She said "congratulations",' Alfred told reporters afterwards, 'and that I had done a very brave thing.'

When the tour moved on to Sydney, the royal couple received a mammoth welcome, with a mixture of adults and schoolchildren all clamouring to see them. As usual, fans climbed on to roofs and shimmied up trees in order to get a better view. One royalist who did not do this, however, was 106-year-old British woman Ellen Cox, whom the Queen met after a concert at the Sydney Entertainment Centre. Ellen was quite blasé about the meeting, since she had once lived near Epsom Racecourse, and had seen Her Majesty pass by many times.

Meeting Ellen was peaceful enough, but the demonstrations never really stopped. There was outrage when a man tried to spray the Queen with water as she arrived at a hotel, and then in Sydney, Francesca D'Espiney leapt on a wall as the Queen and the Duke were boarding a harbour cruise. There was nothing out of the ordinary in climbing a wall, but when the woman exposed her breasts, police stepped in. The woman told reporters that her demonstration was a feminist statement, as she felt that the Queen 'represents a very conservative, very backward image. She can do more to lead women to a much better position.'

When the Queen arrived back in England on 14 March, she headed straight for Windsor, where she was to discuss the romance between her son Prince Andrew and Sarah Ferguson. Fergie, as she was later known, was the daughter of Major Ronald Ferguson, the polo manager for the Duke of Edinburgh and Prince Charles. Five days later, on 19 March, Buckingham Palace announced their engagement. They went on to marry at Westminster Abbey on 23 July 1986.

72

The Mayor Collapses in Canterbury

On 20 March 1987, the Queen and the Duke of Edinburgh travelled to Canterbury for the first time in twenty years. It was a chilly, early spring day, and the Queen was dressed in a long coat and a hat as she was welcomed by a fanfare of trumpets, blown from the Westgate Towers. She was then presented with a key to the city by the mayor, Councillor Peter Baker, and then he accompanied her for the rest of the day. It was a busy one for everyone involved.

There was a £500,000 heritage centre to open at the Poor Priests' Hospital, a visit to the Cathedral House, and then an afternoon of overseeing workshops, attending evensong, and then opening a computer laboratory at the University of Kent. Throughout it all, there were numerous walkabouts, whereby the royal couple met pensioners, families and children clutching flowers and flags.

There were no flags waving outside the Radio Kent studios, however, as the thousand they had ordered were accidentally printed upside down, and had to be sent back. Had he known about it, the Duke of Edinburgh would have no doubt seen the humour in Flag-gate, as his jokes were in full flow throughout the day. At one point he made fun of the mayor's feathered hat, and encouraged others to

THE MAYOR COLLAPSES IN CANTERBURY

do the same, and then he was overheard promising not to sell several books presented to him at the heritage centre.

One of the highlights of the day came when the Queen inspected the guard of honour, made up of local Girl Guides, Scouts, and Army, Sea and Air Cadets. Her Majesty smiled and spoke to many of the youngsters, but behind the scenes, tempers flared when former Boys' Brigade captain Ernest Epps was peeved that the brigade had not been chosen to be part of the guard of honour. 'One would assume the non-presence of these organisations was simply because they were not thought of,' he said. 'Why not?'

The mayor's secretary was called to provide his side of the story, which was that the guard of honour was supposed to be formed by the 3rd Battalion of the Queen's Regiment, but at the last minute they had been sent to Ireland. The secretary assured reporters that there was no reason why the Boys' Brigade was not included, except that they had only a tiny amount of time to organise everything once the 3rd Battalion pulled out.

The fact that news of the battalion's visit to Ulster was actually released in October 1986 – a full five months before the Queen's visit – was not commented on. Besides, the mayor had more pressing issues. Her Majesty's day in Canterbury had been a busy one, and Peter Baker had found himself literally running around when his car was held up in traffic, and he needed to reach the Poor Priests' Hospital before the famous visitor.

Just hours after the Queen had left Canterbury, the man collapsed while attending the annual civic ball. He was rushed first to the intensive care unit, and then transferred to a general ward several days later, where he was reported as being much better. 'The ball came at the end of a very busy week,' his wife Margaret said. 'It proved too much of a strain.'

73

Working Against the Tide at Heysham

Heysham Port is situated on the Lancashire coast, and specialises mainly in cargo ships coming in and out of the Isle of Man and Ireland. The port is not especially used to royalty sailing in, so when rumours began in June 1989 that the Royal Yacht *Britannia* would be arriving in August with the Queen and the Duke on board, there was great excitement.

A reporter from nearby Morecambe was one of the first to hear the story from a 'confidential source', and got straight on the phone to Buckingham Palace. There he spoke to assistant press secretary to the Queen, John Haslam, who assured the journalist that no confirmation could be made. The man pushed further, and asked if he was denying that Her Majesty would be visiting. 'I am not denying it,' he replied, before adding the cryptic comment that it just might be possible.

Rumours swirled throughout the area, mainly based on the fact that it was the Queen's tradition to sail to Balmoral in August each year. With a scheduled visit to Lancashire and the Isle of Man due in the early days of that month, everyone was sure that the boat would stop at Heysham, and lots of bunting and flags were ordered, while civic representatives readied themselves for a call. This would be the first visit to the port by the Queen, so regardless of the time spent there, the very thought of it was a huge deal.

By mid-June, the visit was confirmed. The Royal Yacht *Britannia* would sail into Heysham Port on the morning of 7 August, and then the Queen and the Duke would disembark on their way to visit Duchy of Lancaster tenant farmers based on the Whitewell estate, near Longridge. A trip through Lancaster was planned, they'd board the *Britannia* at 4.45 p.m., and then sail to the Isle of Man shortly after.

The port's general manager, Peter Fenton, was ecstatic to hear the news. 'We are thrilled and very much looking forward to the visit,' he said. 'We shall not let the area down.' Mr Fenton (and a host of dignitaries, including the mayor) would meet the royal couple personally, and his staff would be on-site, but due to the limited space, there would be restricted access to the public. 'We will be making the place look attractive, and we will do whatever we can,' Mr Fenton told reporters.

Behind the scenes, preparations were under way. Staff were seen scrubbing the stairs on to which Her Majesty would step, and everywhere was given a spring clean. But it wasn't just a sprucing up that was required. Port staff also had to work out how to dock the 412-foot ship. A spokesperson decided that it would not be too different to a standard ferry. In the end, however, *Britannia* was anchored offshore, and a launch boat brought the Queen into the port – Philip having decided to fly directly to the Whitewell estate by helicopter.

Her Majesty – wearing an apricot-coloured coat and a cream hat – was greeted by a cheering, flag-waving crowd and various county and city dignitaries. It was only a quick visit before heading off to the Whitewell estate, but the excitement from the public could hardly be contained. One royalist, Joan Bayliss, queued up for two hours to catch a glimpse of Her Majesty. Originally from Heysham, she was now residing in Australia, and it was pure luck that she should schedule her visit to coincide with the Queen's. 'She does a great job,' Joan said, 'and I was delighted when I heard she was coming to Heysham.'

As the Queen's car sped through Lancaster and Morecambe, more fans lined the route, and the Queen waved to everyone. Once at Whitewell, the Queen was reunited with Philip, and the two toured four farms before having lunch in a marquee. The officers from *Britannia*, meanwhile, were given lunch in Lancaster Town Hall while they waited for the royal visitors to head back to the ship. Even Prince Charles made a surprise appearance in Heysham, when he arrived in order to join his parents on *Britannia* for their trip to the Isle of Man.

During the tour of the Whitewell estate, the Queen and the Duke stopped at the farmhouse of Stuart and Kathleen Verity, who served the visitors with a traditional afternoon tea – sandwiches, scones and cake. 'It was a real honour to have been chosen out of all the farms on the estate,' Mrs Verity said.

So popular were the couple that they were a full thirty minutes late getting back into Heysham, sending port managers into a panic. The problem was that the platform specifically made for the Queen's departure was at the perfect place for a 4.45 p.m. getaway. The tide had dropped so much when they actually arrived that quick-thinking staff had to grab some planks of wood to ensure that everything was still level.

Councillor Fred Wilcox was especially pleased to have met the couple, and as they sailed off, he told reporters that meeting them had made 1989 a vintage year. His wife was even more excited. 'You dream about these things,' she said, 'and they always seem to happen to other people. Now we will have something really special to look back on.'

74

The Fire at Windsor

On the morning of 20 November 1992 – the Queen and the Duke's forty-fifth wedding anniversary – a fire broke out in Queen Victoria's private chapel at Windsor Castle. Because of the large rooms, ornate ceilings and lots of wood, it spread quickly, and for a time it looked as though the whole building might be lost.

Thankfully, because there was refurbishment going on in the castle, many works of art had already been removed. However, many more remained in the building, and staff, soldiers and firefighters were seen carrying precious items, including rolled-up rugs and carpets, and also forming human chains to pass smaller items to safety.

Decorator Dean Landsdale and other staff were on the scene as the flames took hold, and they helped to remove paintings from the building. 'I dragged three or four with other people,' Landsdale said, 'then I touched one and felt my hands burning.' The men continued to try and remove items, until eventually the fire became so bad they had to leave.

The Queen, meanwhile, was alerted to the disaster while at Buckingham Palace, and travelled to Windsor to inspect the scene for herself. She was, understandably, distraught at what she witnessed.

When the main fire was eventually put out, tiny fires still burned in various places, so officers had to tackle those before making sure that the rest of the castle was structurally safe. In the hours afterwards, it was estimated that four paintings had been destroyed, but thanks to the quick thinking of staff and firefighters, actually only one painting and one rosewood sideboard were lost. Still, the fire had burned for fifteen hours, and in its wake, 115 rooms were destroyed, including the floors of Brunswick Tower, the roof of St George's Hall, the Crimson Drawing Room, the Star Chamber and the Chester Tower.

In the aftermath of the fire, theories were put forward as to what had caused it. One rumour was that it was the result of a terrorist bomb, while another claimed that inflammable liquid, used by picture restorers, was ignited by a halogen lamp. The former was immediately dismissed, but the second theory was quite close to what actually happened – that a faulty spotlight had ignited a curtain after a picture had pushed the fabric towards the light.

Almost immediately, there was an outcry when it was suggested that the repairs to Windsor would be paid for out of the public purse, since it – like other royal palaces – was not insured. Reporters took to the streets to see what the public thought, and not surprisingly, most felt that since it was the Queen's residence, it should be her who paid for it.

While proposing that taxpayers should foot the bill was not a popular decision, it did reveal a secret that, in summer 1992, the Queen had decided that she would now pay income tax herself. This was a huge announcement, but some wondered if the revelation would have been kept away from the public if not for the controversy surrounding Windsor. Sir Marcus Fox, chairman of the 1992 Committee of Conservative backbenchers, was perturbed by the constant press intrusion. 'Please now leave it alone,' he said. 'We want our monarchy to survive and it will be strengthened by this announcement.'

By late November, the investigation into what caused the fire was complete, and by early December, the Queen had received the report. 'The fire appears to have resulted from an unfortunate combination of circumstances,' Buckingham Palace said, 'with no single factor or individual directly to blame.' The results of the report caused more anger, with some MPs questioning the skimpiness of it, while others demanded more answers. 'It is an insult to the British taxpayer,' Ann Clwyd MP was quoted as saying. 'It leaves far more questions unanswered than are answered.'

In the end, the cost to repair Windsor Castle was said to be over £36 million; £2 million of that came from the Queen, while most of the rest was raised from entrance fees to both Windsor and Buckingham Palace. Repairs were eventually finished on the Queen and the Duke's fiftieth wedding anniversary, five years to the day since the fire had broken out.

75

Annus Horribilis

On 24 November 1992, the Queen attended a Corporation of London lunch to mark her fortieth year as monarch, and delivered what was one of her most famous speeches of all time. After making a toast, Her Majesty looked nervous as she read through the notes in front of her. She then got to her feet, and as she started to speak, her voice cracked – a result maybe of inhaling the smoke at Windsor just days before.

At first, the speech was simple enough, and the Queen thanked the lord mayor for the fortieth anniversary celebration, and for the gift of a picture, which she would cherish. The speech then took a darker turn: 1992, she said, had not been a year that she would look back on with pleasure. '[In the] words of one of my more sympathetic correspondents,' she said, 'it has turned out to be an annus horribilis.' This Latin phrase means a horrible year, and after the Queen spoke it out loud, a smattering of laughter rang out around the room. They could be mistaken for thinking that Her Majesty was making a little joke, but she was deadly serious.

After talking about the fire at Windsor, the Queen went on to speak about her belief in moderation in all things, mentioning her great-great-grandmother, Queen Victoria, who believed the same.

ANNUS HORRIBILIS

Her Majesty wondered how future generations would judge the year 1992, mentioning hindsight, judgement, compassion and wisdom. She then took a swipe at the press by saying that these qualities were often lacking in the reactions of those whose job it was to give their opinions. Criticism could be good for institutions in public life, she admitted, and nobody should expect to be free from it. 'But we are all part of the same fabric,' she said, before urging a gentleness and understanding going forward.

The year 1992 had indeed been a terrible one. First came the announcement that Prince Andrew and his wife Sarah were to separate, and shortly after, Princess Anne divorced her husband, Captain Mark Phillips. One of the biggest shocks, however, happened in June, when the royal family was rocked by a biography of the Princess of Wales. There had been books about the Princess before, of course, but *Diana: Her True Story* by Andrew Morton seemed to have had help from the inside.

The book was a sensation as there were factual quotes from close friends, along with stories and details that nobody but someone close to the family could possibly have known. Rumours swirled that the Princess had been one of the major sources for the biography, but while Buckingham Palace pooh-poohed such stories, years later it was found to be true. As if the book wasn't enough, in the months after its publication there followed a series of tabloid scandals revolving around both Princess Diana and Sarah, Duchess of York.

The Queen was sure to have been most hurt by the fire at Windsor, but the year wasn't finished with her yet. Just weeks after the 'Annus horribilis' speech came the announcement that the Prince and Princess of Wales were to separate. During her Christmas speech that year, the Queen spoke from Sandringham, addressing the difficulties faced around the world, and in her own family, too. 'As some of you may have heard me observe,' she said, 'it has, indeed, been a sombre year.'

76

The Gate of Romantic Candyfloss

The Queen Mother's ninetieth birthday fell on 4 August 1990, and the milestone was celebrated with an array of tribute portraits, poems, competitions, plates, cups and even spoons. For the Queen Mother herself, there were private family celebrations and a tour of the East End, which she still held dear some fifty years after the bombing of Buckingham Palace.

To publicly commemorate her birthday, Prince Michael of Kent – the Queen's cousin, and the Queen Mother's nephew – appealed to the nation to raise £1.5 million in order to build a gate in her honour, behind Apsley House at Hyde Park Corner. These gates would be, he said, 'your chance to show your gratitude to Queen Elizabeth for a long lifetime of service to the country'.

This was a passion project for the Prince, but in a time of recession, it was a battle. As a result of Prince Michael's work, donations came in from individuals, companies, organisations and even some banks, but by 1992, the future of the gates was uncertain, when only half of the money had been raised. The Queen Mother was said to be thrilled when she was presented with a scale model, but her age was against her. Stories came out of Clarence House that she wondered if they would be finished in her lifetime, and whispers abounded that perhaps it would end up being a memorial rather than a celebration of a long life. With all that in mind, more appeals were launched, and eventually enough money was raised for the project to go ahead.

The gate was designed and built by Giuseppe Lund, with a centrepiece by David Wynne. Both the gate and the centrepiece were inspired by the Queen Mother, with the centrepiece particularly representing her interests. Included in the designs were pink roses, a salmon, a tree, birds, a peacock, a lion and a unicorn. A time capsule was to be built into the foundations, and the Queen Mother chose a blue charm salmon fly to go into it. On one of the winged walls flanking the gates were the names of over six hundred donors who had given their support to the project.

On 6 July 1993, the Queen Elizabeth Gate was officially opened by the Queen and the Queen Mother. There was a huge piece of pink material draped over the structure, but because of the elaborate metalwork, when it came time to hoist it off by crane it got stuck and ripped. This did not stop the joy of the two women, however. Together they strolled through the gate, and each pointed out the details woven into the design. The Queen Mother especially seemed thrilled that her birthday gift was now finished and on display, and tourists seemed to agree. 'They are very special gates for a very special lady,' said one visitor.

Giuseppe Lund described the project as a feminine contrast to the black gates in the park, and it was certainly an original, inspired idea. However, while there were many who admired the design, there were some that considered it to be quite vulgar. Comments of 'romantic candyfloss' and 'three-dimensional knitting' were bandied about, and even the British Artist Blacksmiths Association became involved, when representative Raymond Jorden predicted that the gate would likely fall apart. 'We do not think it will last,' he said. 'If it does not decay fairly rapidly, certain parts will probably fall to pieces.'

These comments were dismissed as sour grapes by an equerry to Prince Michael, who predicted that the gate would stand for a long time to come. Sure enough, over thirty years later, the Queen Elizabeth Gate still stands in Hyde Park, and is visited by millions of people every year.

77

Breaking Records, and a Visit to the Fame School

On 7 June 1996, the Queen travelled to Liverpool to open the Liverpool Institute for Performing Arts, founded by former Beatle Paul McCartney and Mark Featherstone-Witty, and based on the site of the school where McCartney and Beatles band member George Harrison were pupils. It was to be a busy day for Her Majesty, who not only opened the school, but afterwards travelled on to Birkenhead, and then back to Liverpool for a concert and plaque-unveiling at the Philharmonic Hall. Later that evening, she would return home to London.

When the Queen – wearing a blue outfit with matching hat, and pearls – arrived at the college, a man who apparently opposed the school tried to break a cordon in order to give her a letter. He didn't get very far, however, and was quickly arrested to prevent a breach of the peace. Paul McCartney then shook the Queen's hand, told her how lovely it was to see her, and introduced her to various members of staff. After that, it was time for a tour of the school.

There were various dance and singing performances on show, and the Queen smiled her way through every display, while McCartney was seen humming and nodding along. She then spoke to the students, asking them about their studies and interests in performing arts.

The pupils of one contemporary dance class had practised their performance for a long time, and although nervous, they enjoyed meeting the Queen. 'Seeing her really got the adrenaline going,' said twenty-year-old student, Beth Olson. The Queen was even given a glimpse of what it was like to be in the Beatles when visiting a recording studio. McCartney spoke about his days in the band, and then showed her some of the equipment.

After hearing a choir sing a medley of showtunes, the Queen then went on to the stage and officially opened the school, much to the delight of everyone in the audience. 'The Queen was very impressed,' McCartney said. 'She was very entertained by all of it.'

When the Queen left the college, reporters flocked to ask McCartney about the visit. He told them that it was all a dream come true, and he was very proud. When asked about the rumour that he would soon be offered a knighthood, the musician smiled and said he knew nothing about it. Six months later, however, it was announced in the New Year's Honours that he would indeed become a sir. 'It is a fantastic honour,' he said on hearing the news, and added that he would be receiving the award on behalf of his fellow Beatles members, and the people of Liverpool.

The Queen received her own honour of sorts a short time after the visit to Liverpool, when it was announced that her reign of 44 years and 127 days was now longer than her namesake, Queen Elizabeth I. Royal scholars thought it to be a wonderful achievement, especially as it now placed the Queen into the top-five longest-reigning monarchs. She was still a long nineteen years away from the 'top spot', however. That record was held by Queen Victoria, who reigned for sixty-three years, seven months and two days.

It was not known what thoughts the Queen had about this new record, but at a time when the family had received criticism over their private lives, as well as the discussion of the repair bill for Windsor Castle, reporters were quick to imagine. 'She must wonder,' pondered journalist Dan O'Neill, 'whether a nation already flirting with thoughts of republicanism really cares.'

78

The Role of Grandmother versus Queen

The date 31 August 1997 is one that most people will never forget. When the news came in that Diana, Princess of Wales had been involved in a car accident in Paris, it was said that companion Dodi Fayed had been killed, and that the Princess had walked away from the vehicle, injured, but still alive.

In Scotland, the Queen and the rest of the royal family – including Diana's sons, fifteen-year-old William and almost-thirteen-year-old Harry – were spending the summer at Balmoral. It was the middle of the night, and the Queen and Prince Charles were initially woken to be told there had been an accident. As the hours passed, it became clear that Princess Diana had not walked away from the car at all, and despite every effort to save her life, she had passed away. Prince Charles was then left with the awful task of telling his sons that their mother had gone.

While arrangements were made to bring the Princess's body home, the Queen and the rest of the family attended Crathie church, as they did whenever they were at Balmoral. As the Queen's car made its way to the church, there was a wave of applause from the mourning crowds,

THE ROLE OF GRANDMOTHER VERSUS QUEEN

but the service did not contain any mention of Princess Diana at all, not in the prayers, not in the sermon, not anywhere. This insistence on sticking to the already-prepared service was confusing to the children, who could be forgiven for wondering if the news of their mother's death had all been a mistake.

The service done, Prime Minister Tony Blair had a meeting with the Queen to discuss the way forward, and then gave a speech where he declared Diana to be the 'People's Princess'. For her part, the Queen was in grandmother mode, and her attention was on protecting her grandsons. They had lost their mother, and she wanted to make sure they were as OK as they could be, and protected from unwanted media attention. In that regard, the Queen thought that she was doing nothing wrong, but the public and the press thought differently.

While flowers, teddy bears, cards and photographs piled up outside Buckingham Palace and Kensington Palace, the country was unified in grief. The newspapers were almost totally dedicated to Diana for the entire week, police officers were seen wiping away tears as they watched over the crowds, and the public queued for hours to sign memorial books peppered around the country. One thing missing, however, was the Queen.

For over forty years, she had been the anchor of the country, but now she was nowhere to be found. Still at Balmoral, her priority remained her grandchildren, but the public attitude towards this decision was chilly to say the least. When there was no flag flying half-mast at Buckingham Palace, and it was revealed that the Queen would likely not return to London before the day of the funeral, emotions reached boiling point. Reporters, keen to hear what the public thought about the Queen not returning to London, were met time and time again with the words, 'disgraceful', 'disgusting' and 'disappointing'. Not even the sighting of the royal family viewing the flowers gathered outside Balmoral was enough to appease the country.

Finally, on the evening before Diana's funeral on 6 September, the Queen and the Duke of Edinburgh arrived at Buckingham Palace. Their greeting by the waiting public was muted, and as they unexpectedly got out of the car at the gates, there was only a faint round of applause. However, when the royal couple stepped forward to look at the tributes, and spoke to members of the crowd, the feelings thawed. There remained a dignified silence amid the calm applause, but some people had the confidence to give their condolences to the Queen, hand over flowers to be placed outside the gates, and even tell Philip to look after the boys.

'That's what we've been doing,' he exclaimed.

Shortly after the Queen had disappeared into Buckingham Palace, she appeared in front of a camera, an open window behind her, showing the public gathered outside the gates. There she spoke to the nation, 'as your Queen, and as a grandmother', about the overwhelming sadness felt after the death of the Princess. Speaking on behalf of the country, the world, her family and herself, the Queen explained how everyone had been trying to cope with the shock, disbelief, concern and anger.

She then spoke from her heart about Diana, calling her a gifted human being, and admiring the fact that no matter what was going on in the Princess's world, she always inspired others. 'I admired and respected her,' Her Majesty said. She then approached the subject of why the family had stayed at Balmoral that week. Everyone had been trying to help the boys come to terms with their loss, she explained, before adding that Diana would never be forgotten, and that lessons could be learned from her life and her death. She then thanked the nation for paying their respects to Princess Diana over the last week, and asked that on the day of the funeral, the nation could come together to express their loss, and 'thank God for someone who made many, many people happy'.

79

'He Has Been My Strength and Stay'

The Queen and the Duke of Edinburgh's fiftieth anniversary – their golden wedding – fell on 20 November 1997, but celebrations took place up and down the country throughout the year. There were bone china commemorative cups and trinket boxes to be collected, new golden wedding postage stamps to be bought, trees to be planted, and souvenir magazines to be read. There was also a special gold crown coin minted, showing the Queen and Prince Philip, which was the first time that they had ever been on a coin together. In addition to that, there was all manner of sponsored events, including a horse ride, where thirty-seven thousand riders raised money for charity.

It wasn't just the Queen and the Duke who were being celebrated that year. Couples who were married during 1947 were invited to apply for tickets to a special golden wedding party, held at Buckingham Palace, on 15 July. Tickets were limited and not every couple was able to get one, but for those left behind, local organisations made sure that they felt special too. All across the country, golden wedding couples were invited to 'golden luncheons' and celebratory parties, while local newspapers and television shows interviewed them about their own big day, fifty years ago.

When July came, four thousand couples bought new suits, frocks and hats, and headed to London. There (once the small matter of checking ID was done), they were admitted into the Buckingham Palace gardens, where they could amble around the grounds before being served afternoon tea. One couple had even stood outside the palace gates, waving up to the balcony when the Queen married Prince Philip in 1947. They had no idea that fifty years later they would be inside the gates, celebrating with Her Majesty.

The Queen – wearing a lemon coat with matching hat, and holding an umbrella just in case – collected flowers and spoke to the happy couples, while the Duke of Edinburgh cracked his usual jokes, and was seen laughing with the Queen throughout the afternoon.

While most left with happy memories of the garden party, there was one tragedy, when seventy-four-year-old guest Dale Rutherford collapsed outside the palace gates while waiting for a taxi. Paramedics rushed to help the man, but he sadly passed away in hospital later that day. The Queen was notified of his passing, and sent a message of sympathy. 'They were both really looking forward to the day,' son Richard told reporters. 'My father was pleased as punch to be chosen and bought a new suit for the occasion.'

By 20 November – the actual wedding anniversary – the country was in a sombre mood after the death in August of Princess Diana. The Queen wanted no huge fuss, but there was a service at Westminster, and a golden anniversary lunch, during which she gave a speech. In it she praised all of the prime ministers who had given her advice over the years. Alluding to the criticism she had received in the aftermath of Diana's death, Her Majesty exclaimed that it was often hard to read public opinion.

'I have done my best,' she said, 'with Prince Philip's constant love and help, to interpret it correctly through the years of our marriage and of my reign as your queen.' She went on to thank the British public for their support during the years, and declared that it had seen them through, and had made their duties enjoyable. Her Majesty also gained a laugh when she exclaimed that there had been many times when the Duke had listened to her speeches as she was rehearsing them, and that his views were always shown in a forthright manner. 'He has, quite simply, been my strength and stay all these years,' she said.

80

'We Must Now Say Goodbye to *Britannia*'

The Royal Yacht *Britannia* had been the Queen's home-from-home for forty years, and it had sailed her and her family around the world on many occasions. However, in 1994, it was decided that in order for her to carry on, the vessel would require £17 million in repairs – and that was only guaranteed to keep her sailing for another five years.

After meetings with the family and the prime minister, John Major, the Queen reluctantly agreed that the ship was no longer necessary for travel, since most royal tours were now done by plane. *Britannia* would, therefore, be decommissioned three years later, in 1997. 'It's a sensible and realistic appointment,' Buckingham Palace said.

When the ship was built in 1953, it had been criticised by numerous MPs because of the cost. Now, however, there was a mixed response. While some decided that *Britannia* was probably best being retired, others couldn't believe what they were hearing. 'I am a traditionalist,' said Aberdeen North MP, Bob Hughes, 'and I do not like to see ships being scrapped.' Other MPs demanded that a replacement be built, but that was unrealistic, and rumours swirled that the government would even sell the ship overseas if it received a lucrative offer. Royalists then hit back and suggested that if the Queen had to part ways with *Britannia*, perhaps the prime minister could say goodbye to the weekend home perk, Chequers.

In the end, however, Chequers stayed, and in 1997 *Britannia* sailed for the last time, when it brought Prince Charles back from handing over Hong Kong to China. There was a continued discussion about whether or not to commission a new ship to take over, but that was met with rejection not only from many MPs but the public too, mainly because the approximate cost of £60 million would come from the public purse.

Plans were put forward for a renovation that would see *Britannia* sail for at least another twenty years but, ultimately, it was decided that there was simply no justification for building a new royal ship or refurbishing the old one. Defence Secretary George Robertson told reporters that the Ministry of Defence must justify everything it spent from the taxpayers' money, 'and in this case,' he said, 'I could not do so, particularly – as the Queen has made clear – since a yacht is not needed for royal travel.'

And so it was that, on 11 December 1997, the *Britannia* crew polished the brass and scrubbed the decks for the last time, in anticipation of the royal farewell. When the Queen arrived in Portsmouth with the Duke of Edinburgh and fourteen members of the family, it was with great emotion. Wearing a long, deep-red coat and matching hat, Her Majesty was piped aboard, and greeted her crew for the final time. Then, standing on the dock as the flags were lowered, the Queen's normally stoic stance faltered, and she was seen lips trembling, weeping and openly wiping away tears.

'It is with sadness that we must now say goodbye to *Britannia*,' the Queen said during a speech. 'Prince Philip and I join you today to pay tribute to *Britannia* and give our thanks to all who have been part of her company.'

While it was said that the Queen was not keen on the idea of her beloved ship becoming a tourist attraction, in May 1998, the Royal Yacht *Britannia* arrived in Leith, Edinburgh, where five months later it was opened to the public. It has remained docked there ever since, and now serves as a popular tourist attraction, as well as a facility for private events.

81

A Very Precious One Hundredth Birthday

On 4 August 2000, the Queen Mother reached her *one hundredth* birthday. To celebrate this milestone, many celebrations were planned on the lead-up to the big day, including a party at Windsor Castle, dinners around the country celebrating the Queen Mother's favourite food, special magazine supplements, charity donations towards cards to send to Her Majesty, treasure hunts, barbecues, special flag-raising events, memories sent to newspapers and, of course, cakes. Many royalists enjoyed the different ways to celebrate the Queen Mother's life, but others worried that the early events might be tempting fate just a little.

Thankfully, there was no need to worry. A couple of weeks before her birthday, a magnificent pageant took place, and was attended by the Queen Mother, her grandchildren and Princess Margaret. Arriving at Horse Guards in a carriage, with Prince Charles at her side, the Queen Mother wore a pink outfit with matching hat, as the crowd sang the national anthem at the top of their voices. Then the displays began. There were marching bands, military events, pipers, veterans, memories from the last one hundred years, covering the First World War, the Second World War, the Eurotunnel and the British film industry, with actor Norman Wisdom waving enthusiastically from the float. As well as all that, there was dancing and singing, and many animals, including horses, camels, one hundred white doves, and even chickens.

At one point the Queen Mother's corgis made an appearance, trotting along and looking over at their owner. Schoolchildren shouted, 'Happy birthday,' as they passed, while others gave a rousing, 'Congratulations!' Throughout it all, the Queen Mother made comments and waved to passersby, and at times even stood to show her appreciation.

At the end of the ceremony, she received a huge card, signed by everyone who had taken part. 'That will be very precious,' she said. She then gave thanks to everyone who had travelled to the event, calling it a great joy, and giving special mention to the music. 'God bless you all,' she said, 'and thank you.'

On 4 August – the actual date of the Queen Mother's birthday – church bells were rung, there were flypasts and the ever-familiar gun salutes. Newspapers, anxious to know what everyone thought of the events, asked readers for their views. Reader Vera Thompson told reporters that she was very fond of the Queen Mother. 'She has been very quiet all her life,' she said, 'and always conducts herself with great decorum. I'm delighted for her.'

The Queen's tradition of sending cards to those lucky enough to celebrate their one hundredth birthday was kept up when an envelope arrived at the Queen Mother's residence, Clarence House. The band of the Irish Guards marched past playing 'Happy Birthday', followed by the Grenadier Guards, and then Her Majesty left Clarence House for Buckingham Palace, where a lunch was planned with her family. She then walked out on to the balcony, wearing a peppermint-green outfit, and waved – with the rest of her family – to the cheering crowds below.

82

Walking into the 'Danger Zone' at Berwick

In July 2001, the Queen and the Duke of Edinburgh visited Northumberland. The primary concern of the tour was to meet those affected by the recent foot-and-mouth outbreak, a contagious disease – mainly affecting farm animals such as pigs, cattle and sheep – that had caused significant harm to farmers and the tourist industry during 2001. Millions of farm animals had been slaughtered, festivals and animal-related shows had been cancelled, and countryside footpaths and fishing areas closed in an attempt to halt the disease. The arrival of the Queen and the Duke of Edinburgh in Northumberland, therefore, created some kind of boost, no matter how little.

On 26 July, the Queen headed to Berwick-upon-Tweed, while the Duke of Edinburgh travelled to Alnwick, thirty-nine miles away. The mayor of Berwick was delighted when it was confirmed that the Queen would visit the town. 'This is certainly a special event,' he said, 'and to mark the occasion the Town Hall bells will be specially rung to welcome our royal visitor.'

Not everyone was happy, however, and disgruntled resident Chris Howsam wrote to the local newspaper with a list of things they should not let the Queen do . . . These included walkabouts, in case she be splattered with seagull poop or dismayed by the number of empty shops, and drive-abouts for fear of potholes. 'Don't let the Queen visit Berwick,' he wrote, 'for she will find a Tin Pot Town, with a Tin Pot Council with no vision, no hope, and nowhere to go.'

He was not the only one to complain. Another resident wrote in to say that the only reason the train station was getting a coat of paint was because of the royal visit, and suggested instead that the council do something about the trees, branches and weeds covering certain footpaths. Yet another resident wondered what the benefits were of the royal visit, complaining about the road closures and the effect they would have on the local trade.

Chris Howsam's mention of the gulls was significant, as many residents had been complaining for some time about the influx of the birds, and the mess they were making of cars, statues and, indeed, people. It was a real problem at the time, and when discovering that the Queen was to visit, Counsellor Neil Simpson was concerned. 'She will walk right into the danger zone,' he said. 'Someone will have to walk alongside her with an umbrella.'

The Queen's last visit to Berwick was on a rainy day in 1956, when she was greeted by thousands and presented with a tin of Berwick cockles and a freshly caught salmon. This time, it was very much a whistlestop tour, and Her Majesty would only be there for an hour, but it was a significant hour, nevertheless. The train station was spruced up, flags decorated the royal route, schoolchildren waved furiously, and newly planted flowers bloomed from hanging baskets and flowerbeds.

The first stop on the visit was to the Tourist Information Centre to discuss the foot-and-mouth crisis with local hoteliers and craftspeople. Carol Lang, owner of some local farm cottages, spoke to Her Majesty for several minutes. 'The Queen was very sympathetic,' she said, 'asking if we were now on the road to recovery and I said we were.'

Next, the Queen went to the Town Hall to find out more about the Berwick Youth Project, an enterprise which offered accommodation and help to young people in the area. During the visit, the Queen spoke to staff and residents, was presented with a glass goblet, and then signed the visitors' book. When she left, the Coldstream Guards played in the street outside. It was a visit that afterwards caused controversy when a local newspaper implied that some of those present had drug and alcohol problems. There then followed some enraged letters to the editor, and then a hasty apology from the newspaper several days later.

At the end of the visit, Her Majesty climbed into a helicopter and flew to Morpeth, where she opened a centre for the blind, and then reunited with Prince Philip for lunch in the County Hall. There, they met farmers and owners of small businesses who had been affected by foot-and-mouth, including the county president of the National Farmers' Union, Malcolm Corbett. 'Throughout,' he said, 'it was all very relaxed and I found her very easy to talk to.'

Back in Berwick, the mini-tour had been so successful that a video of the visit was screened at a coffee morning and raised £600 in aid of the Alzheimer's Society.

83

'In Loving Memory, Lilibet'

The year 2002 was supposed to be one of celebration. It was the Queen's Golden Jubilee, as she had been on the throne for a mammoth half a century. As with other jubilees, there were celebrations and tours around the country and the Commonwealth. The Queen met five surviving prime ministers who had served during her reign, and there was a glittering concert; the highlight of which was when Queen star Brian May played the national anthem on his guitar, standing atop the roof of Buckingham Palace. Unfortunately, 2002 was also a year when Her Majesty was to lose two of the most important people in her life: her mother and her sister, Margaret Rose.

Princess Margaret's health had been in decline for a number of years. Consistently in the newspapers for her partying and so-called scandalous ways, the Princess smoked and drank excessively for most of her life, and had numerous issues as a result. There was surgery on her lungs, bouts of pneumonia, strokes and then, in April 1999, she suffered a bathroom accident so bad that she never fully recovered.

The incident happened while the Princess was at her holiday home in Mustique. She was getting into the bath and the water was so hot that she scalded both feet. After receiving medical treatment, Princess Margaret flew back to England. 'She is getting some nursing care,' a spokesman said, 'helping her change her dressings, and the burns are responding to treatment.' The Princess was said to be in good spirits as she recuperated at Windsor Castle. When she was later spotted at the wedding of Prince Edward and Sophie Rhys-Jones in June 1999, her suffering was clear to see when she entered St George's Chapel in a wheelchair, via a back door, and was unable to stand during the national anthem.

On 9 February 2002, Princess Margaret passed away in her sleep at the age of seventy-one, after suffering another stroke. Her body was cremated and placed next to her father in the vault at St George's Chapel. Around the country, people paid their respects by sharing their memories of the Princess with friends, family and reporters. Mary, a sixty-four-year-old woman from South Shields, remembered meeting Princess Margaret in 1967. 'It was a wonderful day,' she said, 'to me she looked like a movie star, she was beautiful and looked incredible.'

While Her Majesty's stoic attitude was still everywhere apparent, her true feelings about Margaret's passing were revealed days later, when visiting the Salvation Army headquarters in Whitechapel. She was met by representative Bryan Stobart. 'At this time of personal loss,' he said, 'may we also offer our deepest and heartfelt sympathy to you and your family?'

Dressed all in black, the Queen toured the building with as much gumption as she could muster. However, one member of staff was so concerned by her recent loss that he asked if she was OK. 'Yes, thank you very much,' the Queen replied with tears in her eyes, before adding, 'It's very sad, isn't it? It's one of those things that happen in life.'

Unfortunately, just over a month later, the Queen and the royal family were dealt another blow.

Despite being 101 years old, the Queen Mother was still known for her robust health and get-up-and-go attitude. However, there was no doubt that her health was becoming fragile. She had been suffering from a bad cold since Christmas 2001, and the shock of her daughter Margaret's death was too much to bear.

The woman who had been the queen during the war, and who had been part of the royal family for all of her adult life, passed away at Royal Lodge, Windsor, on 30 March 2002. Her lady-in-waiting, Lady Penn, told interviewer Jonathan Dimbleby that she had shared tea with the Queen Mother just weeks before she passed away. She had struggled to get out of her chair on that occasion, but somehow managed to do it, despite her friend's wish that she remain seated. 'It was very, very touching,' Lady Penn said, 'because this was her – she wanted to keep going. That was her strength.'

Around the country, people signed condolence books, and when the Queen Mother lay in state at Westminster Hall, people queued for hours in order to see her coffin. One woman in the queue told reporters that 'After the things the Queen Mother has done for us, it is so little for us to do this for her.' On top of the coffin was a simple message from the Queen, which read, 'In loving memory, Lilibet.'

84

The Queen Meets James Bond

On 18 November 2002, the Queen travelled to the Royal Albert Hall for the premiere of the new James Bond film, *Die Another Day*. The event was a special one because it marked the fortieth anniversary of the film franchise, and the twentieth Bond film overall. To that end, there was a host of stars in attendance, all of whom had been associated with the films over the years. These included four of the actors who had played 007 – Pierce Brosnan, George Lazenby, Timothy Dalton and Sir Roger Moore.

Despite the cold November temperatures, fans turned up at the Albert Hall to catch a glimpse of the stars and, thanks to the gigantic screens outside, were able to see the celebrities arriving, as well as being presented to the Queen. Arrivals included the Bond actors, several Bond girls and Bond villains, along with Dame Shirley Bassey and actors Halle Berry, Rosamund Pike, Rick Yune and Dame Judi Dench. All were given a rapturous welcome, including Queen of Pop, Madonna, who had provided the film's soundtrack and also had a cameo role as Verity, a fencing instructor with attitude. Known for her often-revealing outfits, the star arrived with her husband, Guy Ritchie, wearing an elegant dress, with her blonde hair in a chignon.

As the stars lined up to meet Her Majesty, actor John Cleese told jokes, celebrities chatted among themselves, and Madonna was seen practising her curtsy. When it came time for one queen to meet another, the forty-four-year-old singer had perfected her dip, and told Her Majesty that it was a pleasure to meet her. They then spoke briefly about the film. 'I have never met her before,' Madonna said afterwards, 'but surprisingly I wasn't nervous.'

After shaking hands with John Cleese and sharing a laugh with Rick Yune, the Queen – wearing a floor-length gold evening dress and carrying a matching handbag – made her way down the line, and met Halle Berry and then actor Pierce Brosnan. After shaking hands with Brosnan, she smiled. 'So, you're the modern James Bond, are you?' He replied in the affirmative. 'I've met the other three downstairs,' the Queen told him.

Less than a year later, the Queen made Brosnan an honorary OBE for his contribution to the British film industry. 'I thought they were pulling my leg,' Brosnan told reporters when they asked how it felt when he heard the news. 'I wasn't expecting it and I never dreamt of receiving such an honour.'

85

The Happiest of Happy Birthdays

On 12 April 2006, the Queen was thrilled when she visited Sandhurst military academy to see the passing-out parade of her grandson, Prince Harry. The Prince had been training for a year, and had just been commissioned as an officer in the British Army.

Accompanying Her Majesty was the Duke of Edinburgh, Prince William, Prince Charles and his wife of one year, Camilla, the Duchess of Cornwall. All eyes, however, were on the interaction between the Queen and Prince Harry. As she inspected the line of soldiers, her grandson blushed as she reached him. 'Here's a face I recognise,' the Queen said, and they both grinned broadly at each other.

Another reason to smile was that it was soon to be Her Majesty's eightieth birthday, a date that inspired many celebrations around the country. There were competitions to find chefs who could create a banquet fit for a queen, there was the unveiling of a new portrait, television shows, radio broadcasts, special cover-to-cover magazines and, of course, commemorative coins.

There were also exhibitions to attend. One was held by the Kennel Club, which came up with the brilliant idea of showcasing photographs of the royal dogs. The Queen's dogs were included, of course, but also present were those owned by Queen Victoria and King Edward VII. The other main exhibition was a display of eighty of Her Majesty's dresses, held at Buckingham Palace. The public were treated to outfits worn throughout her life, all colour coordinated, and often embroidered with jewels and pearls.

Two days before her big day – on 19 April 2006 – the Queen entertained ninety-nine guests who were born on the same day as herself. Sitting down to a three-course meal at Buckingham Palace, the 'birthday twins' were treated to a welcome speech by Her Majesty. Talking about the past eighty years, she told guests that while it hadn't been plain sailing, they could all give thanks to those family and friends who had supported them. 'I hope all those of you who are my exact twins will make the most of our special day on Friday,' she said. 'A happy birthday to you all.'

The Queen's actual birthday was spent quietly with her family at Windsor Castle, and in the evening, Prince Charles paid tribute to his mother in a special, televised broadcast. Calling her his 'darling Mama', and wishing her the 'happiest of happy birthdays', the Prince spoke about the coronation, the trips his parents had had over the years, and her dedication to service.

On 23 April, two days after her birthday, the Queen travelled to Westminster Abbey for a thanksgiving service, but the celebrations didn't stop there. During the summer of her eightieth birthday, the Queen and Prince Philip attended a special celebration at the BBC Proms, and she also welcomed children to Buckingham Palace for a special garden party. During the latter, the garden was transformed into scenes from children's books, and attended by a variety of children's authors along with characters such as Bob the Builder, Thomas the Tank Engine, Noddy, Postman Pat and Paddington.

The Queen made an appearance, of course, and was introduced to the attendees by author Jacqueline Wilson. 'Children's characters are an enduring part of our culture,' the Queen said, before adding that she hoped the literary-themed garden party would encourage children to go home and 'discover the pleasure of reading'.

86

Why Doesn't the Queen Like Tennis?

In June 2010, the Queen arrived at the All England Lawn Tennis and Croquet Club to watch the Wimbledon Championships. Her match on that day was the second-round game between British tennis player Andy Murray and Finnish player Jarkko Nieminen.

Wearing a white dress, turquoise coat and matching hat, she greeted her cousin, the Duke of Kent, with a kiss, accepted a bouquet, spoke to those involved in the sport, including players, umpires and ball boys and girls, and then made her way through the clapping crowds to take her seat in the Centre Court's royal box. There, she waved at the public and then watched Andy Murray beat Jarkko Nieminen in three clear sets. 'It's probably a once in a lifetime opportunity for all of us,' Murray said, adding that he did not know if the Queen would return to Wimbledon in the coming years.

He was correct. Her Majesty never attended Wimbledon again. In fact, in all her years as sovereign, she only ever visited the club on three other occasions – in 1957, 1962 and 1977. When she stepped down from being patron of the club in 2016, chairman Philip Brook thanked the Queen for her service. 'It was a great honour to welcome Her Majesty to Wimbledon in 2010,' he said, before adding how proud they all were of her role in their history.

WHY DOESN'T THE QUEEN LIKE TENNIS?

Before attending her first ever Wimbledon match, there were already rumblings as to why she did not wish to watch tennis. During a 1956 talk at Bradford Rotary Club, C. W. Banks, chairman of the Lawn Tennis Association, put forward the theory that it was because of an experience her father, George VI (still the Duke of York at the time) had endured while playing a match at Wimbledon in 1926. A keen tennis player, he participated in the championship with his doubles partner Sir Louis Greig, but they went out in the first round to A. W. Gore and H. R. Barrett.

The story went that the Duke had not wanted to play on Centre Court, but was persuaded to by the committee. According to Banks, the Duke had felt foolish afterwards. 'He never forgave the committee,' he said. 'He never once again went to Wimbledon. Whether the Queen is following that unfortunate example we don't know.'

Her father's experience may have had something to do with her unwillingness to watch tennis, though more likely is the fact that she never had any particular liking for the sport, except for playing occasionally as a child. Instead, Her Majesty preferred to watch horse racing, along with polo matches when Prince Philip was playing.

When she did attend her first Wimbledon championship in 1957, Her Majesty was in for something of a shock. While watching Australians Lew Hoad and Neale Fraser play against Americans Gardnar Mulloy and Budge Patty, a woman climbed over the barrier and ran on to the court, holding a banner with the words 'Save Our Queen', along with captions about wanting women electors and wishing for no world government.

In front of where the Queen was sitting, the woman – dressed all in white with a matching straw hat – shouted and waved her flag before marching around the court. The match stopped, everyone stared in disbelief, and Gardnar Mulloy calmly turned his racquet upside down, and sat on it. The Queen sat quietly, watching the scene unfolding below the royal box, but others in the crowd began clapping and booing, and shouting for someone to take control of the situation.

Finally, the woman was marched off the court by a policeman and the referee, shouting as she went. She was later taken to the local police station, where she was given a warning. 'The taxpayer demands an honest charter to kill war today,' she shouted, as she was hauled out of the club.

87

A Royal Wedding and a Familiar Ring

The Queen's grandson, Prince William, met Catherine Middleton in 2001 while studying at the University of St Andrews. They were friends and then flatmates for a while, before finally becoming boyfriend and girlfriend several years later. Since they were only young when they met, their relationship had been slightly rocky at times, and they made headlines when they broke up in 2007, though they got back together shortly afterwards. The Prince later explained that the reason for the break-up was that they were still young, and finding themselves and their own way. While Catherine was understandably heartbroken by the break-up, she did come to believe that it made her a stronger person in the long run.

A year later, Catherine met the Queen for the first time. The date was 17 May 2008, and the occasion was the wedding of Princess Anne's son Peter to Autumn Kelly. Her Majesty had wanted to meet the young woman for a while, and Catherine later remembered her to be, 'Very friendly.'

During a trip to Kenya in October 2010, Prince William proposed to Catherine, using the sapphire and diamond engagement ring that his mother, Princess Diana, had once worn. The Prince had hidden the ring in his rucksack during their holiday, and by his own admission, he had carried it everywhere he went, in the fear that if it went missing, he'd be in trouble. Since the Princess's death in 1997, Prince William was aware of all the life moments that she would miss out on, and so giving the ring to Catherine ensured that the essence of Diana could be kept close by.

While the couple had talked a little about getting married in the past, when Prince William took the opportunity to propose while on the Kenya holiday, Catherine was in shock. She accepted straight away, and on 16 November 2010 – after informing the Queen that Catherine had said yes – Clarence House, the home of Prince Charles, announced the engagement.

The wedding of the most talked-about couple in the United Kingdom came five months later, on 29 April 2011. While still a grand event in keeping with other royal marriages, Prince William and Catherine were determined that they would make the ceremony as personal as they could. The Queen was in agreement, and while their guest list still included Commonwealth and religious leaders, Armed Forces representatives, dignitaries, politicians and the like, it also included friends from showbusiness, such as singer Sir Elton John, footballer David and Spice Girl Victoria Beckham, and film director Guy Ritchie.

Unusually for royal weddings, both the bride and groom arrived at Westminster Abbey in cars. Prince William, with his brother Harry acting as best man, was in a Bentley State Limousine, while Catherine and her father arrived in a Rolls-Royce Phantom. On the insistence of the Queen, the groom wore the Irish Guards full dress uniform, but he did change several times during the course of the day.

Catherine was glittering in a white lace gown with a long train, designed by Sarah Burton for Alexander McQueen, along with a Cartier tiara. Like Prince William, she changed into another outfit later in the day, this time a strapless dress with cardigan, again designed by Alexander McQueen. The Queen, meanwhile, wore a beautiful lemon frock coat with matching hat, and pearls. She had previously said that she was delighted that William and Catherine were to be married, and her happiness was everywhere apparent on the day. She spoke animatedly to other guests, and smiled at various times throughout the ceremony.

After the couple were pronounced man and wife, the now Duke and Duchess of Cambridge made their way down the aisle and out into the spring, London sunshine. This time it wasn't cars that picked them up. Instead, they made their way to Buckingham Palace in an open coach – the 1902 State Landau, which was the same one Prince Charles and Lady Diana had used on their wedding day. There, joined by their family, they appeared (and kissed) on the balcony, and then attended the wedding breakfast, hosted by the Queen.

Later, much to the delight of the crowds, the couple drove out of Buckingham Palace, down the Mall to Clarence House in Prince Charles's prized blue Aston Martin. The car was adorned with red, white and blue ribbons, an L plate on the front, a JU5T WED registration plate at the back, and towed a selection of helium balloons, all bobbing in the wind.

88

'Good Evening, Mr Bond'

The year 2012 was a sparkling one for the United Kingdom. Not only was it the year of the Queen's Diamond Jubilee (the first since Queen Victoria celebrated hers in 1897), but it was also Britain's time to host the Olympics. The two events came at a time of financial hardship for much of the country, and while the Jubilee celebrations were scaled back to reflect this, the summer of 2012 brought a little brightness to the hard times.

As with other jubilees over the years, events were held around the country for much of the year. There were royal visits, thanksgiving services, dinners and tea parties, and then on 4 June, beacons were lit across the Commonwealth, including one lit by the Queen outside Buckingham Palace. Her Majesty even managed to make a newlywed couple's day when she and the Duke of Edinburgh were at an official event in Manchester.

Frances and John Canning invited the Queen along to their wedding when they heard that the royal couple would be in their area, but received a reply to say that unfortunately they would be unable to attend. However, unknown to them, Buckingham Palace arranged it so that the Queen made a surprise entrance just after the ceremony, and didn't just meet them, but posed for photographs, too.

'She was beautiful, a really nice woman, and wished us all the best,' Mrs Canning said.

The Jubilee weekend was a busy one, and included a river pageant, where members of the royal family stood on a barge on the Thames, watching the flotilla of one thousand boats go by. Although it was early summer, the day was a chilly, wet one, and Prince Philip ended up in hospital afterwards, suffering from a bladder infection.

The concert which ended the bank holiday weekend of celebrations was held outside Buckingham Palace, and attended by most of the royal family – except the Duke of Edinburgh, who remained ill. The event was opened by UK popstar Robbie Williams, and then continued with performances from many of the day's stars, including Jessie J, Cliff Richard, Ed Sheeran, Kylie Minogue, Stevie Wonder, Elton John and Gary Barlow. The latter had arranged the event, and sang a special song, which was composed by himself and Andrew Lloyd Webber.

While Paul McCartney sang a medley of hits, including 'Let it Be' and 'Live and Let Die', he was joined on stage by the Queen's Guards and many of the acts who had performed that evening. Afterwards, the Queen, Prince Charles and his wife, Camilla, Duchess of Cornwall, took to the stage. Wearing a long, gold dress, Her Majesty watched as Prince Charles thanked everyone who had performed, and called on the audience to cheer so loud that his father could hear it from hospital. When he called the Queen 'Mummy', the crowd cheered enthusiastically, and Her Majesty laughed.

Less than two months later, the Olympics came to Britain, and at the opening ceremony, the Queen surprised people in a way that nobody expected. While thinking of ways to entertain the crowd, director Danny Boyle thought about the possibility of merging two very British institutions – the Queen and James Bond. The idea was that the production company could hire a double to play the part of the monarch, but when they wrote to the palace to tell them their idea, they were surprised to discover that the Queen herself wanted to play the role. Another surprise came when she suggested dialogue, and then improvised her lines.

In the skit – entitled 'Happy and Glorious' – James Bond (Daniel Craig) is seen arriving at Buckingham Palace by taxi, where he heads up the stairs and straight past the Queen's corgis. As he goes into the room, Her Majesty sits with her back to him, engrossed in her private papers. He coughs, she turns, and says the immortal words, 'Good evening, Mr Bond.' She then leads James Bond, her equerry and the corgis out of the door, before she and Bond climb into a waiting helicopter.

Off it goes, leaving the dogs behind, and heads straight over to the Olympic Stadium, where the Queen (actually skydiver Gary Connery in an identical dress) parachutes out of the chopper, and then makes her way to her seat. The crowd – as could be expected – went wild, not only because the Queen was playing a role in a special James Bond episode, but also because she had shown such a terrific sense of humour.

Shortly after the event, the Queen joked that it took Danny Boyle to convince her to 'jump' out of a helicopter. Then, some years later, Daniel Craig told Stephen Colbert on *The Late Show* that Her Majesty was very funny. He also added that during the making of the skit, he got to spend time with the corgis, and even played with them between takes.

89

The Queen's Horse Wins the Gold Cup

As the Queen grew older, her love for horses and horse racing never diminished. She continued to ride in Windsor Park, and was often photographed meeting horses, feeding them carrots, and reprimanding those that tried to take a bite out of her hat or her bouquet. She owned many race horses over the years, and as an avid Ascot fan, in June 2013 her horse, Estimate – an eightieth birthday present to Her Majesty from the Aga Khan – was entered into the Gold Cup, as 7–2 odds-on favourite.

After appearing in the traditional carriage ride around the course, the Queen settled into the royal box alongside her racing manager John Warren. Dressed in a purple suit (to match her racing colours of purple, scarlet and gold) with matching hat and signature pearls, she leaned forward and watched the race with a worried scowl. It was a close call, but as Estimate eventually romped home in first place, Her Majesty clapped her hands, beamed, and excitedly spoke to a delighted John Warren and the people around her. She then stood up and gave jockey Ryan Moore an enthusiastic wave.

This was the first time in history that the race had been won by a reigning monarch, and everyone was anxious to hear what Ryan Moore had to say. He was calm as he described riding the Queen's horse, but later described it as a very special event. Before the race, he had been sure that Estimate was the best horse racing that day, and he was proved correct. 'The reaction after she won was probably unlike anything else I've heard on the track,' he said.

Trainer Sir Michael Stoute seemed in shock when he was asked about the race. Describing Estimate as 'a pain in the backside at times', he went on to say what an honour and a thrill it was to train the Queen's Ascot winner. 'We know how much she loves this game,' he said.

The Queen was due to present the trophy for the Gold Cup, but as the winner herself, that wasn't possible. As she stepped into the winner's enclosure, the crowd roared and the Queen spoke to Moore, laughed at his jokes and rubbed Estimate's nose. It was rumoured that Princess Anne would present the trophy to her mother, but in the end it was the Duke of York who stepped in. The crowd that gathered around to see the historic presentation was so thick that the television cameras could barely get close as the Queen and Ryan Moore received their prizes. Throughout it all, however, Her Majesty's smile did not fade.

The Queen's grandson, Peter Phillips, told Channel 4 news that his grandmother was thrilled. 'To win the big one at Royal Ascot means so much to her,' he said. 'Everyone is just thrilled, it's very close to her heart and today is very special.'

Someone who wasn't quite as thrilled was bookmaker William Hill, as so many punters bet on the Queen's horse that the company estimated that they would be saddled with a £1.5 million payout. Her Majesty herself won £155,960 in prize money, not as a gambler, but as the owner of the horse itself.

90

'A Source of Inspiration and Pride for Us All'

On 4 July 2014, the Queen and the Duke of Edinburgh travelled to the Rosyth Dockyard in Fife in order to christen the largest warship ever built in the UK. Not only that, but it was named after the first HMS *Queen Elizabeth* ship, which served during both world wars. The idea for the new aircraft carrier had been bandied about since the early 2000s, but risk evaluations and cutbacks meant that the actual commissioning of the ship was pushed back until 2007. There was also criticism of the project, with some believing that the only reason the ship was being called the *Queen Elizabeth* was to gain favour with fans of the royals, in the hope that the commission would not be cancelled.

Criticism or not, by 2014 the aircraft carrier was completed, and at 65,000 tonnes and taking five years to build, it was considered the nation's flagship. The event to launch her, therefore, was a huge deal, and filled with pomp and ceremony, marching bands, sailors, a cheering public and flypasts.

The Queen wore a long turquoise coat and black gloves, and as the wind whipped around her, she held on to her hat before taking her seat between her husband and Prime Minister David Cameron. Aircraft Carrier Alliance representative Ian Booth welcomed Her Majesty to the shipyard, and then the Red Arrows flew overhead, leaving behind red, white and blue vapour. Admiral Sir George Zambellas spoke about the history of British sea power, and then the Queen took to her feet for the official christening.

'I believe that *Queen Elizabeth*, as flagship for the Royal Navy, will be a source of inspiration and pride for us all,' she said, before wishing all who sailed and served in her a safe journey. With the press of a button, a bottle of whisky smashed into the ship's hull, and as helicopters flew overhead and the national anthem was played, the *Queen Elizabeth* was named. Three years later, the ship was officially commissioned into the Royal Navy, after successfully completing sea trials. As of 2025, HMS *Queen Elizabeth* is still in service, and still considered the most important and powerful warship in the United Kingdom, along with her sister ship, HMS *Prince of Wales*.

Eight months later, on 10 March 2015, the Queen and the Duke of Edinburgh arrived at Southampton for the official christening of P&O Cruises' biggest cruise ship, *Britannia*. Although there was still the pomp and ceremony expected at such events, this one was more informal, with a host of entertainment for the waiting crowds. Rock band Queen's 'We Will Rock You' was played on the bagpipes, acrobats contorted themselves in huge plastic balls, comedian Rob Brydon told jokes, and dancers from *Strictly Come Dancing* worked through a routine.

The person the crowd most wanted to see, however, was the Queen. As she arrived at the venue, wearing a long, peach coat and matching hat, she spoke animatedly to captain Paul Brown before he invited her to take to the podium.

'I name this ship *Britannia*,' the Queen said. 'May God bless her, and all who sail in her.' As the sparkling wine bottle smashed against the hull of the ship and 'Rule Britannia' was played, red, white and blue confetti rained down, before Her Majesty went onboard to have a guided tour of the ship. When asked about the bottle used to christen the boat, the Queen gave a broad smile. 'It exploded rather successfully,' she laughed.

91

Time Marches On

The five years before the Covid lockdown in 2020 saw many changes in the Queen's life. On 9 September 2015, she became the longest-reigning British monarch, taking over the record previously set by her great-great-grandmother, Queen Victoria. It was a big deal for royalists, and was marked by a thirty-minute tribute in the House of Commons, a gun salute, and a procession of boats along the Thames.

Thanking well-wishers in Scotland, the Queen seemed non-perturbed by the event, and told them that, actually, the title was not one to which she had ever aspired. 'Inevitably,' she said, 'a long life can pass by many milestones – my own is no exception – but I thank you all and the many others at home and overseas for your touching messages of great kindness.'

Seven months later, in April 2016, the Queen turned ninety years old, and there followed a series of events leading up to her official birthday in June. These included a service of thanksgiving at St Paul's Cathedral, London, the Trooping of the Colour on Horse Guards Parade, an appearance by the royal family on the Buckingham Palace balcony, and a giant street party in the Mall, London.

Perhaps the most popular of all the events, however, happened in May, when a birthday tribute was held in the grounds of Windsor

Castle. Hosted by television duo Ant and Dec, the celebration gave various artistic representations of the Queen's life, stories and memories from actors, biographers and family members, and songs from the likes of Kylie Minogue, Gary Barlow, James Blunt and Dame Shirley Bassey. There were also acrobats, dancing, bagpipes, and animal and military-related displays.

When Her Majesty entered the arena in the Scottish State Coach to the tune of the national anthem, the crowd roared. Wearing a turquoise suit, white gloves and pearls, she looked happy as she kissed Prince Charles, who was waiting to greet her. Sitting in the royal box with the rest of her family, the Queen watched the displays with great attention, and at one point – when cows entered the arena – she was seen pointing. 'Cows!' she squealed, and then laughed. This obvious delight has been turned into a popular gif and meme in the years since.

The event ended with a display around a gigantic birthday cake, and a rendition of 'Diamonds Are Forever' from Dame Shirley Bassey. Then, after the crowd sang 'Happy Birthday' and the national anthem, the Queen and the Duke of Edinburgh left their seats in the royal box and thanked the performers who had entertained them that evening. It was a mammoth celebration, and one that brought together all aspects of the Queen's life and reign.

A year later, in May 2017, rumours abounded that there was about to be an important announcement from Buckingham Palace. There was speculation that the Queen could be stepping down from the throne, or that possibly there had been some kind of health crisis, but in the end, the news was that the almost ninety-six-year-old Duke of Edinburgh was to retire from public duties, with the full support of the Queen. It was a historical moment, especially as he had been by Her Majesty's side for all of her sixty-five-year reign.

Prince Philip moved to Sandringham shortly after the announcement but continued to support the Queen publicly at various events, such as the opening of the Queensferry Crossing in Scotland,

and Remembrance Day and Christmas services at Sandringham. Privately, the couple celebrated their seventieth wedding anniversary, and then the 2018 weddings of Prince Harry and Meghan Markle, and Princess Eugenie and Jack Brooksbank. But failing health was never far away, and as well as having hip surgery in London, Prince Philip also created headlines when he crashed his Land Rover into the car of Emma Fairweather in January 2019. The collision happened as he pulled out of a side road near Sandringham, and left his car on its side and all parties shaken. Fairweather also suffered a broken wrist.

There was a media uproar when the news broke, with film crews arriving in Norfolk from around the world, and much discussion about whether or not the Duke should still be driving at ninety-seven years old. Prince Philip was adamant, however, that the reason for the crash was because of the low sun shining over the main road. Things were made no better when he was seen driving without a seatbelt just days after the collision. The Duke later wrote to Emma Fairweather, apologising for his part in the accident, and wishing her a speedy recovery.

Later that year, in June 2019, the Queen attended a seventy-fifth anniversary of D-Day event in Portsmouth, without Prince Philip by her side. Instead, she was with Prince Charles and a host of world leaders, including US President Donald Trump. Calling her generation resilient, Her Majesty expressed her delight in being able to attend the event, and spoke about the brave men who fought for freedom during the Second World War. 'Many of them would never return,' she said, 'and the heroism, courage and sacrifice of those who lost their lives will never be forgotten.'

92

The Queen... 'Quite Cantankerous' But Also Hilarious

As a child, Princess Elizabeth was known for her quick wit, her jokes and her imitations. As she grew up and the enormity of her future role became apparent, her fun side – for the most part – was hidden from public view. However, as she became older, her playfulness was once again revealed, and she was not scared to have a laugh at her own expense.

In 2018, the TV documentary *The Queen's Green Planet* was filmed with Sir David Attenborough. As they walked around the Buckingham Palace garden, the philanthropist pointed out that a sundial was placed firmly in the shade. 'Isn't it good, yes,' she said before smiling and asking staff if 'we' had thought of that at the time it was erected. When a helicopter was heard flying overhead, her eyes darted from left to right, before deciding that the racket sounded as though President Trump or President Obama were about to land in the garden.

Over the years, cakes have caused more than their fair share of hilarity. There was the time when the Queen got her knife stuck in the cake, which prompted a laughing Princess Anne to step forward to stop the whole thing being dragged off the table, and there were many times when Her Majesty couldn't quite work out how to cut the extravagantly decorated sponges. On occasions like those, Prince Philip would often step forward to give his help, which was often as haphazard as the Queen's. Then there was the time when four generations of the royal family came together to make a Christmas pudding. As Prince George stirred the bowl, the Queen smiled, until he became so enthusiastic that she had to move away for fear of being splattered with mixture.

Another bakery moment occurred in 2021 when Her Majesty was asked to cut a cake for 'The Big Lunch' – a community event at the Eden Project. Accompanied by the Duchess of Cornwall and Duchess of Cambridge, the Queen attempted to cut the cake with a sword, only to come into difficulties with the size of it. While the Duchess of Cornwall told her to use two hands, a lady stepped forward to announce that there was a knife nearby, should the Queen need it. 'I know there is,' she exclaimed. 'This is something that is more unusual.'

When presented with a cake to celebrate the Platinum Jubilee, the Queen was perplexed as to why it was upside down. When it was explained that it was so that the press could get a good view of it, the Queen jokingly retorted, 'I don't mind, I don't matter.'

While the Queen and her family are not meant to have any political leanings, meetings and dinners with politicians could lead to more jokes. When Canada's Prime Minister Justin Trudeau gave the Queen a lengthy introduction, her reaction was to thank him for making her feel so old. Then, during the G7 summit in Cornwall, she posed for photographs with various politicians, including Prime Minister Boris Johnson. 'Are you supposed to be looking as though you're enjoying yourself?' she asked.

In 2022, Protection Officer Richard Griffin told a story about going on a picnic with Her Majesty at Balmoral. After the lunch, they went for a walk and came across a couple of American tourists, who did not recognise her at all. They gave the Queen a rundown of the activities they had been doing on their walking holiday, before asking her where she lived. When she replied that she had a holiday home nearby, they asked if she knew the Queen, and she said no, but then pointed to her protection officer, exclaiming that he met her regularly. Knowing that she wouldn't mind a joke, Griffin told the tourists that she could be quite cantankerous at times, and then they all had photographs taken together, the couple still none the wiser that they had just met the Queen.

93

'Better Days Will Return'

In early 2020, reports circulated that a mysterious flu-like illness had reached the shores of Great Britain. Covid-19 was a new virus, especially dangerous to the older generations and those with other health or immune-system challenges.

While at first the government encouraged the public to wash their hands and refuse handshakes, by March it became clear that something else had to be done. Finally, Prime Minister Boris Johnson made the announcement that the country was all but shutting down, that people must stay at home, schools would close, and all but essential workers should carry out their work remotely.

These limitations affected not just the British public, but the working royals, too. While families around the country got used to home schooling, PE with Joe Wicks, working via Zoom and making bread, the Queen retreated to Windsor Castle with the Duke of Edinburgh. The awful circumstances meant that the couple were now living together full time for the first time since Philip had retired to Norfolk. Not only that, but because official engagements were made via the internet, and there was no travelling required, they could now live something resembling a quiet life for the first time since Elizabeth had become queen.

Her Majesty's circle grew smaller, there was a skeleton crew at Windsor Castle, and most of her work was carried out virtually. This she seemed to enjoy a great deal. During one call, Princess Anne asked the Queen if she could see everyone properly. When Her Majesty said that she could see some, Princess Anne responded, 'Actually, you don't need me. You know what I look like!'

As when Princess Diana passed away, the British public looked to their monarch for some reassurance during such a time of uncertainty. This came on the evening of 5 April, when a pre-recorded speech was broadcast from Windsor Castle.

During the programme, the camera panned the outside of the castle, before the Queen appeared on-screen. Wearing a green dress, with pearls and a brooch, Her Majesty noted that she was speaking to everyone in a challenging, disrupting time. Footage then appeared of those on the frontline, as the Queen thanked the doctors, nurses, carers and essential workers for the dedication to their duties, and for the support they had shown to everyone who needed it. The camera returned to Her Majesty, as she thanked everyone for staying indoors to protect the vulnerable. 'Together, we are tackling this disease,' she said, 'and I want to reassure you that if we remain united and resolute, then we will overcome it.'

The speech was a warm one, full of hope and the sense that every single person would one day be proud of the strength shown during the pandemic. There was an emphasis on the coming together of the public to help others, footage of children displaying drawings of rainbows in their windows, and the weekly applause and banging of pans in appreciation of the essential workers.

Towards the end of the broadcast, the Queen told viewers that it reminded her of the very first speech she had given, during the war in 1940. It had been eighty years since she had sat behind the desk at Windsor Castle and addressed the public as a fourteen-year-old child, and now a photo of the young Queen and her late sister appeared on the screen.

The Queen had come full circle, and while the circumstances may have been different, the feelings of anxiety of the unknown were the same. Her words, therefore, gave great comfort to many.

'Better days will return,' she said. 'We will be with our friends again, we will be with our families again, we will meet again.'

94

Princess Beatrice Borrows a Dress

On 17 July 2020, the Queen's granddaughter, Princess Beatrice, married Edoardo Mapelli Mozzi at the Royal Chapel of All Saints, Windsor. The world was in lockdown because of the Covid-19 virus, and so the ceremony was small, simple and socially distanced.

Surprisingly, the bride had chosen not to buy a new dress, and instead went to her grandmother to borrow one of hers. The gown decided on was from the 1960s, designed by Norman Hartnell, and made from ivory taffeta embroidered with jewels. The Queen's dresser, Angela Kelly, helped to adjust the dress for Beatrice, which included adding short puffed sleeves. The bride also wore her grandmother's tiara – the same one she had worn when marrying Prince Philip in 1947 – and which had originally belonged to Queen Mary. It was an inspired decision. The bride looked stunning, and the Queen and the Duke were both photographed beaming at the sight of their granddaughter, after the ceremony.

The first time the Queen had worn that particular dress was on 10 December 1962, when she attended the premiere of *Lawrence of Arabia* and met the star of the film, Peter O'Toole. Columnist John London from the *Evening News and Star* predicted that the event would be 'the most glittering film premiere of the season', and he was right.

Wearing long white gloves, a fur stole over her shoulders, diamonds around her neck, and a tiara on her head, Her Majesty literally shimmered, and as she got out of the car, the thousand people crowded into Leicester Square gasped and cheered. Over two thousand guests paid for tickets to the sold-out event, and many more begged to be allowed in, but were left disappointed. The evening was a huge success, however, and raised money for the Soldiers', Sailors', and Airmen's Families Association and Save the Children.

The second time the Queen wore the dress was on 21 April 1966, her fortieth birthday. Birthdays were usually kept free of official engagements, but on that day, Her Majesty and the Duke of Edinburgh attended the State Opening of Parliament, and then Prince Philip travelled on to open a wildlife exhibition at Alexandra Palace in north London.

Forty was – and still is – considered a milestone birthday, and mostly male columnists were eager to argue that it would be a formidable, tough anniversary for the Queen. They decided that she would now be conscious of how she looked in front of the live television cameras, and that the speech would come with a level of maturity. Dramatically, they predicted that Her Majesty would be looking back on her life and her reign, and could possibly be heading for some kind of personal crisis that could rock her authority.

Whether or not the Queen thought anything like this is questionable. Regardless, she looked every inch her normal self, wearing the white, jewelled dress, the Imperial State Crown and crimson robes over the top. The sight was – according to those present – a brilliant scene, and the gun salutes were in overdrive. There were forty-one fired as the Queen arrived at the House of Lords, and another forty-one fired in Hyde Park. Many others were launched from Royal Navy ships, and the Tower of London was exceptionally busy, with a forty-one-gun salute at midday, and then a sixty-two-gun salute just minutes later.

95

'With Grateful Hearts, We Remember'

On 9 April 2021 it was announced that Prince Philip had passed away. The Duke was just two months shy of his one hundredth birthday, and had been in poor health for some time. But while the news wasn't altogether unexpected, the loss of someone who had been in the public eye – and by the Queen's side – for over seventy years felt unsettling. The world was still in the grip of the Covid-19 pandemic, and just as her parents had done during the Second World War, the Queen had provided a sense of security at a time when the country felt uprooted. Now, however, her own 'strength and stay' was gone.

Tributes to the Duke came in from all over the world, and flags were lowered to half-mast. Gun salutes went off, and Westminster Abbey tolled the bell ninety-nine times to honour each year of Prince Philip's life. Flowers then began to arrive at the royal palaces, which lead to a request that donations should be made to charity, instead, for fear of people gathering during the ongoing pandemic.

While the royal family could not all come together, they each posted tributes to the Duke on Instagram. Calling him 'Grandpa', Princess Eugenie remembered him teaching her how to cook and paint, and listening to the stories of his life. Prince William posted a photograph of his son, Prince George, sitting with the Duke in a carriage, along with a tribute to his life. Both Eugenie and William promised the same thing – to support the Queen in the years ahead.

Prince Philip's funeral was held on 17 April 2021 at St George's Chapel, Windsor. Because of the lockdown, guests were minimal, though it was always his wish to have the least amount of fuss possible. There was still the pomp and ceremony of marching bands and military personnel, but they were as socially distanced as possible, and many – including the pallbearers – wore masks outside, and everyone else wore them inside.

However, in spite of the stripped-down ceremony, the Duke's personality shone through. His coffin arrived atop a personally selected custom Land Rover, his family marching behind. The Duke was famous in later years for his love of carriage riding, and as his coffin headed towards the chapel, his black ponies and carriage stood silently by.

When the Queen arrived, she was accompanied by her lady-in-waiting, though the woman did not sit with Her Majesty in the chapel. Instead, as the sound of the national anthem rang out, the Queen took her seat alone. Dressed in black, with a matching face mask, she kept her head bowed. Then, as the coffin was carried up the steps to the chapel, a gun salute rang out, and the country fell silent.

When the funeral began, it was with speeches, prayers, bible readings and a socially distanced four-person choir singing hymns chosen by the Duke himself. After a lone piper played 'The Flowers of the Forest', the buglers of the Royal Marines sounded the 'Last Post', the Archbishop of Canterbury read the blessing, and then the choir sang the national anthem.

'With grateful hearts, we remember the many ways in which his long life has been a blessing to us,' said the Dean of Windsor, the Rt Rev David Conner. 'We have been inspired by his unwavering loyalty to our queen . . .'

96

'Thank You, Ma'am ... For Everything'

Paddington, the little bear known for his red hat, blue duffel coat and battered suitcase, was created by author Michael Bond in 1958. His various scrapes have made him a favourite of children and their parents for six decades, but perhaps the most beautiful connection in recent years was when he teamed up with the Queen to create a short film to celebrate her Platinum Jubilee.

The skit began with actor and writer Simon Farnaby, as a Buckingham Palace footman, bringing tea through the corridors of the palace. When he finally reaches the set table, Paddington is unveiled as the guest waiting to be served. He thanks his as yet unknown companion for inviting him to tea, and then the camera turns to reveal the Queen, wearing a colourful floral dress and her trademark pearls.

When Her Majesty asks if the little bear would like tea, he accepts, drains the teapot, and is then embarrassed when there's none left for the Queen. 'Never mind,' she says, before Paddington embarrasses himself further by almost falling out of his chair, juggling the teapot and then accidentally splashing cream all over the footman's cheek.

The Queen looks suitably amused, and then the two discuss marmalade sandwiches – Paddington having kept his in his hat, and the Queen's in her handbag. 'Happy Jubilee, ma'am,' says Paddington, tipping his hat. 'And thank you, for everything.' The two then join in on the opening bars of Queen's 'We Will Rock You' by playing the beat on their teacups.

The shoot wasn't without difficulties, mainly because the Queen had to react to all of Paddington's quirky behaviour despite him not actually sitting in front of her. The scene where she tells the bear that she keeps her marmalade sandwich in her handbag also caused a slight problem, because the director thought that she should be gentler in her approach. After several attempts, the Queen nailed the scene, and the shoot was finished successfully.

Simon Farnaby later spoke on the Richard Herring podcast, *RHLSTP*, and told a story about the making of the film. According to him, after filming ended, he approached the Queen and told her that she was fantastic, and a great actress. 'Well, I do it all the time,' she said, alluding to the fact that she was frequently called upon to give speeches. However, Farnaby assumed that she meant that she put on the role of queen when required, and commented on it. 'You know I am the Queen?' she asked the embarrassed actor.

The film was created with the utmost secrecy, and not even her family knew anything about it. This was confirmed at the opening of the Jubilee party, when Prince Charles and Prince William were both seen in the royal enclosure, looking completely gobsmacked. For the Queen, it was a chance once again to perform, just as she had done during her teenage years, when she and Princess Margaret took to the stage to entertain friends and family, during the Second World War.

Since then, the 'friendship' between the Queen and Paddington has become a beautiful and fitting tribute to Her Majesty. The twosome has been painted by artists such as Eleanor Tomlinson and Lucy Claire, and reposted thousands of times on social media. After the Queen's passing, there were so many Paddington soft toys and

'THANK YOU, MA'AM . . . FOR EVERYTHING'

marmalade sandwiches left outside the palace and in parks that the public had to be ever-so-politely asked to stop.

In 2022, co-writer James Lamont gave his opinion of the sketch to BBC Radio 5 Live. He said that it felt very natural that the Queen and Paddington could spend time together. 'They would both welcome each other,' he said, 'because they're both cut from the same cloth.'

97

One Last Time on the Balcony

The Queen's Platinum Jubilee, celebrating seventy years on the throne, fell in 2022. In keeping with past jubilees, there were parties, a special coin, flags, parades and, of course, bunting. There was also a special photograph released on Accession Day, which showed the Queen smiling joyfully, with a red box of papers sat before her, and a photograph of her beloved father on a table next to her. Her Majesty was also filmed opening cards from well-wishers, during which time she playfully spoke to her oldest dog Candy the dorgi – a cross between a dachshund and a corgi. Candy was to pass away in the summer of 2022, bringing sadness to what was otherwise a season of celebration.

In a letter to the British people, the Queen renewed her promise to devote her life to service, and wrote about the extraordinary events that had happened in the seventy years since she ascended the throne. She gave thanks to the people around the country and the world, who had supported her during her reign, and gave special mention to her husband, the late Duke of Edinburgh.

'I was blessed that in Prince Philip I had a partner willing to carry out the role of consort and unselfishly make the sacrifices to go with it,' she wrote, before adding that she hoped that when Prince Charles

ONE LAST TIME ON THE BALCONY

ascended the throne, the public would give his wife, Camilla, the same support that they had given to Her Majesty.

Along with the letters, photos and memorabilia, there were also special events to follow. These included a Platinum Pudding competition, along with 'The Queen's Green Canopy', which was an initiative in Her Majesty's honour to encourage people around the country to plant a tree. To celebrate the start of the programme – nicknamed the Treebilee – the Queen joined Prince Charles as he planted his own tree. While he did most of the work, Her Majesty supervised, dressed in a warm winter coat, wellies and her headscarf. Afterwards, she spoke to local children, who presented her with an album full of tree-inspired artwork. 'I shall look at it in the car on my way down to Edinburgh,' Her Majesty said. 'Thank you very much, that's very kind.'

Prince Charles spoke about the Canopy project on a video for the Royal Family Instagram account. 'Planting a tree,' he said, 'is a statement of hope and faith in the future.'

While the commemorative events were in full force during the first half of the year, the major celebrations happened during a special four-day weekend in June. Street parties were held, beacons were lit, and the Queen was seen lighting her own at Windsor, using a sparkly globe. A special concert was held at Buckingham Palace – before which the Queen's Paddington skit was broadcast – and pageants were made all the more interesting when Prince Louis – the son of William and Catherine, the Duke and Duchess of Cambridge – danced along to the music and sat on his grandfather's knee.

Perhaps the most poignant of all the events, however, came at the end of the Jubilee celebrations, when the Queen and the royal family went on to the Buckingham Palace balcony. Dressed all in green, and leaning on a cane, Her Majesty was given a beautiful welcome from the thousands of people outside the palace, and all the way down the Mall. It was a wonderful sight, and as the national anthem played below, the crowds sang along at the top of their voices.

The Queen smiled and waved, and looked genuinely happy to be there. She was now ninety-six years old, her health was not what it once was, and she had problems with her legs and feet, but her determination and strength were everywhere apparent. Still, there was also a sense of an ending, a nostalgic feeling of all the times she had been on that balcony, from a tiny baby all the way up to her nineties. It was as if every important event had been witnessed on that space.

As she gave one last wave, and walked back into Buckingham Palace, one had to wonder if Her Majesty knew that this would be the last time she'd ever be out there. Afterwards, she released a message to the people. 'While I may not have attended every event in person,' she wrote, 'my heart has been with you all; and I remain committed to serving you to the best of my ability.'

98

The Passing of the Queen

For many years, there had been a plan in place for when the Queen eventually passed away. Called Operation London Bridge, it was a blueprint of events that would be called to action in the minutes, hours and weeks after her death. The plan was intricate, and involved the prime minister, the police, the Armed Forces and many others who would have to come together to guide and support the country through the period of mourning.

On 6 September 2022, new prime minister Liz Truss arrived at the Queen's Scottish residence, Balmoral, to be officially asked to form a government. This came after the resignation of former PM Boris Johnson, whose leadership had been questioned after so-called Partygate – a scandal caused by the revelation that while the rest of the country was under strict lockdown rules, there had been several social gatherings within the Conservative Party.

Unknown to anyone at the time, Liz Truss would resign just forty-nine days later, but for now, she was photographed meeting the Queen at Balmoral. Her Majesty had been in Scotland for her traditional summer break, but the photographs taken that day showed that the monarch was in fragile health. Wearing a kilt, cardigan, shirt and her pearls, the Queen leaned on a walking stick, and there was some bruising on the back of her hand. Press photographer Jane Barlow told *Sky News* that the Queen was 'frail' but 'in good spirits' during their meeting. The two made small talk about the rainy Scottish weather, but Her Majesty was full of smiles, nevertheless, as she spoke to the photographer, and then greeted Liz Truss.

There was no inkling that the Queen would pass so soon after her last meeting and photos, but at 12.39 p.m. on 8 September 2022, television show *Bargain Hunt* was interrupted to bring the news that Her Majesty was under medical supervision at Balmoral. The urgency of the statement, the reading from paper instead of autocue and the words 'comfortable' and 'family members have been informed', made it clear that this was much more than a trivial matter. Still, the idea of the Queen passing away – even at the age of ninety-six – seemed something of an exaggeration, given the amount of time she had been on the throne. Around the country, therefore, fans hoped that, somehow, she would rally.

As the afternoon went on, newsreaders changed into black formalwear, and it seemed inevitable that the news was looking bleak. Sure enough, at 6.31 p.m., *BBC News* showed the flag above Buckingham Palace being lowered, and then it was officially announced that Her Majesty had passed: 'The Queen died peacefully at Balmoral, this afternoon,' the newsreader said. 'The King and the Queen Consort will remain at Balmoral this evening, and will return to London tomorrow.'

Television shows and bulletins were interrupted to deliver the sad news of the Queen's death, and tributes poured in from around the world. Pilots broke the news to passengers travelling to far-off places, supermarkets announced it over the loudspeakers, and across the world, people picked up the telephone to inform and console family and friends. Flags were lowered, books of condolence were opened, and local newspaper reporters delved into the archives to find photographs and stories of the Queen visiting their area.

THE PASSING OF THE QUEEN

Buckingham Palace has always been a magnet for tourists, but as soon as it had been announced that Her Majesty's health was faltering, more and more people had arrived. By the time the official news of her death was broken, there were thousands of people standing outside, laying flowers, leaving notes and flags, and taking photographs. In order to centralise the laying of flowers in London, a memorial garden was created in Green Park. The scene was replicated outside the Queen's beloved Windsor, Sandringham, at city halls, and at Balmoral, where she had passed.

After the official announcement, the United Kingdom went into a ten-day period of national mourning. The main focus during this period was on Westminster Hall, where Her Majesty lay in state between 14 and 19 September. The procession to the hall was a long one, and some members of the royal family – including the new king, Charles, Princess Anne, Prince William and Prince Harry – marched behind the gun carriage carrying the coffin. The Queen's children would return to Westminster Hall on 16 September to hold vigil, and her grandchildren did the same, a day later.

During much of the time that the Queen lay in state, visitors were able to file past her coffin, bowing or silently reflecting. The desire to see the coffin was so great that members of the public queued for two miles and many hours, making friends with others in the line, and spotting famous people such as footballer David Beckham and actress Tilda Swinton. Politicians paid their respects, as did dignitaries and council officials. All had a story to tell, and a memory to share.

'Her Majesty reigned for seventy years,' said one visitor. 'I can give her twenty-four hours of my time, to pay respects and to say thank you for an incredible reign.'

99

'Sleep, Dearie, Sleep'

The funeral for Queen Elizabeth II was held on 19 September 2022, at Westminster Abbey. The service was designed to pay tribute to the Queen's long reign, and it gave people around the world the opportunity to say goodbye. The funeral day began when the Queen's coffin, followed by the royal family, was transported by gun carriage to Westminster Abbey. The coffin was draped in the Royal Standard Flag, and atop it was the Imperial State Crown, along with the Orb and the Sceptre – all of which were used during the Queen's coronation in 1953.

The flowers that were laid on the coffin were all very personal to the Queen, and included foliage and blooms from the gardens of Buckingham Palace, Clarence House and Highgrove House. There was rosemary, chosen to represent remembrance, myrtle grown from a sprig from the Queen's wedding bouquet, and English oak, a symbol of strength. There were also roses, hydrangeas, sedum, dahlias and scabious, chosen in colourful shades of pink, gold and burgundy. In the middle of it all, a card from Her Majesty's son, Charles, reading, 'In loving and devoted memory.'

Once the coffin had arrived at Westminster, it was carried in by the 1st Battalion Grenadier Guards. Then it was time for the first ceremony of the day. Conducted by the Dean of Westminster, the state funeral service included lessons read by Prime Minister Liz Truss, and the secretary general of the Commonwealth, the Rt Hon. Patricia Scotland. Political leaders, foreign royal families, dignitaries, volunteers and representatives from all over the world sat quietly in Westminster as the funeral took place, and at the end, after the 'Last Post' was played, they, and the rest of the country, sat in quiet reflection during the two minutes' silence.

The state funeral service over, the Queen's coffin was placed on the State Gun Carriage, and taken through the streets to Wellington Arch. The carriage was not pulled by horses. Instead, it was pulled by ninety-eight Royal Navy sailors with forty others following behind, and following them were the family. The procession included thousands of military personnel, all marching, some playing instruments, and all intent on making Her Majesty's final journey a safe, respectful and memorable one.

The most sentimental part of the London procession was when the cortège passed Buckingham Palace. The site of so many events in the Queen's life, from her childhood with her grandparents, to her move there when her parents became king and queen. The bombing of the palace while the then-princess was in Windsor, and then the jubilant celebrations, as Princess Elizabeth and Princess Margaret Rose danced around the Queen Victoria Memorial. All the wedding breakfasts, the balcony appearances, the garden parties and the state visits, all had a part to play in the Queen's life, and now here was her cortège, passing by for the very last time.

When the procession reached Wellington Arch, the coffin was placed in the State Hearse, and off it went to Windsor for the committal. The route took the car through the countryside, where farmers had lined up their tractors in tribute. Once in Windsor, the hearse went up the Long Walk, lined with thousands of people, their heads quietly bowed. Along the way, the Queen's pony, Emma, stood with her groom, and as the coffin came past, she lifted her front leg. Inside the castle quadrangle, the two corgis, Muick and Sandy, waited with a footman.

The final part of the funeral was the committal service, which was attended by the Queen's household as well as political figures. The service was conducted by the Dean of Windsor, prayers were said and hymns sung. The Crown, the Orb and the Sceptre were all removed from the coffin, and then the lord chamberlain 'broke' his wand, signifying the end of his service to the Queen as sovereign. As prayers were said, the Queen's coffin was then lowered into the Royal Vault.

Finally, the Queen's piper, Pipe Major Paul Burns of the Royal Regiment of Scotland, played for Her Majesty one last time. As he marched out of the chapel, the tune of choice was the Scottish lament, 'Sleep, Dearie, Sleep'.

100

The Queen's Lasting Legacy

Although she was ninety-six years old, the passing of Queen Elizabeth II seemed too soon in many ways. It was as if she had been in this world for so long that she would never leave. Every single person in the United Kingdom and beyond had some memory to share, even if it was just an article in a newspaper, or a random thought or observation.

However, while the Queen has now been gone for over three years, in many ways she is still with us. Books are still published, pictures are printed, and a quick trip to London still shows her image on mugs, plates, flags, calendars, Christmas tree decorations and even bobble-head ornaments. The souvenirs are still bought by tourists, all eager to take something of the Queen back home.

So, what of her lasting legacy? Queen Elizabeth's motto of never complain, never explain, is not something most people can put into action, since all of us have to let off steam at some point in our lives. But it is likely that away from prying eyes, the Queen complained occasionally, too, and perhaps that's a good lesson to be learned. Maybe we should all take her stance of holding our heads high in public, of quietly dealing with issues that come our way, but not to make a big deal of every little thing – until we're back in our own homes, anyway.

Elizabeth II may not have held power in the way that Elizabeth I did, but that does not mean that she had no power at all. Far from it. During her reign, the Queen had fifteen British prime ministers, and met and spoke with each of them regularly – from Winston Churchill in 1952, right up to Liz Truss, just days before the Queen's passing in 2022. Her position meant that she must remain neutral to all things political, but there is no doubt that her ministers held her care and listening skills in high regard. There are lessons to be learned here for all of us; that maybe it is OK not to have an opinion on everyone and everything, and instead just to offer an ear, a kind word and some compassion, regardless of whether or not we agree.

In 1947, while still a princess, Elizabeth gave a speech at St Mary's College for Women in Durham. Talking about women's rights, she expressed her opinion that, 'Women can learn and prove that there need be no conflict between the part they want to play in the world and their traditional duties in the home.' She went on to mention how many women (including herself) had taken part in the war effort, but, 'If we have established our rights we have multiplied our duties.'

During a visit to Cardiff a year later, she delved further into the subject, explaining that the claims of women to be equal and fair in opportunity and earnings were no longer in dispute. 'Once these claims are accepted,' she said, 'there is found to be no conflict between the rights women have won, and the duties to which they are born.' She then expressed her view that the love of a family was a natural instinct, which would never take second place.

While some of the Princess's opinions were very much of her time – and some may say a little out of touch since she herself had access to nannies and staff – it was a bold step to talk about women's rights in the 1940s. Not only that, but as princess and then queen, Elizabeth proved that women could work even as mothers to young children

– something which was still frowned upon into the 1980s and far beyond. Perhaps the lesson here is that no matter what your age or your position, it is OK to speak out and be supportive of others, even if their lives do not necessarily imitate your own.

No matter what stage of life the Queen was at, she had the knack of putting anyone at ease, and could always find a question to ask or an observation to share. She did not receive a formal school education, but she remembered names, details and history with ease. She was not afraid to speak her mind and tell people off occasionally. She was serious, but funny at the core – her childhood love of theatre returning in later life. She was a person who lived by the rules, and created them, too, and when she spoke, everyone listened.

After reigning over her people for seventy years, there is, perhaps, a little of the Queen in all of us, and the stoic, determined way she approached her work no matter what her age is an inspiration to us all. She once promised that her whole life would be devoted to service, and she did just that. Perhaps that is Queen Elizabeth's legacy . . . to remind us to treat others with humility, to be kind, to share our lives and, most of all, to be true to our word.

Bibliography

General sources

Bradford, Sarah, *George VI*, Penguin, 2002
Brandreth, Gyles, *Elizabeth: An Intimate Portrait*, Michael Joseph, 2022
Brown, Craig, *A Voyage around the Queen*, 4th Estate, 2024
Brown, Craig, *Ma'am Darling: 99 Glimpses of Princess Margaret*, 4th Estate, 2018
Clark OBE, Stanley, *Palace Diary: The Authorized Account of the Queen's Official Engagements*, George G. Harrap & Co., 1958
Crawford, Marion, *The Little Princesses*, Seven Dials, 2003
Dennison, Matthew, *The Queen*, Head of Zeus, 2021
Dimbleby, Richard, *Elizabeth Our Queen*, University of London Press, 1953
Eastoe, Jane, *Queen Elizabeth II: A Lifetime Dressing for the World Stage*, Pavilion, 2022
Elizabeth II: Princess, Queen, Icon, National Portrait Gallery, 2022
Ferrier, Neil, *The Queen Elizabeth Coronation Book*, R. T. A. Robinson, 1953
Hardman, Robert, *Queen of Our Times*, Macmillan, 2022
Heald, Tim, *Princess Margaret: A Life Unravelled*, Weidenfeld & Nicolson, 2007
Holt, Bethan, *The Queen: 70 Years of Majestic Style*, Ryland Peters & Small, 2022
Hughes, Sali, *Our Rainbow Queen*, Square Peg, 2019
Kelly, Angela, *The Other Side of the Coin: The Queen, the Dresser and the Wardrobe*, HarperCollins, 2019
Lacey, Robert, *The Crown: The Inside History*, Blink, 2017
Larman, Alexander, *Power and Glory: Elizabeth II and the Rebirth of Royalty*, Weidenfeld & Nicolson, 2025
Morgan, Michelle, *When Marilyn Met the Queen*, Robinson, 2022

Morton, Andrew, *Diana: Her True Story – In Her Own Words*, revised edition, Michael O'Mara, 2017

Morton, Andrew, *The Queen*, Michael O'Mara, 2022

Pope-Hennessy, James, *The Quest for Queen Mary*, Zuleika, 2018

The Queen's Speeches, Hardie Grant, 2023

Ring, Anne, *The Story of Princess Elizabeth*, John Murray, 1930

Sebba, Anne, *That Woman: The Life of Wallis Simpson Duchess of Windsor*, Weidenfeld & Nicolson, 2011

Shawcross, William, *Queen Elizabeth The Queen Mother: The Official Biography*, Macmillan, 2009

Smith, Sally Bedell, *Elizabeth the Queen: The Woman. The Family. The Life*, Penguin, 2016

Strober, Deborah Hart and Strober, Gerald, *Queen Elizabeth II: The Oral History*, September, 2021

Vickers, Hugo, *Elizabeth the Queen Mother*, Hutchinson, 2005

Warwick, Christopher, *Princess Margaret: A Life of Contrasts*, André Deutsch, 2018

Wulff MVO, Louis, *Queen of To-morrow*, Sampson Law, Marston & Co., 1946

Sources of quotations

1. One of the Prettiest Babies

'The Duchess of York has had some rest' – 'A royal baby', *Hampshire Telegraph and Post*, 23 April 1926.

'Elizabeth Alexandra Mary, I baptise thee' – 'Princess Elizabeth', *Crewe Chronicle*, 5 June 1926.

'And not in the heavy manner' – 'Princess Elizabeth', *Penrith Observer*, 28 December 1926.

'We hope that this porringer' – 'For Princess Elizabeth', *Scotsman*, 21 December 1926.

'You see she likes it at once' – 'For Princess Elizabeth', *Birmingham Gazette*, 21 December 1926.

2. 'Baby Betty' Visits Her Grandparents

'Thank you. I am terribly thrilled' – 'New Zealand doll for Princess Betty', *Evening News*, 23 February 1927.

3. The Most Popular Baby in the Land

'We must not forget the youngest member' – 'Princess Elizabeth', *Belfast News-Letter*, 21 June 1929.

'the most remarkable child' – 'Princess Elizabeth', *Sunday Dispatch*, 8 June 1930.

'Nice man' and 'Speak to pretty boy' – 'Meet the Duchess of York!', *Sunday Post*, 2 September 1928.

'How frightfully untidy' – 'Little Princess and "Sandy"', *Sheffield Independent*, 19 November 1930.
'Naughty Mummy!' – 'Princess Elizabeth imitates sea lions', *Daily Independent*, 18 October 1932.
'all grown-up ladies wear hats' – 'Princess Elizabeth', *Sheffield Daily Telegraph*, 26 April 1929.
'You forgot to shut the door after you' – 'When the King was "reproved"', *Sunday Dispatch*, 27 October 1929.

4. Margaret Rose Makes Four

'fine chubby-faced little girl' – 'Infant princess "doing fine"', *Halifax Daily Courier & Guardian*, 22 August 1930.
'Oh, but why Bud?' – 'Princess Elizabeth "Just like any other little girl," says biographer', *Western Morning News and Daily Gazette*, 19 October 1932.

5. Lilibet Loves Animals

'Oh, how charming' – 'Princess Elizabeth', *Paisley Daily Express*, 9 July 1928.
'She always goes to the bird house' – 'Princess Elizabeth visit to the London Zoo', *Scotsman*, 10 July 1934.
'While I was painting her' – 'Princess Elizabeth', *Taunton Courier and Western Advertiser*, 6 May 1931.
'Her tutors declare' – 'Princess Elizabeth', *Civil and Military Gazette*, 8 July 1931.
'Have you watched him?' – 'Royal puppy causes a stir', *Daily Mirror*, 9 November 1933.
'And the enlightened public' – Jane Bevan, 'The latest in pet dogs', *Dundee Evening Telegraph*, 8 December 1933.
'All the same, he bled all over the floor' – quoted in Marion Crawford, *The Little Princesses*, p. 93.

6. The Little House with the Straw Roof

'It is in no sense a doll's house' – 'Princess Elizabeth's own house', *Daily News*, 25 May 1931.
'We gladly accept it on behalf' – 'Welsh nation's gift to princess destroyed', *Leicester Evening Mail*, 21 March 1932.
'I could play in it for ever myself' – 'Princess's house burned', *Belfast Telegraph*, 21 March 1932.
'Everyone in Cardiff is terribly sorry' – 'Royal "house" destroyed', *Sunderland Echo*, 21 March 1932.
'One needs to be a child' – 'A London diary', *Portsmouth Evening News*, 22 March 1932.
'The Duchess of York desires me to say' – 'Gift for Princess', *Birmingham Gazette*, 26 March 1932.

BIBLIOGRAPHY

'She is a very pretty little girl' – 'Auntie Muriel's Treasure Chest: Princess Elizabeth', *Liverpool Echo*, 17 February 1934.

'I've had the most awful meals here' – 'Royal Special: The Queen Mother interview on 90th Birthday (1990)', ITN Archive YouTube channel. Accessed 17 April 2025.

7. The Quiet Before the Storm

'I must have that for Elizabeth' – 'Queen aids trade', *Sheffield Daily Independent*, 18 February 1931.

'She sat there with ink trickling down' – 'When Princess poured ink on herself', *Edinburgh Evening News*, 30 December 1949.

'I am ten and I often ride a bicycle' – 'Princess Elizabeth', *Courier*, 27 April 1932.

'red hot' – 'Death of Whimsical Walker', *Leeds Mercury*, 13 November 1934.

'greatly pleased the little Princess' – 'Our London Letter', *Western Mail and South Wales News*, 24 January 1934.

'The people, too, cannot help being interested' – 'Princess Elizabeth', *Nottingham Journal*, 21 April 1934.

8. The Heavy Burden of Responsibility

'God save our King – Long may he reign' – 'Edward VIII – The man who is King', *Banbridge Chronicle*, 1 February 1936.

'He has shared the sorrows' – 'Death of the King', *Daily Express*, 21 January 1936.

'The Associated Press requests' and 'a middle-aged American brunette' – 'English King as co-Respondent?', *Galway Observer*, 14 November 1934.

'I ask everyone' – 'Pray for Mrs. Simpson', *Daily Mirror*, 7 December 1936.

'It is emphasised that there has never' – 'No clash between the King and Cabinet!', *Daily Mirror*, 7 December 1936.

'impossible to carry the heavy burden' – 'Abdication speech by Edward VIII (1936)', British Pathé YouTube channel. Accessed 24 March 2025.

9. Times Are Changing

'After all, childhood is short enough' – 'Princess Elizabeth training according to royal precedent', *Edinburgh Evening News*, 25 January 1937.

'There is no doubt that in present circumstances' – 'Princess Elizabeth sole heir to the throne', *Western Mail and South Wales News*, 29 January 1937.

'[I can] do six strokes' – 'Princess Elizabeth to learn ballet', *Civil and Military Gazette*, 26 October 1937.

'Princess Elizabeth is always a little chatterbox' – 'The top-hatted stationmaster', *Belfast Telegraph*, 4 March 1937.

'That shows her precocity' – 'A princess and a sermon', *Lynn News*, 12 January 1937.

10. The Coronation . . . 'a Pageant, a Show'

'That's a good idea' – 'Royal visit to fair', *Hartlepool Northern Daily Mail*, 16 February 1937.

'the Coronation could have taken place' – 'The coronation', *Falkirk Herald and Scottish Midlands Journal*, 8 May 1937.

'Cannot we just try and bring a little ray of light' – 'The coronation and the poor', *Worthing Gazette*, 24 March 1937.

'a dignity and charm' – 'It was a fairyland to the royal children', *Daily Mirror*, 13 May 1937.

'God crown you with a crown of glory' – 'Long may they reign!', *Leader*, 14 May 1937.

'Please convey to them our heartfelt thanks' – 'The King's thanks for "wonderful reception"', *Daily Mirror*, 13 May 1937.

'There was only empty, ritualistic pomp' – 'The coronation: Welsh clergyman's criticism of the service', *Belfast News-Letter*, 1 June 1938.

11. Camp Fires and Map Reading at Buckingham Palace

'a good friend and a sister' – 'The Guide Law', found on the Girlguiding website, www.girlguiding.org.uk. Accessed 19 June 2025.

'They will join just as ordinary children' – 'Princesses to be Girl Guides', *Sunday Pictorial*, 27 June 1937.

'the most exclusive little group' and 'To do my duty to God' – 'Princess Elizabeth as Girl Guide', *Civil and Military Gazette*, 2 December 1937.

'great fun, and we taught them' – 'Princesses do their bit – as Girl Guides', *Birmingham Daily Gazette*, 13 January 1940.

'It was very nice of Princess Elizabeth' – 'Princess Elizabeth salute for Girl Guide cripple', *Belfast News-Letter*, 19 July 1947.

12. Accidents, Illness and a Trip to the Zoo

'Apart from the fact' – 'Queen Mary: Eye injury "Painful but not source of anxiety"', *Leicester Evening Mail*, 24 May 1939.

'One could imagine their excitement' – 'Tremendous welcome home for the King and Queen', *Shields Evening News*, 22 June 1939.

13. 'The King Will Never Leave'

'The children won't go without me' – 'Queen Elizabeth The Queen Mother', www.royal.uk. Accessed 19 June 2025.

'It went off like a 16-inch shell' – 'Buckingham Palace damaged by time bomb', *Liverpool Echo*, 11 September 1940.

'We think you are all wonderfully brave' – 'Buckingham Palace damaged by bomb', *Midland Daily Telegraph*, 11 September 1940.

'There was something sisterly' – 'London Letter for Women. Queen's sympathy', *Liverpool Daily Post*, 12 September 1940.

'It is entirely possible' – 'The palace bomb', *Edinburgh Evening News*, 12 September 1940.

14. 'I Am Glad We Have Been Bombed'

The letter from Queen Elizabeth to Queen Mary was found on the Royal Collection Trust website, www.rct.uk. Accessed 19 June 2025.

'I heard the plane coming down' – 'Buckingham Palace bombed. King and Queen there but unhurt', *Derby Evening Telegraph*, 13 September 1940.

'It is an amazing scene of devastation' – 'Royal chapel wrecked', *Leicester Evening Mail*, 14 September 1940.

'Like so many other people' – 'Buckingham Palace bombed', *Express and Echo*, 13 September 1940.

'We are impressed by the calm' – 'Buckingham Palace', *Walsall Observer*, 14 September 1940.

'The German plane was flying very low' – 'Buckingham Palace bombed', *Dumfries and Galloway Standard and Advertiser*, 18 September 1940.

'great psychological blunder' – 'Buckingham Palace bombing', *Express and Echo*, 14 September 1940.

'I am glad that we have been bombed' – David Niven, 'I'm glad we've been bombed said the Queen. Now, we can look the East End in the face', *Daily Mirror*, 29 July 1980.

15. 'All Will Be Well'

'We should very much welcome the opportunity' – 'Princess Elizabeth may broadcast', *Dundee Evening Telegraph*, 1 March 1935.

'My sister, Margaret Rose, and I', 'All will be well' and 'She speaks just like the Queen' – 'Princess Elizabeth's broadcast', *Lurgan Mail*, 19 October 1940.

'I thought myself this young British girl' – 'The royal heiress message of true sympathy', *Belfast Telegraph*, 14 October 1940.

'One of the most important days' – 'Message of hope for children', *Edinburgh Evening News*, 14 October 1940.

'One of the most effective broadcasts' – 'USA praises Princess', *Daily Record and Mail*, 14 October 1940.

'You will agree, I am sure' – 'Children's Corner conducted by Uncle Charlie', *Gloucester Journal*, 19 October 1940.

17. Princess 230873

'It is so very hard to part with one's toys' – 'Broadcast by Princess', *Daily Record*, 31 January 1945.

'The first or Grenadier Regiment' and 'showed no sign of nervousness' – 'Princess Elizabeth reviews Grenadier Guards at Windsor', *Portsmouth Evening News*, 21 April 1942.

'The King has granted to Her Royal Highness' – 'Princess Elizabeth joins A.T.S.', *Dundee Courier*, 5 March 1945.
'I couldn't understand why' – Princess Margaret to interviewer Richard Astbury, broadcast on the BBC, 8 May 1995; YouTube video from the Forgotten TV channel. Accessed 17 March 2025.

18. Conga at the Palace
'Our gratitude to our splendid Allies' – 'Mr Churchill's broadcast', *Newry Reporter*, 10 May 1945.
'He was quite naughty' – 'The Princess Margaret memories of VE Day P1', DigitaliseMe YouTube channel. Accessed 29 April 2025.
'refused to be seen in the company' – 'The Queen remembers VE Day 1945', RandomRadioJottings YouTube channel. Accessed 29 April 2025.
'Never give up, never despair' – 'Watch in full: The Queen's VE Day 2020 address.' The Telegraph YouTube channel. Accessed 29 April 2025.

19. Joy and Good Fortune in Northern Ireland
'I would like to wish happiness' – 'Giant carrier launched by Princess Elizabeth', *Yorkshire Post*, 20 March 1946.
'This was of great assistance to me' – 'Princess Elizabeth: Delighted with her stay in Ulster', *Belfast News-Letter*, 23 March 1946.

20. The Princess Meets a Prince
'We both love dancing' – quoted in Andrew Morton, *The Queen*, pp. 80–1.
'Princess Elizabeth is not engaged' and 'He is a blond Greek Apollo' – A. J. Cummings, 'The case of Prince Philip of Greece', *London Daily News*, 10 December 1946.

21. 'I Declare Before You All . . .'
'I declare before you all' and 'I know that your support' – 'Princess Elizabeth's dedication vow', *Western Morning News*, 22 April 1947.
'Your Royal Highness has lived' – 'Princess pledges life of service to people', *Birmingham Gazette*, 22 April 1947.
'Cape Town is the most envied city' – 'Smuts hands South Africa's gift to the princess', *Halifax Daily Courier & Guardian*, 22 April 1947.
'We have learned to admire her' – 'Commonwealth "Admiration and Love"', *Gloucestershire Echo*, 22 April 1947.
'I am deeply grateful' – 'General Smuts expresses empire wishes to Princess', *Coventry Evening Telegraph*, 22 April 1947.
'Please convey to the citizens' – 'Princess vows to serve empire', *Western Daily Press*, 22 April 1947.

BIBLIOGRAPHY

22. Wedding Plans at Buckingham Palace

'It is with the greatest pleasure' – 'Princess Elizabeth engaged', *Dundee Courier*, 10 July 1947.

'Soon' – 'Princess Elizabeth's wedding', *Civil and Military Gazette*, 17 July 1947.

'He got into trouble once' – letter from Sandie Bradley, 25 April 2025.

'This is a present which we shall use' – letter from Princess Elizabeth to James Jackson, 26 November 1947, from the collection of Sandie Bradley.

'The Princess was all the better' – 'Princess Elizabeth chooses wedding dress', *Belfast Telegraph*, 18 August 1947.

23. An Ivory Gown and Nine-Foot Wedding Cake

'We can find no words to express what we feel' – 'Unforgettable send-off in our married life', *Yorkshire Post*, 27 November 1947.

'we knew contentment' – 'Princess Elizabeth's wedding', *North Star*, 22 November 1947.

24. Parties in Paris

'We are taking exhaustive precautions' – 'Threat to Princess Elizabeth', *Western Daily Press*, 11 May 1948.

'The warmth of your welcome' – 'Princess Elizabeth thanks Paris: "This exciting visit"', *Daily Mirror*, 15 May 1948.

'According to the protocol' – 'Princess's tears as Paris crowds wildly cheer', *Leicester Evening Mail*, 14 May 1948.

'We will welcome her' – 'Paris is happy about Princess Elizabeth visit', *Yorkshire Observer*, 2 April 1948.

'with much dismay' – 'Princess Elizabeth: Fifth protest', *Dublin Evening Herald*, 22 May 1948.

'We were profoundly shocked' – 'Princess Elizabeth', *Belfast News-Letter*, 24 May 1948.

'a handful of misery-mongers' – 'Elizabeth and the misery-mongers', *Sunday Pictorial*, 23 May 1948.

25. A Baby at Buckingham Palace

'Her Royal Highness is taking life' – 'Princess Elizabeth', *Northern Whig*, 10 April 1948.

'the leaders in medical knowledge and research' – 'Princess Elizabeth amusing encounter with mechanical man', *Belfast News-Letter*, 7 May 1948.

'In Court circles it is understood' – 'Princess Elizabeth', *Aberdeen Press and Journal*, 5 June 1948.

'No previous Royal announcement' – 'H.R.H. Princess Elizabeth', *Belfast News-Letter*, 5 June 1948.

'Her Royal Highness and her son' – 'Son for Princess Elizabeth', *Kirriemuir Observer*, 18 November 1948.

'Oh, my word, what splendid news' and 'a lovely boy, a really splendid baby' – 'Son for Princess', *Aberdeen Press and Journal*, 15 November 1948.

26. A 'Normal' Life in Malta

'Her Royal Highness Princess Elizabeth' – 'Princess Elizabeth has a daughter', *Portsmouth Evening News*, 15 August 1950.

'Words cannot express my gratitude' – 'The wish Princess Elizabeth remembered', *Daily Mirror*, 25 June 1951.

27. How Do You Clean a Kettle?

'Can you help me?' – 'The Princess asks: How do you clean kettles? Dad wants to know', *Daily Mirror*, 11 May 1949.

'I could only tell the princess' – 'Princess and Duke visit Castle Bromwich Fair', *Coventry Evening Telegraph*, 10 May 1949.

'She certainly knows what she is talking' – Dennis Irving, 'The domestic interest', *Birmingham Gazette*, 11 May 1949.

28. Cheering Crowds, Tea and a Gold-mounted Riding Crop

'From where we were on the second floor' – 'Cheers from start to end of royal day', *Evening Despatch*, 10 May 1949.

'It is perhaps a little premature' – 'John gives riding whip for prince', *Evening Despatch*, 10 May 1949.

'I am eight and a half, your Royal Highness' and 'How dreadful' – Jack Hill and Ivor Jay, 'Princess and people', *Birmingham Gazette*, 11 May 1949.

'Not at all' and 'I could do with a week' – 'Yes – A thousand times', *Sunday Post*, 22 May 1949.

29. The Scandal of Marion 'Crawfie' Crawford

'You would lose all your friends' – letter from Queen Elizabeth to Marion Crawford, dated 4 April 1949, quoted in Hugo Vickers, *Elizabeth*, p. 283.

'Every British family should read' – full-page advert for *Woman's Own* magazine, *Aberdeen Press and Journal*, 2 March 1950.

'The demand is colossal' – 'The loving, human, authentic story of the Little Princesses', *Sunday Pictorial*, 5 March 1950.

'charming volume' – advert for *The Little Princesses*, *Gloucestershire Echo*, 25 October 1950.

'has done the finest service' – Ephraim Hardcastle, 'What's going on', *Sunday Express*, 19 November 1950.

'She must have gone off her head' – 'Teacher's tales out of class', *Northamptonshire Evening Telegraph*, 21 May 1986.

BIBLIOGRAPHY

'I have no comment to make' – 'Whatever became of "Crawfie"?', *Sunday Express*, 20 February 1977.
'The Queen certainly knows about her death' – 'Governess who lifted the lid on Palace secrets', *Dundee Courier*, 18 February 1988.
'She was not bitter' – Lady Olga Maitland, 'Crawfie's shoe box goes to the Queen', *Sunday Express*, 21 February 1988.

30. 'An Extremely Strenuous Tour Awaits'

'The King's voice has not yet' – 'King's speech recorded', *Derry Standard*, 24 December 1951.
'I have learned once again' – 'The King's message', *Scotsman*, 26 December 1951.
'a huskiness of the lower notes' – 'The King sits with family to hear his recorded speech', *Yorkshire Observer*, 27 December 1951.
'Through it could be sensed' – 'The King's Speech', *Lytham Times*, 28 December 1951.
'I have never seen a man enjoy it more' – 'Royal family at theatre', *Belfast News-Letter*, 31 January 1952.
'An extremely strenuous tour awaits' – 'The royal tour', *Yorkshire Post and Leeds Mercury*, 31 January 1952.

31. The King Is Dead

'but the lions would not play' – Dudley Hawkins, 'Princess Elizabeth "shoots" a lioness', *Sunday Mail*, 3 February 1952.
'I have had a thoroughly enjoyable day' – '"I'll see you Thursday," the King said', *Daily Mirror*, 7 February 1952.
'Such sorrow is a very strange experience' – quoted in Sarah Bradford, *George VI*, p. 610.
'A model of dignity' and 'The responsibilities of Queen' – 'World shocked by the news', *Evening News*, 6 February 1952.
'Now the country goes forward' – 'The King', *Norfolk and Suffolk Journal and Diss Express*, 8 February 1952.

32. Gold Lace and Diamonds at the Opening of Parliament

'I pray that the blessing of Almighty God' – Joan Reeder, 'One thing was different', *Daily Mirror*, 5 November 1952.
'It is entirely a Court Circular affair' – 'London Notes', *Yorkshire Post and Leeds Mercury*, 5 November 1952.

33. The Death of Queen Mary

'Queen Mary never faltered' – 'Queen Mary', *Inverness Courier*, 27 March 1953.
'Her passing strikes deep home to us all' – 'Queen Mary', *Bucks Advertiser*, 27 March 1953.

'Her very appearance was symbolic' – 'Queen Mary', *Banbury Advertiser*, 25 March 1953.
'Queen Mary's dearly loved grandchild' – 'Queen Mary', *London Evening News*, 24 March 1953.

34. 'I Name this Ship *Britannia*'

'I name this ship *Britannia*' – 'Queen launches new royal yacht "Britannia" (1953)', British Pathé YouTube channel. Accessed 14 April 2025.
'Had he been here today' – 'King chose the name for the Royal yacht', *Newcastle Journal*, 17 April 1953.
'a full crew of 22 officers and 225 ratings' – '*Britannia*'s Base: Royal Yacht service to be revived', *Belfast News-Letter*, 18 April 1953.
'This yacht is to enable Her Majesty' – 'Cost of Royal Yacht. MP's questions', *Belfast News-Letter*, 30 April 1953.

35. Bunting, Tea Parties, Crowns and Complaints

'All supplied in Coronation Souvenir Covers' – advert for A. Primrose & Son, *Morpeth Herald and Reporter*, 29 May 1953.
'It was a wonderful and never-to-be forgotten' – 'Letters to the Editor', *Mid-Ulster Mail*, 16 May 1953.
'I wonder how many workers' houses' – 'Letters to the Editor', *Barnoldswick & Earby Times*, 19 June 1953.
'I should be most grateful if they could' – 'Letters to the Editor', *Hampstead News*, 23 April 1953.
'There will be something for everybody' – 'Sibford's plan Coronation Day', *Banbury Advertiser*, 11 March 1953.
'Owing to various duties' – 'Coronation decorations – The citizen's protest', *Nottingham Evening Post*, 10 June 1953.

36. 'I Shall Strive to Be Worthy of Your Trust'

'horrible' – 'Queen Elizabeth speaks candidly about her coronation', clip from BBC programme, *The Coronation*, CBS Mornings YouTube channel. Accessed 16 May 2025.
'Vivat Regina Elizabetha!' and 'God Save Queen Elizabeth!' – Gerard Worcester, 'Coronation year', *Fife Free Press*, 23 May 1953.
'Because if you did' – 'Queen Elizabeth's advice on wearing a crown', *BBC News* YouTube channel. Accessed 16 May 2025.
'I thank you from a full heart' – 'Happy palace climax to memorable day', *Dundee Courier*, 3 June 1953.

37. The Princess and the Equerry

'Let the truth be made known' – 'Princess Margaret: Scandalous stories of her romance', *People*, 14 June 1953.

BIBLIOGRAPHY

'If she is having a romance' – 'Princess Margaret: their views', *People*, 21 June 1953.

'Princess Margaret is a credit' – Rex North, 'Would you marry them?', *Sunday Pictorial*, 12 July 1953.

'unwarrantable and disgusting intrusion' – 'Africa – By the Queen Mother', *Evening News*, 13 July 1953.

38. A Surge of Crowds in Scotland

'the hot-heads' – 'The Queen and Scotland', *Inverness Courier*, 23 June 1953.

'I return you these keys' – 'Roaring crowds welcome Queen to Scotland', *Lancashire Evening Post*, 23 June 1953.

'[We've had a] very nice journey' – 'The Queen back from Scotland', *Northamptonshire Evening Telegraph*, 30 June 1953.

39. Aureole, a Difficult Horse

'The Queen has an encyclopaedic knowledge' – Brigadier Stanley Clark OBE, 'Palace Diary', *Peterborough Evening Telegraph*, 5 September 1957.

'The Queen has many Derby years' – '"My luckiest Week," says Gordon – At 28th attempt', *People*, 7 July 1953.

'There was a little bit of wire' – 'Queen ducks and misses wire during canter', *Yorkshire Observer*, 19 June 1954.

'He was a difficult horse' – 'The Queen's horse Aureole wins the King George in 1954', AscotRacecourse YouTube channel. Accessed 5 March 2025.

40. Princess Margaret Decides Between Love and Duty

'I am sorry' – 'Crowds mass at Clarence House', *Sunderland Echo*, 14 October 1955.

'I would like it to be known' – 'Princess Margaret: I have put my duty before all else', *Daily Mail*, 1 November 1955.

'He is a man of dignity' – Keith Waterhouse, 'This must not wreck two lives', *Daily Mirror*, 2 November 1955.

41. Rain, No Umbrellas and a Dirty Red Carpet

'It will be difficult for the crowds' – 'Royal visit: No forest of umbrellas, please', *Birmingham Gazette*, 3 November 1955.

'Don't surge across the road' – 'The Royal route to Shard End', *Chronicle and Advertiser*, 29 October 1955.

'to give the impression of sunshine' – 'Birmingham offers the Queen "sunshine"', *Birmingham Post*, 3 November 1955.

'I used to be a buyer for a fashion shop' – 'Hospital reporters for the Royal visit', *Birmingham Gazette*, 1 November 1955.

'Her Majesty said that she thought the church' – 'The Queen's visit to Shard', *Chronicle and Advertiser*, 5 November 1955.

'As she passed by' – 'Brilliant day', *Birmingham Post*, 4 November 1955.
'The Queen and Duke of Edinburgh' – 'The Queen sends her thanks to the city', *Birmingham Gazette*, 8 November 1955.

42. When the Queen Met Marilyn

'She asked how I liked living in Windsor' and 'The Princess laughed' – Diana Narracott, 'Monroe plimsoll line takes a dip', *Daily Herald*, 30 October 1956.
'I thought Miss Monroe was a very sweet person' – 'Love and babies at Buckingham Palace', *People*, 22 October 1961.

43. Scandal on *Britannia*, and a Trip to Portugal

'He has told me' – 'Parker of the palace quits', *Daily Express*, 5 February 1957.
'Thank you for a wonderful time' – 'Queen ends Portugal visit', *Northern Daily Mail*, 21 February 1957.
'Elizabeth conquered Lisbon' – 'Elizabeth conquered Lisbon as woman and Queen', *Londonderry Sentinel*, 19 February 1957.

44. Opening Parliament in Canada

'my gratitude and that of my husband' – 'A coronation Queen enchants new world', *Liverpool Daily Post*, 15 October 1957.
'the most exciting broadcast' – 'The Queen captivates Canada', *Aberdeen Evening Express*, 14 October 1957.
'We didn't talk to her about television' – 'The Queen scores a TV triumph in Canada', *Leicester Mercury*, 14 October 1957.
'It has been lovely' – 'Royal visit to Canada and the US', *Mid-Ulster Mail*, 19 October 1957.
'to emerge in Britain as the regal' – 'Across the Atlantic', *Shields Evening News*, 14 October 1957.

45. The Queen Meets the President

'As the Queen of Canada' – 'President Dwight Eisenhower delivers short speech to Queen Elizabeth II (October 17, 1957)', Foggy Melson YouTube channel. Accessed 7 April 2025.
'I cannot leave without saying' – 'Queen addresses UN Assembly', *Birmingham Post and Gazette*, 22 October 1957.

46. Happy Christmas from Sandringham

'a priggish schoolgirl' – 'Peer attacks The Queen', *Daily Express*, 3 August 1957.
'I very much hope' and 'I can give you my heart' – 'Queen's call for "special kind of courage"', *Belfast News-Letter*, 27 December 1957.
'Though with great difficulty' – John Bunyan, *The Pilgrim's Progress*, 1678.

BIBLIOGRAPHY

47. Thunder, Umbrellas and the Magna Carta in Lincoln

'I'm going to see them' and 'I hope you will say what a wonderful' –
'The Queen opens new bridge', *Lincolnshire Echo*, 27 July 1958.
'This will greatly simplify the work' – 'The Queen in London: Pictures', *Lincolnshire Echo*, 30 June 1958.

48. The Queen Meets the Kennedys

'Tomorrow, I am about to assume' – 'Kennedys hustle in to a big welcome', *Daily Mirror*, 5 June 1961.
'a good old English dinner' – 'Chaos as the Kennedys see Queen', *Daily Record*, 6 June 1961.
'But that's what she's there for' – quoted in Andrew Morton, *The Queen*, p. 178.
'How dare you' – 'Dear Sir', *Daily Express*, 12 June 1961.
'In the deep purple of martyrdom' and 'My people shared his triumphs' –
'An English hillside . . . for ever America', *Daily Mirror*, 15 May 1965.

49. Trees, Tea and Soapy Suds in Corby

'The royal car came into view' – interview with Annette Finn Moffat, 10 March 2025.
'Look, Mummy' – 'A royal shampoo hat', *Daily Mirror*, 28 June 1961.
'She did not sit down at all' – 'Queen drops in for tea', *Leicester Evening Mail*, 19 June 1961.
'We all stood there wearing our plastic aprons' – interview with Richard Morgan, 10 March 2025.

50. Sympathy and Kindness at Addenbrookes

'The professions of medicine and nursing' – 'Queen visits boy hit by royal car', *Evening Express*, 28 May 1962.
'slightly improved . . . but remains serious' – 'Royal car accident', *Liverpool Echo and Evening Express*, 26 May 1962.
'She said she would be keeping in touch' – 'Boy of five injured by royal car', *Daily Express*, 26 May 1962.
'The decision was the Queen's alone' – 'Her care', *Sunday Express*, 3 June 1962.
'A most wonderful piece of work' – 'Queen sees "Adoration of the Magi" at Cambridge', *Belfast News-Letter*, 29 May 1962.
'[He is] in good health and spirits' – *Halifax Daily Courier & Guardian*, 22 June 1962.
'It may seem strange' – 'Royal driver quits', *Daily Express*, 2 July 1962.

51. Prince Charles and the Cherry Brandy

'It made life very difficult for me' – 'Prince Charles and the cherry brandy', *Arbroath Herald*, 21 June 1963.

'It does now appear' – Robin Parkin, 'Palace says "we were wrong"', *Daily Mirror*, 20 June 1963.
'To read some reports of the incident' – 'Viewpoint', *Daily Mirror*, 22 June 1963.
'it was the end of the earth' and 'And hardly had I taken a sip' – 'This is my life – by Charles', *Liverpool Echo*, 1 March 1969.
'Oh, shut up' – 'Prince's query: "Where's the pub?"', *Stornoway Gazette*, 6 July 1985.

52. One More Baby at Buckingham Palace
'It is announced from Buckingham Palace' – 'Queen expecting in the New Year', *Belfast News-Letter*, 17 September 1963.
'Both the Queen and the Duke' – 'Very happy about it', *Birmingham Post*, 17 September 1963.
'The girls all look so alike' – 'New girl Anne shakes hands with the Head', *Daily Express*, 21 September 1963.
'as a normal precaution' – 'Royal midwife moves in', *Eastbourne Gazette*, 4 March 1964.
'The Queen has had a comfortable night' – 'Queen and baby (5lb) are well', *Peterborough Evening Telegraph*, 11 March 1964.
'She looks a super baby' – '6lb. 2oz. Margaret and baby both "doing well"', *Daily Express*, 2 May 1964.

53. When the Beatles Met the Queen
'If you want a detailed description' – 'Ringo gets a haircut for the Queen', *Daily Mirror*, 25 October 1965.
'I've never seen anything like it' – 'Beatles' fans besiege Palace', *Halifax Daily Courier & Guardian*, 26 October 1965.
'drilled by the guards' – 'Palace "besieged"', *London Evening News and Star*, 26 October 1965.
'They were the life and soul of the party' – 'A laugh with the Beatles and a chat with the Queen', *Lancaster Guardian and Observer*, 29 October 1965.
'She was so very sweet' – 'Queen laughs with the Beatles', *Liverpool Echo*, 26 October 1965.
'The Queen was like a mum' – 'Beatles a wow at the palace', *Wolverhampton Express and Star*, 26 October 1965.

54. Heartache at Aberfan
'It has always been there' – 'Queen and Duke to visit Aberfan', *Peterborough Evening Telegraph*, 25 October 1966.
'Your grief is shared by everyone' and 'It was like thunder' – 'The Queen tours stricken village', *Evening Chronicle*, 29 October 1966.
'I cannot understand the silence' and 'There were tears in the Queen's eyes' – 'Queen weeps in Aberfan', *Evening Post*, 29 October 1966.

BIBLIOGRAPHY

'very upset' and 'I told the Duke' – 'The Queen shares Aberfan sorrow', *Sunday Post*, 30 October 1966.
'I think the visit of the Queen' and 'from the remaining children' – 'Queen's visit of sympathy', *Liverpool Echo*, 29 October 1966.
'deeply grieved' – 'The Queen's wreaths for Aberfan dead', *Halifax Evening Courier*, 29 October 1966.
'A gathering like this' – 'Queen remembers Aberfan', *Scotsman*, 10 May 1997.

55. A Royal Photo Scandal

'They were almost certainly' – 'Royal family snaps printed in French magazine', *Daily Express*, 1 October 1968.
'Since the photographs are of such a personal kind' – 'Personal pictures that the Queen did not want to be printed', *Daily Record*, 2 October 1968.
'it is only fitting' – 'The picture that Anne took', *Daily Express*, 2 October 1968.
'The story that the *Daily Mirror*' – 'The naughty, naughty, *Daily Express*', *Daily Mirror*, 4 October 1968.
'A fuss' – 'That picture of the Queen with Edward', *Aberdeen Evening Express*, 12 October 1968.
'Her Majesty trusts' – 'Complaints against Express rejected', *Wolverhampton Express and Star*, 26 November 1968.

56. Prince Charles Comes of Age

'There was no point' – 'This is my life – by Charles', *Liverpool Echo*, 1 March 1969.
'This is a comparatively small group' – Terence Blocksidge, '"Anarchy not monarchy" taunt by 100 angry Welsh students', *Birmingham Post*, 13 March 1969.
'If the Prince and his bodyguard' – Susan Anderson, 'University prepared to be friendly', *Birmingham Post*, 13 March 1969.
'I shall not show any hostility' – 'What waits for Prince?', *Wolverhampton Express and Star*, 13 March 1969.
'His pronunciation was very good indeed' – Michael Henfield, 'Cheering holidaymakers greet student Prince', *Birmingham Post*, 21 April 1969.
'I didn't know whose car it was' – Bruce Myles, 'Charles is "booked" for parking', *Daily Mirror*, 24 April 1969.

57. Eggs and Bomb Threats at the Investiture

'I shall be glad when it's over' – R. Gomer Jones, 'My life', *Daily Mirror*, 6 June 1969.
'It was because of the idea of the Investiture' – 'Explosion near castle raises tension after several incidents', *Birmingham Post*, 2 July 1969.
'I, Charles Prince of Wales,' – Geoffrey Parkhouse, 'Caernarvon – It's like preparing for the bride', *Sunday Express*, 8 June 1969.

'Prince Charles is just the right man' – 'Prince's day was Rosie's too', *Coventry Evening Telegraph*, 2 July 1969.

58. A Different Side to the Royal Family

'A fine memento' – 'Tribute to the royal family', *Daily Mirror*, 21 November 1969.

'a film which, through the perceptive' – 'Royal Family', *Staffordshire Newsletter and Guardian*, 20 June 1969.

'disappointing' – 'TV robs music festival', *Bexhill-on-Sea Observer*, 9 August 1969.

The *Royal Family* documentary, described and quoted from here, was found on the Sean M. King, Sr. YouTube channel. Accessed 19 May 2025.

'It has had the effect' – 'The Royal Family', *Hartlepool Northern Daily Mail*, 1 July 1969.

'Her Majesty has therefore decided' – Tom Brown, 'The Queen cancels Christmas broadcast', *Daily Express*, 21 October 1969.

59. Walkabouts and Ruined Frocks in Coventry

'The biggest problem is not security' – Roger Williams, 'Coventry may set pattern in royal "walkabouts"', *Coventry Evening Telegraph*, 29 June 1970.

'I know she will not be passing' – 'Royal visit decorations are torn to shreds', *Coventry Evening Telegraph*, 29 June 1970.

'She is so natural' – 'The Queen – so at ease – delights the hospital', *Coventry Evening Telegraph*, 30 June 1970.

'When I arrived' – 'Crowds greet Queen on first visit for eight years', *Coventry Evening Telegraph*, 30 June 1970.

'She was really looking forward' – 'Gail, 17, misses her chance to meet the Queen', *Birmingham Post*, 29 June 1970.

'It is disgusting that this should happen' – 'In a right mess', *Coventry Evening Telegraph*, 30 June 1970.

60. The Princess Anne Kidnap Attempt

'a discussion about where' – 'Princess Anne speaks openly on 1974 kidnap attempt – Parkinson Interview', Royal Reviewer News Show YouTube channel. Accessed 9 May 2025.

'Get down' – 'I'm fine thank you, says the Princess', *Birmingham Post*, 21 March 1974.

'I lost my rag at that stage' – 'Princess Anne talks about – kidnap attempt', Bubblegum YT YouTube channel. Accessed 9 May 2025.

'Your daughter has been kidnapped' – 'QC tells of royal kidnap bid', *Belfast News-Letter*, 23 May 1974.

'we are deeply disturbed' – 'Princess Anne escapes shots in kidnap attempt', *Birmingham Post*, 21 March 1974.

BIBLIOGRAPHY

'draw attention to the lack of facilities' – Nick Garnett, 'Anne shots – why I did it', *Reading Evening Post*, 4 April 1974.

'without limit of time' – 'The Jackal of Bayswater's two years' plotting', *Birmingham Post*, 23 May 1974.

'They do a vital and often dangerous job' – 'Queen thanks kidnap police', *Wolverhampton Express and Star*, 1 June 1974.

'The Queen is taking the opportunity' – 'Princess Anne gets bravery award', *Scotsman*, 15 August 1974.

'One thing about horses and sport' – 'Princess Anne recalls the moment she survived a kidnapping attempt', Listen to genius people YouTube channel. Accessed 9 May 2025.

61. A Most Boring Dresser in the USA

'Proclaim liberty throughout all the land' – 'Why we lost US – by the Queen', *Daily Record*, 7 July 1976.

'Well, I think they would have been extremely surprised' – 'WBZ Archives: Queen Elizabeth II speaks in Boston, 1976', CBS Boston YouTube channel. Accessed 7 April 2025.

'it is good to know that the people' – 'I could hug you, baby', *Daily Express*, 13 July 1976.

'Her Majesty is quite aware' and 'These are backed up' – 'The Queen criticised as "dull and dowdy"', *Scotsman*, 9 July 1976.

62. Street Parties and Downpours at the Silver Jubilee

'All your bulk requirements in flags' – 'Home and Business Services', *Rugeley Times*, 28 May 1977.

'Although that vow was made in my salad days' – 'Sovereign recalls when she was 21', *Hartlepool Mail*, 8 June 1977.

'Everyone was determined' – 'It's drip, drip, hooray for Silver Jubilee', *Lichfield Mercury*, 10 June 1977.

63. Stray Dogs and Gigantic Cheese in Chester

'The Trades Council' – 'Outlay not extravagant', *Chronicle*, 26 October 1979.

'The Queen's visit is a great honour' – 'Councils "No" to royal service', *Chester Observer*, 26 October 1979.

'Had we been so, we would have said' – 'Trades Council and royal visit', *Cheshire Observer*, 2 November 1979.

'Did you put it there?' – Tony Riley, Ian Callister and Carolyn Taylor, 'Thousands greet the Queen', *Liverpool Echo*, 2 November 1979.

'I should be sitting there' – Tony Riley, Larry Neild, and Carolyn Taylor, 'Cheshire cheers and cheese for the Queen', *Liverpool Daily Post*, 3 November 1979.

64. Prince Charles Finds a Wife

'Well, I suppose this is awfully difficult' – Ken Irwin, 'The girl I will marry', *Daily Mirror*, 27 June 1969.

'began to realise then' – Grania Forbes, 'How I proposed – Charles', *Newcastle Evening Chronicle*, 24 February 1981.

'The Queen is very angry' – Ashley Walton, 'Hot-shot Edward takes to camouflage', *Daily Express*, 5 January 1981.

'It is with the greatest pleasure' – 'Charles to wed Lady Diana', *Newcastle Evening Chronicle*, 24 February 1981.

65. A Trip to the Cobbles

'It must be a very worrying time' – 'It's a worrying time says the Queen', *Daily Express*, 6 May 1982.

'I said I would pull him a pint' – 'A royal day down at Rover's Return', *Liverpool Echo*, 5 May 1982.

'[The Queen] smiled when she saw the earrings' – 'A royal stroll down *Coronation Street*', *Belfast Telegraph*, 5 May 1982.

'I doubt whether she has the Buck House sets' – Janet Buckton, 'Streets ahead', *Coventry Evening Telegraph*, 5 May 1982.

'No, I know' and 'Well, ma'am' – 'Queen visits *Coronation Street* set to mark 60 years of soap', *BBC News*, 8 July 2021, www.bbc.co.uk.

'You're like a ray of sunshine' – 'The Queen meets *Coronation Street* cast on set in Manchester', The Royal Family Channel, YouTube. Accessed 19 March 2025.

66. 'It's Always Lovely to Have a New One.'

'My goodness' – Michael Parry and John King, 'Booties for the baby as Diana puts her feet up', *Daily Express*, 7 November 1982.

'A baby will be marvellous' – Geoffrey Levy, 'What wonderful news!', *Daily Express*, 6 November 1981.

'You have all got wives' – 'Princess Diana still not well', *Wolverhampton Express and Star*, 10 November 1981.

'I told her it would get worse' – Lucy Orgill, 'Gifts galore for the royal mum-to-be', *Derby Evening Telegraph*, 13 November 1981.

'The Princess feels totally beleaguered' – Allan Guy, 'Lay off Diana, press is told', *Bristol Evening Post*, 9 December 1981.

'Very bad labour' – quoted in Andrew Morton, *Diana: Her True Story – In Her Own Words*, revised edition, p. 46.

'It's a rather grown-up thing I've found' – 'Royal family celebrates the birth of Prince William;, ITN Archive YouTube channel. Accessed 20 March 2025.

'It's always lovely to have' – 'Off home with Mum and Dad', *Liverpool Daily Post*. 23 June 1982.

BIBLIOGRAPHY

67. An Intruder at Buckingham Palace

'She just said "get out"' – '"Get out" Queen told intruder', *Shropshire Star*, 25 March 1993.

'The incident was reported fully' – 'Palace silent on Queen intruder', 2 February 1987.

68. Controversy at the Opening of Parliament

'No member of the royal family' – John Merritt and Jack McEachran, 'Who's to blame?', *Daily Mirror*, 4 November 1982.

'Until that is achieved' – 'Queen's Speech: "A chilling document"', *Stornoway Gazette and West Coast Advertiser*, 13 November 1982.

'It would be a shot in the arm' – H. Hunter, 'Letter to the Editor: The Queen's speech – Letters to the Editor', *Fife Free Press*, 12 November 1982.

69. Faux Pas and 'Dowdy' Clothes in Canada

'at 58 [the Queen] looks tired at times' and 'You can't have both' – 'The royal defenders: The Queen is not dowdy, say her fashion experts', *Liverpool Daily Post*, 8 October 1984.

'She has attracted big crowds' – 'Our Queen dowdy? Britain hits back', *Hartlepool Mail*, 5 October 1984.

'downright insulting to her Majesty' – Paul Connew, 'Prison if you pester Queen!', *Daily Mirror*, 8 October 1984.

'I did not touch her back' – 'Minister in Queen row says sorry', *Liverpool Echo*, 1 October 1984.

'Nobody told me that it was wrong' and 'a matter of common sense' – '"Hands off the Queen" move', *Daily Express*, 1 October 1984.

'The last time I saw the Queen' – 'Crowds wait in rain for Queen', *Burton Mail*, 8 October 1984.

70. Complaints and Crying Children in Scotland

'It is essential for teachers' – 'Summer's end?', *Inverness Courier*, 13 August 1985.

'What annoyed us was the fact' and 'I am well aware of the comfort' – 'The Queen's visit', *Inverness Courier*, 16 August 1985.

'The visit went like clockwork' – Gordon Fyfe, 'Saying it with flowers', *Inverness Press and Journal*, 16 August 1985.

71. Eggs and Demonstrations Down Under

'outrageous insult' – 'Arrests as 5 bare bottoms at the Queen', *Sandwell Evening Mail*, 1 March 1986.

'New Zealand has long been' – Jean Rook, 'Her unflappable Majesty', *Daily Express*, 4 March 1986.

'She said "congratulations"' – 'Queen presents award to boy', *Dundee Evening Telegraph*, 3 March 1986.

'represents a very conservative, very backward image' – 'Boob demo at Queen', *Torbay Express and South Devon Echo*, 5 March 1986.

72. The Mayor Collapses in Canterbury

'One would assume the non-presence' – 'Treasured memories for guard of honour', *Kentish Gazette*, 27 March 1987.

'The ball came at the end' – 'Mayor rushed to hospital', *Kentish Gazette*, 27 March 1987.

73. Working Against the Tide at Heysham

'I am not denying it' – 'Queen to visit Heysham?', *Visitor*, 7 June 1989.

'We are thrilled and very much looking forward' – 'Royal Yacht will dock at Heysham', *Morecambe Guardian*, 16 June 1989.

'We will be making the place look' – Diane Mangan, 'Heysham prepares for royal visitors', *Visitor*, 21 June 1989.

'She does a great job' – Gerrie Burns, 'The Queen sails in', *Lancashire Evening Post*, 7 August 1989.

'It was a real honour to have been chosen' – 'Farmhouse tea fit to set before a Queen', *Lancashire Evening Post*, 8 August 1989.

'You dream about these things' – Alan Sandham, 'Joyous welcome to royal farms', *Morecambe Guardian*, 11 August 1989.

74. The Fire at Windsor

'I dragged three or four with other people' – 'Dean's heroic rescue effort', *Shropshire Star*, 21 November 1992.

'Please now leave it alone' – John Hipwood, 'Windsor fire brought secret into open', *Shropshire Star*, 27 November 1992.

'The fire appears to have resulted' – Robert Bedlow, 'Windsor fire: No one to blame', *Irish Independent*, 5 December 1992.

'It is an insult to the British taxpayer' – 'Windsor Castle fire report "whitewash"', *Scotsman*, 5 December 1992.

75. Annus Horribilis

'[In the] words of one of my more' and 'But we are all part' – '1992: Queen Elizabeth II's famous "Annus Horribilis" speech', ITN Archive YouTube channel. Accessed 28 March 2025.

'As some of you may have heard me observe' – 'The Queen's Christmas message 1992', Reelsarency YouTube channel. Accessed 28 March 2025.

76. The Gate of Romantic Candyfloss

'your chance to show your gratitude' – John McEntee and Cathy Scott-Clark, 'Queen Mother: My dearest wish', *Sunday Express*, 3 May 1992.

BIBLIOGRAPHY

'They are very special gates' – 'Queen Mother unveils nation's gift', *Western Daily Press*, 7 July 1993.
'romantic candyfloss' and 'three-dimensional knitting' – 'Gates honour life of Queen Mother', *Scotsman*, 7 July 1993.
'We do not think it will last' – 'Blacksmiths "appalled" by Queen Mum's gate', *Journal*, 11 August 1993.

77. Breaking Records, and a Visit to the Fame School
'Seeing her really got the adrenaline going' – 'Paul welcomes Queen to Fame school', *Dundee Courier*, 8 June 1996.
'The Queen was very impressed' – Tom Leonard, 'Beatle welcomes Queen', *Irish Independent*, 8 June 1996.
'It is a fantastic honour' – 'A Hard Day's Knight for ex-Beatle', *Dundee Courier*, 31 December 1996.
'She must wonder' – Dan O'Neill, 'The last to reign over us?', *South Wales Echo*, 13 June 1996.

78. The Role of Grandmother versus Queen
'That's what we've been doing' – *The Princess*, documentary, 2022. Accessed 24 May 2025.
'as your Queen' and succeeding comments – 'Queen Elizabeth II's tribute to Princess Diana' (1997), ITN Archive YouTube channel. Accessed 26 March 2025.

79. 'He Has Been My Strength and Stay'
'They were both really looking forward' – 'Golden wedding party tragedy', *Shropshire Star*, 19 July 1997.
'I have done my best' – Jane Kerr and Christian Fraser, 'I try so hard to listen', *Mirror*, 21 November 1997.
'He has, quite simply' – 'A speech by the Queen on her Golden Wedding Anniversary', 20 November 1997, www.royal.uk.

80. 'We Must Now Say Goodbye to *Britannia*'
'It's a sensible and realistic' – '*Britannia* loses admiral', *Daily Express*, 23 September 1994.
'I am a traditionalist' – '*Britannia* will rule the waves no more', *Aberdeen Press and Journal*, 24 June 1994.
'and in this case' – '*Britannia* "will not be replaced"', *Shropshire Star*, 10 October 1997.
'It is with sadness that we must now' – 'For *Britannia*, tears that the royals couldn't hide', *Daily Express*, 12 December 1997.

81. A Very Precious One Hundredth Birthday

'That will be very precious' and 'God bless you all, and thank you' – 'The Queen Mother's 100th Birthday Pageant (2000); Royal Specials', ITN Archive YouTube channel. Accessed 25 April 2025.

'She has been very quiet all her life' – 'Castle does the old lady proud with jets and guns', *Aberdeen Press and Journal*, 5 August 2000.

82. Walking into the 'Danger Zone' at Berwick

'This is certainly a special event' – 'Itinerary is announced for royal visit', *Berwick Advertiser*, 19 July 2001.

'Don't let the Queen visit Berwick' – 'Don't let the Queen', *Berwick Advertiser*, 19 July 2001.

'She will walk right into the danger zone' – 'Action to be taken over gulls', *Berwick Advertiser*, 28 June 2001.

'The Queen was very sympathetic' – 'Queen lends sympathetic ear to farmers', *Berwick Advertiser*, 9 August 2001.

'Throughout, it was all very relaxed' – 'A right royal day for Northumberland', *Northumberland Gazette*, 2 August 2001.

83. 'In Loving Memory, Lilibet.'

'She is getting some nursing care' – 'Scalded princess may be at wedding', *Belfast News-Letter*, 12 April 1999.

'It was a wonderful day' – Iain Smith, 'She was like a movie star', *Shields Daily Gazette*, 9 February 2002.

'At this time of personal loss' – 'Brave Queen back on duty', *Belfast News-Letter*, 13 February 2002.

'Yes, thank you very much' – '"Are you okay, ma'am?" Queen Elizabeth's emotional exchange with member of the public', ITN Archive YouTube channel. Accessed 14 May 2025.

'It was very, very touching' – 'She battled to the last week', *Belfast News-Letter*, 8 April 2002.

'After the things the Queen Mother' and 'In loving memory' – 'In loving memory, Lilibet – Queen's personal tribute', *Belfast News-Letter*, 6 April 2002.

84. The Queen Meets James Bond

'I have never met her before' – 'Queen meets Bonds old and new', *Aberdeen Press and Journal*, 19 November 2002.

'So you're the modern James Bond' – 'James Bond at Her Majesty's Service', *Chronicle & Echo*, 19 November 2002.

'I thought they were pulling my leg' – 'Embassy does the honours as Brosnan collects OBE', *Irish Independent*, 21 July 2003.

85. The Happiest of Happy Birthdays

'Here's a face I recognise' – 'I'm just wild about Harry', *Dublin Evening Herald*, 13 April 2006.

'I hope all those of you' – Laura Elston, '80 years young . . . Queen hosts "twins" party', *Irish Independent*, 20 April 2006.

'darling Mama' – 'Charles leads 80th birthday tributes to "darling Mama"', *Irish Independent*, 22 April 2006.

'Children's characters are an enduring part' – Caroline Horn, 'Charity launched at the palace', *Bookseller*, 30 June 2006.

86. Why Doesn't The Queen Like Tennis?

'It's probably a one in a lifetime' – 'Queen graces Wimbledon courts', ESPN, 24 June 2010.

'It was a great honour to welcome' – Ainhoa Barcelona, 'The Queen has only attended Wimbledon four times in her life – here's why', *Hello!*, 8 July 2021.

'He never forgave the committee' – 'Why does Queen stay away from Wimbledon?', *Edinburgh Evening News*, 21 July 1956.

'The taxpayer demands an honest charter' – 'An amazing scene at Wimbledon', *Football Gazette*, 6 July 1957.

87. A Royal Wedding and a Familiar Ring

'Very friendly' – 'In full: William and Kate's 2010 engagement interview', ITV News YouTube channel. Accessed 15 May 2025.

88. 'Good Evening, Mr Bond'

'She was beautiful' – 'Queen's wedding visit at Manchester Town Hall "the best present"', *BBC News*, 24 March 2012, www.bbc.co.uk.

'Good evening, Mr Bond' – 'James Bond and the Queen London 2012 Performance', Olympics YouTube channel. Accessed 13 May 2025.

89. The Queen's Horse Wins the Gold Cup

'The reaction after she won' – 'I Know How Much It Means to the Queen/ Ryan Moore', Ascot Racecourse YouTube channel. Accessed 23 April 2025.

'A pain in the backside at times' – 'History is made as the Queen wins the Ascot Gold Cup with Estimate – full Channel 4 reaction', Royal Central YouTube channel. Accessed 23 April 2025.

'To win the big one at Royal Ascot' – 'Royal Ascot: The Queen's horse Estimate wins historic Gold Cup', *BBC News*, 20 June 2013, www.bbc.co.uk.

90. 'A Source of Inspiration and Pride for Us All.'

'I believe that *Queen Elizabeth*' – 'Queen christens Britain's biggest ever warship with whisky', Telegraph YouTube channel. Accessed 16 April 2025.

'I name this ship *Britannia*' – 'Queen launches Britain's biggest cruise ship', ITN Archive YouTube channel. Accessed 16 April 2025.

'It exploded rather successfully' – 'Queen names new PO Cruise Liner *Britannia* at Southampton Ceremony', Last Wording YouTube channel. Accessed 16 April 2025.

91. Time Marches On

'Inevitably, a long life can pass' – 'Queen Elizabeth II becomes longest-reigning UK monarch', *BBC News*, 9 September 2015, www.bbc.co.uk.

'Many of them would never return' – 'D-Day 75: Queen Elizabeth praises the resiliency of "my generation"', Global News YouTube channel. Accessed 24 April 2025.

92. The Queen . . . 'Quite Cantankerous' But Also Hilarious

'Isn't it good, yes' – 'Queen shows funny side in conversation with Sir David Attenborough for ITV documentary', ITV News YouTube channel. Accessed 19 May 2025.

'I know there is' – 'Queen cuts cake with sword at G7 event', Reuters YouTube channel. Accessed 19 May 2025.

'I don't mind, I don't matter' – 'Queen Elizabeth cuts cake to mark 70 years of rule', Reuters YouTube channel. Accessed 19 May 2025.

'Are you supposed to be looking' – '"Enjoying yourself?" Queen jokes with G7 leaders in family photo', Guardian News YouTube channel. Accessed 19 May 2025.

'The story of the American tourists' – 'Platinum Jubilee: Richard Griffin on the Queen's sense of humour', Sky News YouTube channel. Accessed 19 May 2025.

93. 'Better Days Will Return.'

'Actually, you don't need me' – 'The Queen learns how to use Zoom from Princess Anne', Fabulous Magazine YouTube channel, 29 July 2020. Accessed 12 March 2025.

'Together, we are tackling this disease' and 'We will meet again' – '"We will meet again" – The Queen's coronavirus broadcast', BBC YouTube channel, 5 April 2020. Accessed 12 March 2025.

94. Princess Beatrice Borrows a Dress

'the most glittering film premiere of the season' – John London, 'Glittering', *Evening News and Star*, 10 December 1962.

BIBLIOGRAPHY

95. 'With Grateful Hearts, We Remember.'

'With grateful hearts, we remember' – 'Prince Philip funeral: How the day unfolded', *BBC News* YouTube channel. Accessed 15 April 2025.

96. 'Thank You, Ma'am . . . For Everything.'

'Never mind' – 'Queen Elizabeth II and Paddington share love of marmalade sandwiches over Jubilee tea', SBS News YouTube channel. Accessed 14 March 2025.

'Well, I do it all the time' – Jacob Stolworthy, 'Simon Farnaby shares hilariously blunt reply Queen gave him while filming Paddington sketch', *Independent*, 21 October 2023.

'They would both welcome each other' – 'The Queen and Paddington: How a bear became an unlikely mascot', *BBC News*, 15 September 2022, www.bbc.co.uk.

97. One Last Time on the Balcony

'I was blessed that in Prince Philip' – letter from the Queen to her public, written at Sandringham House, 5 February 2022, www.royal.uk.

'I shall look at it in the car' – 'The Queen and Prince Charles plant tree ahead of Platinum Jubilee', Telegraph YouTube channel. Accessed 8 May 2025.

'Planting a tree' – 'The Queen and Prince Charles "Plant a Tree for the Jubilee" to Kickstart Green Canopy Project', Royal Family YouTube channel. Accessed 8 May 2025.

'While I may not have attended every event' – 'A thank you message from Her Majesty the Queen following the Platinum Jubilee weekend', 5 June 2022. www.royal.uk.

98. The Passing of the Queen

'frail' but 'in good spirits' – Siba Jackson, 'Photographer reveals story behind Queen's last public picture, *Sky News*, 9 September 2022, www.news.sky.com.

'comfortable' and 'family members have been informed' – 'BBC interrupt live broadcast for update on Queen's health', Telegraph YouTube channel. Accessed 16 April 2025.

'The Queen died peacefully' – 'BBC announces the death of Queen Elizabeth II', Guardian News YouTube channel. Accessed 16 April 2025.

'Her Majesty reigned for seventy years' – 'Hundreds queue overnight in the rain as Queen's lying in state nears', Sky News YouTube channel. Accessed 16 April 2025.

100. The Queen's Lasting Legacy

'Women can learn and prove' – 'Princess and women's rights', *Derby Evening Telegraph*, 23 October 1947.

'If we have established our rights' – 'Home comes first, says princess', *Manchester Evening News*, 23 October 1947.

'Once these claims are accepted' – 'Princess speaks up for women's rights', *Gloucester Citizen*, 27 May 1948.

Index

Aberfan disaster (1966), 168–70
Abergele, Conwy, 178
Aberystwyth University, 174–6
Adams, Marcus, 9
Adamson, Peter, 203
Addenbrookes Hospital, Cambridge, 159–60
Aga Khan IV, 271
Air Raid Precautions, 43
Aircraft Carrier Alliance, 274
Albert, Prince consort, 104
Alexander, Jean, 203
Alexandra, Princess, 53
Alexandra Palace, London, 286
Alice's Adventures in Wonderland (Carroll), 199
All England Lawn Tennis and Croquet Club, 262–4
Alnwick, Northumberland, 251
Altrincham, John Grigg, 2nd Baron, 147, 148
Alturlie Point, Inverness, 218
Alzheimer's Society, 253
Andrew, Duke of York, 163–4, 219, 203, 223, 233, 272
animals, 15–17, 40
Anne, Princess Royal
    Ascot Gold Cup (2013), 272; Aureole, memories of, 127; birth (1950), 84; cake incident, 279; Christmas broadcast (1957), 148; coronation of Elizabeth II (1953), 116; Covid lockdowns (2020–21), 283; divorce (1992), 233; education, 163–4; George VI's death (1952), 99; kidnapping attempt (1974), 187–90; mother's death (2022), 297; *Royal Family* documentary (1969), 182; State Opening of Parliament (1952), 105
Anne, Queen, 52
'Annus Horribilis' speech (1992), 232–3
Argyll and Sutherland Highlanders, 123
Armstrong-Jones, Antony, 130
Ascot, 95, 271–2
Aston, Michael Parker, Bishop, 133
Astor, Nancy, Viscountess, 94
Attenborough, David, 279
Attlee, Clement, 68
Aureole, 125–7
Auriol, Vincent, 77, 78
Australia, 6, 7, 97, 183, 211, 222–3, 227–8
Austria, 138, 181
Auxiliary Territorial Service (ATS), 55–7, 59

Baker, Peter, 224, 225
Baldwin, Stanley, 26
Ball, Ian, 187–90
Ballygawley, County Tyrone, 62
Balmoral Castle, Aberdeenshire, 217, 220, 226
    American tourists incident (2022), 280; Charles's birth (1948), 81, 82; Diana's death (1997), 240–42; Diana's visit (1980), 201; Elizabeth II's death (2022), 296, 297; George VI's death (1952), 101;

Girl Guides at, 36–7; Margaret's birth (1930), 13; *Royal Family* documentary (1969), 181–2; Simpson's visit (1936), 27; Truss's visit (2022), 295–6; wedding of Elizabeth and Philip (1947), 76
Banks, C. W., 263
Bardot, Brigitte, 135
Barlow, Jane, 296
Barrett, H. R., 263
Battle of the River Plate, The (1956 film), 135
Bayliss, Joan, 227–8
Beatles, The, 166–7, 237, 238
Beaton, James, 187, 190
Beatrice, Princess, 285
Bedells, C. Herbert, 9
Belfast, Northern Ireland, 9, 61–2
Berwick-upon-Tweed, Northumberland, 251–3
Bexhill-on-Sea, East Sussex, 181
Big Lunch, The (2021), 280
Binfield, Berkshire, 129
Birkenhead, Merseyside, 34, 237
Birkhall, Balmoral, 52, 76, 82
Birmingham, West Midlands, 87, 89–91, 121, 131–4
Blackwell, Richard, 193
Blair, Tony, 241, 254
Bloomberg, Abe, 69
Bond, Michael, 289
Bonham Carter, Mark, 119
Booth, Ian, 274
Boston, Massachusetts, 192–3
Bowden, Janet, 199
Bowes-Lyon, David, 60
Bowes-Lyon, John, 15–16
Bowlby, Geoffrey, 40
Boyle, Danny, 269, 270
Boys' Brigade, 225
Bradford Rotary Club, 263
Brassey, Rowena, 189
Brighton bombing (1984), 216
Bristol, England, 15
Britannia, HMY, 109–11, 138–40, 191–3, 217–20, 226, 246–8
Britannia, MV, 274
British Army, 225, 259
British Broadcasting Corporation (BBC), 48–50, 154, 180–82, 194, 200, 210, 260, 283, 291, 296
British Industries Fair, 22, 32, 86–8
British Legion, 62
British Steel, 157
British Telecom, 212
Broadlands, Hampshire, 76
Brook, Philip, 262
Brooksbank, Jack, 278
Brosnan, Pierce, 257, 258
Bruton Street, London, 3, 7
Brydon, Rob, 274
Buchan family, 157
Buckingham Palace, London, 7, 8, 29, 39, 65
   chapel, 4, 14, 36, 45–6; Charles's birth (1948), 81–2; Diamond Jubilee celebrations (2012), 268–9; eightieth birthday celebrations (2006), 260; Fagan's break-in (1982), 208–10, 211–12; Girl Guides at, 35–6, 40; golden anniversary celebrations (1997), 244; ninetieth birthday celebrations (2016), 276–7; Royal Mews, 211; Second World War bombings (1940), 42–4, 45–7, 234; Silver Jubilee celebrations (1977), 195; VE Day (1945), 58–60
Bulteel, J. C., 126
Bunyan, John, 149
Burman, J. C., 87
Burns, Paul, 300
Burton, Sarah, 266
Buthlay, George, 92
Bwthyn Bach, Y, 18–21

Caithness, Scotland, 217
cakes, 279–80
Cambridge University, 159
Cameron, David, 274
Camilla, Queen consort, 201, 202, 259, 269, 280, 293
Campbell, Duncan, 88
Canada, 39, 41, 42, 48, 141–3, 193, 214–16, 280
Canning, Frances, 268–9
Canning, John, 268
Canterbury, Archbishop of
   Fisher, Geoffrey, 75, 107, 119; Lang, Cosmo, 14, 34; Welby, Justin, 288
Canterbury, Kent, 224–5
Cape Town, South Africa, 67–9
Cardiff, Wales, 8, 18–19, 177, 302
Carrington, John, 33
Carroll, Lewis, 199
Castle Bromwich, Solihull, 87–8
Catherine, Princess of Wales, 265–7, 280
Cawston, Richard, 180

INDEX

Ceylon, 97
Charles III, King
  birth (1948), 80–82; Camilla, relationship with, 201, 202, 259, 293; cherry brandy incident (1963), 161–2; Diana, relationship with, 200–202; Diana's death (1997), 240–42; education, 161–2, 174, 219; Hong Kong handover (1997), 247; Prince of Wales investiture (1969), 174–6, 177–9, 180; riding crop gift (1949), 89; State Openings of Parliament, 105, 212; tonsilitis (1948), 84; wedding (1981), 202, 204, 267; William's birth (1982), 205–7
Charlottesville, Virginia, 192
Charteris, Martin, Baron, 170
Chatto, Sarah, 165
Chequers, Buckinghamshire, 247
Chester, Cheshire, 197
Chesterfield, Derbyshire, 206
Children's Hour speech (1940), 48–50, 283
Christian, James, 62
Christmas, 25, 32, 36, 52, 55, 84, 138, 201, 278, 280
Royal messages on, 1, 96–7, 147–9, 164, 182, 233
Church of England, 120, 130
Churchill, Winston, 43, 46, 58–9, 100, 104, 120, 128, 302
Circo's, London, 65
Clapperton, Nellie, 37–8
Clarence House, London, 81, 84, 118, 129, 234, 250, 266, 267, 298
Clark, Stanley, 125
Clarke, Elizabeth, 164
Cleese, John, 258
clothing, 22, 132–3, 181, 193, 215, 218
Clwyd, Ann, 231
Clydeside, Scotland, 109
Cocks, Freda, 132–3
Colbert, Stephen, 270
Coldstream Guards, 253
Collins, Alfred, 222
Comber, County Down, 62
Commonwealth, 67–8, 97, 111, 130, 194, 268
Conner, David, 288
Connery, Gary, 270
Constitution, USS, 192–3
Cooper, Gary, 52
Corbett, Malcolm, 253
Corby, Northamptonshire, 156–8
corgis, 17, 39, 181, 209, 270, 292

Cornwall, England, 280
Coronation Cup, 127
coronation
  Elizabeth II (1953), 112–14, 115–17, 194, 298; George V (1911), 112; George VI (1937), 32–4
Coronation Street, 203–4
Coventry, West Midlands, 183–6
Covid-19 crisis (2020–22), 60, 204, 282–4, 285, 287, 295
Cox, Ellen, 222
Craig, Daniel, 270
Craigweil House, West Sussex, 23
Cranage, David, 31
Crathie church, Balmoral, 240
Craveiro Lopes, Francisco, 140
Crawford, Joan, 135
Crawford, Marion, 17, 23, 30, 65, 74, 92–5
Crown, The, 154
Crown Hotel, Stornoway, 161–2
Cuthbert, David, 154

D-Day commemorations (2019), 278
D'Espiney, Francesca, 223
Daimler Motor Company, 90
Dalkeith, Midlothian, 55
Dalton, Timothy, 257
Dartmouth, Devon, 64
Davies, Edmund, 169
Davies, Helen, 205
Davis, Bette, 52
Davison's Footwear Ltd, 184
Dench, Judi, 257
Derby, Derbyshire, 85
Devlin, Patrick, Baron, 172
Diamond Jubilee (2012), 268–9
Diana, Princess of Wales, 200–202, 204, 240–42, 265
  death (1997), 240–42, 244; Morton's biography (1992), 233; Scotland holiday (1985), 217; State Opening of Parliament (1982), 212; wedding (1981), 202, 204, 267; William's birth (1982), 205–7
Die Another Day (2002 film), 257
Dimbleby, Jonathan, 256
divorce, 26–8, 118–21, 128, 139
Dodd, E. J., 132
dogs, 17, 39, 181, 209, 259–60, 270, 292
Donnelly, Declan, 277
dorgis, 292
Dromore, County Down, 62
Duchy of Lancaster, 227

333

Dukakis, Michael, 192
Dungannon, County Tyrone, 62–3
Durham, County Durham, 302

Eagle, HMS, 63
Earl's Court, London, 201
Eden, Anthony, 128
Eden Project, Cornwall, 280
Edinburgh, Scotland, 55, 122–4, 248
Edward, Duke of Edinburgh, 171, 181, 219, 255
Edward, Duke of Kent, 53, 262
Edward I, King, 152
Edward VII, King, 140, 260
Edward VIII, King, 25–8, 119
Eisenhower, Dwight, 143, 144–6
Elizabeth, Queen Mother
  Australia visit (1927), 6, 8; Bwthyn Bach tour (1990), 21; Canada visit (1939), 39, 41; Charles's birth (1948), 81; coronation (1937), 34; death (2002), 255–6; Elizabeth's birth (1926), 3–5; Elizabeth's engagement (1946), 66, 70; Elizabeth's wedding (1947), 75; George's death (1952), 99–102; John's death (1930), 15–16; Margaret's birth (1930), 12–14; ninetieth birthday (1990), 234–6; one hundredth birthday (2000), 249–50
Elizabeth I, Queen, 31, 140, 238
Elizabeth II, Queen
  accession to throne (1952), 101–2; Andrew's birth (1963), 163–4; animals, love of, 15–17, 40; Anne's birth (1950), 84; 'Annus Horribilis' speech (1992), 232–3; birth (1926), 3–5, 46; Bwthyn Bach, 18–21; Cape Town speech (1947), 67–9; Charles's birth (1948), 80–82; Charles's wedding (1981), 202; cheekiness, 10–11, 279–81; *Children's Hour* broadcast (1940), 48–50, 283; Christmas speeches, 1, 147–9, 182, 233; clothing, 22, 132–3, 181, 193, 215, 218, 285–6; comic talent, 11, 279–81; coronation (1953), 112–14, 115–17, 194, 298; Covid-19 speech (2020), 283–4; Crawford's writing on, 92–5; death (2022), 295–7, 298–300; Diamond Jubilee (2012), 268–9; Diana's death (1997), 240–42, 244; driving lessons, 56–7; education, 23, 30, 92, 303; Edward's birth (1964), 171; eightieth birthday (2006), 259–61; equestrianism, 16, 125–7, 263, 271–2; Fagan's break-in (1982), 208–10, 211–12; father's death (1952), 101–2; film making hobby, 39; funeral (2022), 298–300; Girl Guides membership, 35–8, 40, 56, 57, 62; golden anniversary (1997), 243–5; Golden Jubilee (2002), 254; heirship (1936), 29–30; Lilibet nickname, 10; Margaret's birth (1930), 12–14; Mary's death (1953), 107; ninetieth birthday (2016), 276–7; personality, 10–11, 180, 279–81; pets, 15–17, 39, 181, 209; Philip, relationship with, 64–6, 70–73, 74–6, 292; Philip's death (2021), 287–8; Platinum Jubilee (2022), 280, 289–91, 292–4; pregnancy (1948), 78, 80–81; Second World War (1939–45), 42–4, 48–50, 55–7; Silver Jubilee (1977), 182, 194–6; State Openings of Parliament, 103–5, 116, 211–13, 286; temper, 11, 281; theatre, love of, 51–4, 290; UN address (1957), 145–6; wedding (1947), 70–73, 74–6, 285
Ellesmere Port, Cheshire, 199
Elliott, S. S., 86
Empire Theatre, London, 135
Englefield Green, Surrey, 136
Enniskillen, County Fermanagh, 62–3
Epps, Ernest, 225
Epsom, Surrey, 125, 223
equestrianism, 16, 125–7, 263
Estimate, 271–2
Eugenie, Princess, 278, 287
Evans, Geraint, 175
Evans, William Lloyd, 170

Fagan, Michael, 208–10, 211–12
Fairweather, Emma, 278
Fairweather, Graeme, 216
Falklands War (1982), 203
Farnaby, Simon, 289, 290
Faure, Edgar, 101
Fawkes, Guy, 212
Fayed, Dodi, 240
Fenton, Peter, 227
Ferguson, Ronald, 223
Ferguson, Sarah, 223, 233
Fermoy, Maurice Roche, 4th Baron, 99
film industry, 249, 257–8
Finch, Gail, 185
Finch, Peter, 135
Finn, Annette, 156
First World War (1914–18), 249

INDEX

floods (1953), 113
foot-and-mouth outbreak (2001), 251
Forbes, Grania, 201
Ford, Betty, 191
Ford, Edward, 133–4
Ford, Gerald, 191, 193
Fox, Freddie, 215
Fox, Marcus, 230
Fox, Paul, 180
France, 77–9, 101
Fraser, Neale, 263
Fredericton, New Brunswick, 214
Frost, David, 172
Fullerton, Steve, 176

G7 summit (2021), 280
Galliera Museum, Paris, 78
Gardner, Ernest, 167
George, Duke of Kent, 7, 25, 64
George of Wales, Prince, 280, 287
George V, King, 3–4, 6–8, 11, 13, 16, 23, 25–7, 48, 107, 112
George VI, King
  accession to throne (1936), 28, 29; Australia visit (1927), 6, 8; Canada visit (1939), 39, 41; Charles's birth (1948), 81; Christmas speech (1951), 96–7; coronation (1937), 32–4; death (1952), 99–102; Elizabeth's birth (1926), 3–5; Elizabeth's engagement (1946), 66, 70; Elizabeth's wedding (1947), 75; father's death (1936), 25; horse breeding, 125; lung removal operation (1951), 96; Margaret's birth (1930), 12–14; Second World War (1939–45), 42–4, 45–7; *South Pacific* viewing (1952), 98; theatre performances and, 52–3; Wimbledon Championships (1926), 263
Girl Guides, 7, 35–8, 40, 56, 57, 62, 68, 225
Glamis Castle, Angus, 10, 12–14, 51
Glasgow, Scotland, 37, 61, 124
Glass Coach, 75
Gold Cup, 271–2
Golden Jubilee (2002), 254
Goodyear, Julie, 204
Gordonstoun School, Elgin, 161, 219
Gore, A. W., 263
Gough, Jean, 170
Gould Foundation, 49
Graham-Hodgson, Sonia, 52
Granville, Rose Leveson-Gower, Countess, 13, 61

Granville, William Leveson-Gower, 4th Earl, 61
Green Park, London, 59, 297
Greenock, Inverclyde, 61
Greig, Louis, 263
Grenadier Guards, 55–6, 57, 250, 298
Griffin, Richard, 280–81
Griffith, Derek, 20
Guildhouse, London, 27, 195
Gunpowder Plot (1605), 212
Gwinnutt, Charles and Dorothy, 85

Halifax, Dorothy Wood, Countess, 40
Hameringham, Lincolnshire, 113
Harcourt, Brace and Company, 94
Hardcastle, Ephraim, 94
Hardwicke Stakes, 127
Harland & Wolff, 62
Harriman, W. Averell, 145
Harrison, George, 166–7, 237
Harry, Duke of Sussex, 217, 240, 242, 259, 278, 297
Hartnell, Norman, 72, 75, 193, 285
Haslam, John, 226
Hawke's Bay, New Zealand, 221
Health of the People exhibition (1948), 80
Herring, Richard, 290
Heseltine, William, 173, 183
Hewins, Beatrice, 186
Heysham, Lancashire, 226–8
Highgrove House, Gloucestershire, 298
Hind-Smith, Michael, 142
Hoad, Lew, 263
Hong Kong, 247
Hoover, Herbert, 146
Horse Guards Parade, London, 276
horses, 16, 125–7, 263, 271–2, 299–300
Hôtel de Lauzun, Paris, 78
Household Cavalry, 55, 74
Howsam, Chris, 251–2
Hoyle-Hansen, Taral, 185
Hoyle, David, 299
Hudson River, 145, 192
Hughes, Bob, 246
Hughes, Geoffrey, 203
Hughes, J. G. Moelwyn, 34
Huxley, Julian, 40
Hyde Park, London, 12, 234–6, 286

Ideal Home and Building Exhibition, 19
Imperial State Crown, 116, 286, 298
Imperial War Graves Commission, 85

Inverness, Highland, 107, 122, 218–20
Irish Guards, 16, 250, 266
Irish Republican Army (IRA), 216
Irish State Coach, 75, 211
Isle of Man, 226, 227
ITV, 180, 200

Jackley, George, 51
Jackson, James, 71–2
James Bond films, 257–8, 269–70
Jamestown, Virginia, 146
Jefferson, Thomas, 192
Johnson, Boris, 280, 282, 295
Jones, Colin, 169
Jones, Gareth, 170
Jorden, Raymond, 236
Joseph, G. L., 5
Judd, Harold G., 113

Kelly, Angela, 285
Kelly, Autumn, 265
Kennedy, Jacqueline, 153–5
Kennedy, John Fitzgerald, 153–5
Kennel Club, 259–60
Kensington Palace, London, 92, 94, 241
Kentucky, United States, 216
Kenya, 97, 99, 100–101, 265
King, Elizabeth, 62
King George VI and Queen Elizabeth Stakes, 127
King's Lynn, Norfolk, 159
Kissinger, Henry, 191
Knox, Barbara, 204

Lamont, James, 291
Lancaster, Lancashire, 227, 228
Landsdale, Dean, 229
Lang, Carol, 252
Lascelles, Alan, 66
Lawrence of Arabia (1962 film), 285
Lazenby, George, 257
Lennon, John, 166–7
Libya, 111
Lichfield, Staffordshire, 196
Light, George, 91
Lincoln, Lincolnshire, 150–52
Little Cottage, The, 18–21
Little Princesses, The (Crawford), 94
Liverpool, Merseyside, 20, 44, 237–9
Lloyd Webber, Andrew, 269
London Airport, 101, 138
London Zoo, 16, 40

London, John, 285
Longridge, Lancashire, 227
Louis of Wales, Prince, 293
Lowndes Place, London, 129
Lund, Giuseppe, 235
Lurgan, County Armagh, 62
Lyons, R. Nevil, 79

MacGraw, Ali, 193
Macmillan, Harold, 153
Madden, Catherine, 184
Madonna, 257, 258
Magna Carta, 152
Major, John, 246, 254
Mall, London, 4, 8, 116–17, 166, 187–90, 195, 267, 276
Malta, 83–5
Manchester, England, 268
de Manio, Jack, 176
Margaret, Countess of Snowdon, 12–14, 254–6
 Armstrong-Jones, marriage to, 130; birth (1930), 12–14, 46; Bwthyn Bach, 20; Crawford's writing on, 94; death (2002), 254–6; driving lessons, 57; education, 23, 30; Elizabeth's wedding (1947), 75; George's death (1952), 99–102; Girl Guides membership, 35–7, 40; heirship (1936), 29–30; London Zoo visit (1939), 40–41; Mary, relationship with, 107; Monroe, meeting with (1956), 136–7; Sarah's birth (1964), 165; scalding accident (1999), 254–5; Scotland holiday (1985), 217; Second World War (1939–45), 42, 49; theatre, love of, 52–4, 290; Townsend, relationship with, 118–21, 128–30; VE Day (1945), 58–60
Marina, Duchess of Kent, 64, 65
Markle, Meghan, 278
Marks, Derek, 172
Martineau, C. L., 133
Mary, Princess Royal, 7–8, 25, 35
Mary of Teck, Queen consort, 3–4, 5, 6–8, 11, 22, 285
 British Industries Fair visits, 22, 86; car accident (1939), 39–40; childhood, views on, 29; Craigweil House visits, 23; Crawford's writing on, 94; death (1953), 106–8; Elizabeth's birth (1926), 3–4; Elizabeth's Cape Town speech (1947), 68; George's death (1952), 100; horse riding skills, 16; Margaret, relationship

INDEX

with, 107; Margaret's birth (1930), 13; Second World War (1939–45), 45; Simpson, relationship with, 27
Maryland, United States, 146
Mature, Victor, 135, 136
McCartney, Paul, 166–7, 237, 238, 269
McCulloch, Derek, 49
McLeish, Dorothy, 206
McLellan, W. A., 88
McPartlin, Anthony, 277
McQueen, Alexander, 266
Meghan, Duchess of Sussex, 278
Melbourne, Victoria, 138
Michael of Kent, Prince, 234–6
Middleton, Catherine, 265–7, 280
Miller, Arthur, 136–7
Miller, St James, 122
Millward, Edward, 176
Mitchell, Philip Euen, 99
Mollington, Cheshire, 198–9
Monroe, Marilyn, 1–2, 135–7
Monticello, Charlottesville, 192
Montreal Olympics (1976), 193
Moore, Roger, 257
Moore, Ryan, 271–2
Moore, W. N. R., 86–7
Morecambe, Lancashire, 226, 228
Moreton, John, 193
Morgan, Richard, 158
Morpeth, Northumberland, 253
Morrah, Dermot, 68
Morris, Nicholas Douglas, 136
Morton, Andrew, 233
Mountbatten, Edwina, Countess, 84
Mountbatten, Louis, 1st Earl, 65
Mozzi, Edoardo Mapelli, 285
Mulloy, Gardnar, 263
Mulroney, Brian, 215
Murray, Andy, 262
Murray, Francis, 159–60
Mustique, 254–5

Naseby Hall, Northamptonshire, 15–16
New Orleans, Louisiana, 154
New York, United States, 145, 192
New Zealand, 6, 97, 183, 221–2
Newcastle-upon-Tyne, 205
Nicholls, Graham, 197, 198
Nieminen, Jarkko, 262
Nixon, Richard, 180
Noble, Allan, 110
Noble, Bernadette, 156

Norfolk, Bernard Fitzalan-Howard, 16th Duke, 33
North, Rex, 120
Northern Ireland, 61–3, 193
Northumberland, England, 251–3
Norwich Cathedral, 31
Norwich, David Cranage, Dean, 31
Nottingham Cottage, Kensington Palace, 92
Nova Scotia, Canada, 142, 193

O'Neill, Dan, 239
O'Toole, Peter, 285
Ogilvie, Helen, 184
Olivier, Laurence, 135–6
Olson, Beth, 238Olympia, London, 22, 24, 32, 86–7
Olympic Games
London (2012), 268, 269–70; Melbourne (1956), 138; Montreal (1976), 193
Operation London Bridge, 295
Owens-Kay, Derek, 198

P&O, 274
Paddington Bear, 260, 289–91, 293
Papworth Everard, Cambridgeshire, 160
Paris, France, 77–9
Paris Match, 171–3
Parker-Bowles, Camilla, 201, 202, 259, 269, 280, 293
Parker, Michael, 139
Parliament
Canada, 141–3; United Kingdom, 103–5, 116, 211–13, 286
Parris, J., 162
Patterson, Richard, 145
Patty, Budge, 263
Pelham Bridge, Lincoln, 150, 152
Penley, Charles, 136
Penn, Prudence, 256
Philadelphia, Pennsylvania, 191
Philip, Duke of Edinburgh, 64–6, 70–73, 74–6, 292
Andrew's birth (1963), 163–4; Anne's birth (1950), 84; Antarctica tour (1957), 138; Charles's birth (1948), 81; Chester visit (1979), 197–9; Commonwealth tour (1954), 111; coronation (1953), 116; death (2021), 287–8; equestrianism, 126, 263; golden anniversary (1997), 243–5; Malta, life in, 83–5; polo matches, 263; Portugal visit (1957), 138–40; Prince of Wales investiture (1969), 178; retirement

337

(2017), 277; State Openings of Parliament, 103–5, 286; wedding (1947), 70–73, 74–6, 285
Phillips, Mark, 187–90, 233
Phillips, Peter, 265, 272
Pike, Rosamund, 257
Platinum Jubilee (2022), 280, 289–91, 292–4
polo, 263
Portadown, County Armagh, 62
Portsmouth Evening News, 20
Portsmouth, Hampshire, 6, 278
Portugal, 138–40
Powner, Rose, 179
Preen, Thomas, 15
Prescott, J. A., 56
Press Council, 172–3, 206
Price, W. H., 91
Prince and the Showgirl, The (1957 film), 135, 136
Prince of Wales, HMS, 274
Prince, William, 164
Putney, London, 39–40

Quayle, Anthony, 135
Queen (band), 274, 290
Queen Elizabeth Gate, Hyde Park, 234–6
Queen Elizabeth, HMS, 273–5
Queen of Hearts, 51
Queen's Green Canopy, The, 293
Queen's Green Planet, The (2018 documentary), 279
Queen's Guards, 269
Queen's Regiment, 225
Queensferry Crossing, 277–8
Quinn, Edward Aloysius, 146

Radziwiłł, Anna Christina, 153
Radziwiłł, Caroline Lee, 154
Raigmore Hospital, Inverness, 218, 219
Raleigh, Walter, 140
Ramsay, David, 16
Reagan, Nancy, 208
Reagan, Ronald, 208
Red Arrows, 274
Renown, HMS, 6
republicanism, 221, 239
Rhys-Jones, Sophie, 255
Richards, Gordon, 126
Richmond Park, London, 16
Ring, Anne, 10
Rizzo, Frank, 191
Roache, Bill, 204

Robens, Alfred, Baron, 168–9
Robertson, George, 247
Robey, George, 52
Roosevelt, Eleanor, 101
Rosyth Dockyard, Fife, 273
Rowe, Helen, 164
Royal Ascot, 95, 271–2
Royal British Legion Pipe Band, 218
Royal College of Heralds, 192
Royal Command Performance, 135–7
Royal Family (1969 documentary), 180–82, 194
Royal Household Wool Fund, 53
Royal Humane Society, 222
Royal Lodge, Windsor, 20–21, 256
Royal Marines, 288
Royal Navy, 64, 83, 273–5, 286, 299
Royal Regiment of Scotland, 300
Royal Vault, 300
Royal Victorian Order, 93
Royden, Maude, 27
Rubens, Peter Paul, 159
Runnymede, Surrey, 155
Rutherford, Dale, 244
Rutland, Kathleen Manners, Duchess, 23

Sandhurst, Berkshire, 259
Sandringham, Norfolk
    Christmases at, 84, 97, 147–9, 201, 233, 278; Diana's birth (1961), 200; Elizabeth II's death (2022), 297; George V's death (1936), 25; George VI's death (1952), 99–101; Girl Guides at, 36; mumps outbreak (1927), 7; Murray's car accident (1962), 159; Philip's retirement (2017), 277; St Mary Magdalene Church, 31
Sarah, Duchess of York, 223, 233
Sassoon, Victor, 126
Save the Children, 286
Scotland, 122–4, 212, 217–20
Scotland, Patricia, Baroness, 299
Scottish State Coach, 277
Scouts, 225
Scrabster, Caithness, 217
Second World War (1939–45), 42–50, 52, 55–60, 68, 71, 72, 101, 234
memorialisation, 78, 85, 249, 278
Setúbal, Portugal, 139
Shaftesbury, Anthony Ashley-Cooper, 9th Earl, 52
Shaftesbury, Constance Ashley-Cooper, Countess, 52

INDEX

Shakespeare, William, 51
Shea, Michael, 202, 206
Shediac, New Brunswick, 214
Shew, Betty, 65
Sibford Gower, Oxfordshire, 113–14
Silver Jubilee (1977), 182, 194–6
Simon, John, 29
Simpson, Neil, 252
Simpson, Wallis, 26–8
Sleeping Prince, The (1957 film), 135, 136
Smith, Bruce, 95
Smith, F. Walker, 23
Smith, Jean, 23–4
Smith, Tom, 30
Smuts, Jan, 69
Snow, James, 215
Snowdon, Antony Armstrong-Jones, 1st Earl, 130, 165, 168
Soldiers', Sailors', and Airmen's Families Association, 286
Solihull, West Midlands, 87–8
Soper, Donald, 121
Sophie, Duchess of Edinburgh, 255
South Africa, 66, 67–9, 73, 97
South Shields, Tyne and, Wear, 255
Spencer, Edward, 8th Earl, 200
Spencer, Frances, Countess, 200
St Edward's Crown, 116
St George's Chapel, Windsor, 107, 255, 288
St George's Road Boy's School, Wallasey, 20
St James's Palace, London, 71, 72
St Mary's College for Women, Durham, 302
St Mary's Hospital, Paddington, 206–7
St Paul's Cathedral, London, 276
St Paul's Walden Bury, Hertfordshire, 8
Stamford, Leicestershire, 157
Stapleton Station, Staten Island, 145
Starr, Ringo, 166–7
State Gun Carriage, 299
State Landau, 267
State Openings of Parliament, 103–5, 116, 211–13
Stewart, Donald, 212
Stobart, Bryan, 255
Stornoway Gazette, 161
Stornoway, Outer Hebrides, 161–2
Story of Princess Elizabeth, The (Ring), 10
Stoute, Michael, 272
Strathmore, Cecilia Bowes-Lyon, Countess, 5, 6, 7
Strathmore, Claude Bowes-Lyon, 14th Earl, 6, 13

Summer, Eric R., 139
Superb, HMS, 61, 63
Swing, Raymond Gram, 47
Swinton, Tilda, 297
Sydney, New South Wales, 222
Synge, Violet, 36

Tagus River, 140
Tanner, Hubert, 53
tennis, 262–4
Thatcher, Margaret, 202, 212, 216, 254
Theatre Royal, Drury Lane, 51–2, 98
Thompson, Vera, 250
Thornton, Frances, 161
Thornton Heath, London, 32–3
Titania's Palace, 10
Tobruk, Libya, 111
Toronto, Ontario, 214
Tower of London, 12, 286
Townsend, Peter, 118–21, 128–30
Trooping of the Colour, 95, 276
Trudeau, Justin, 280
Trump, Donald, 278
Truss, Liz, 295–6, 299, 302
Turner, Helen, 90

United Nations, 145–6
United States, 47, 48, 68, 143, 144–6, 153–5, 180, 191–3, 208, 216, 278
University of Cambridge, 159–60
University of Kent, 224
University of St Andrews, 265
University of Virginia, 192
Usher Art Gallery, Lincoln, 150

Vanguard, HMS, 67
Verity, Kathleen and Stuart, 228
Victoria Memorial, London, 4, 45, 166, 299
Victoria, Queen, 14, 46, 104, 181, 222, 229, 232–3, 238, 260, 268, 276
Vidal, Gore, 154
Virginia, United States, 143, 146, 192

Wade, William Oulton, 199
Wagner, Robert, 145, 146
Wales, 174–6, 177–9, 180
Wallasey, Merseyside, 20
Walsall, West Midlands, 47, 195
Warren, John, 271
Warrington, Cheshire, 199
Wellington Arch, London, 299

West Bromwich, West Midlands, 86
Westminster Abbey, London, 12, 33–4, 75–6, 115–17, 223, 260, 266–7, 287, 298–9
Westminster Hall, London, 256, 297
Whimsical Walker, 24
Whitechapel, London, 255
Whitewell estate, Lancashire, 227, 228
Wilcox, Fred, 228
William, Prince of Wales, 205–7, 217, 240, 242, 259, 265–7, 287–8, 290, 297
William II, King of England, 26
Williams, Beatrice, 169–70
Williams, T. D., 46
Williamsburg, Virginia, 146
Willmott, Edmund Charles Morgan, 18
Wilson, Harold, 86, 155, 168, 188
Wilson, Jacqueline, 260–61
Wimbledon Championships, 262–4
Windsor Castle and Estate, Berkshire, 7, 8, 16, 20–21, 22, 36, 39, 52, 68
  Children's Hour broadcast (1940), 48–50; Covid lockdowns (2020–21), 282–4; Elizabeth II's death (2022), 297; fire (1992), 229–31, 232, 239; Great Park, 37, 136; Queen Mother's death (2002), 256; Reagan's visit (1982), 208; Royal Chapel of All Saints, 285; Second World War (1939–45), 42, 43, 48–50, 52–3, 56, 58; Silver Jubilee (1977), 195; St George's Chapel, 107, 255, 288
Winter, H. W. R., 40
Wisdom, Norman, 135, 249
women's rights, 302
Woods, Cyril, 53
Wynne, David, 235

York, William Temple, Archbishop, 34
Youens, Bernard, 203
Youth Service Scheme, 56
Yune, Rick, 257, 258

Zambellas, George, 274
Ziegler, Ronald, 180